Literature in Context

Related Palgrave titles:

History of English Literature   *Michael Alexander*
The Practice of Reading   *Derek Alsop and Chris Walsh*
Reading Fiction: Opening the Text   *Peter Childs*
Mastering English Literature (second edition)   *Richard Gill*
Thinking About Texts   *Chris Hopkins*
How to Begin Studying English Literature (second edition)
   Nicholas Marsh
Literary Terms and Criticism (second edition)   *John Peck and
   Martin Coyle*

Literature in Context

Edited by Rick Rylance and Judy Simons

palgrave

First published 2001 by
PALGRAVE
Houndmills, Basingstoke, Hampshire RG21 6XS
and
175 Fifth Avenue, New York, N.Y. 10010
Companies and representatives throughout the world

PALGRAVE is the new global academic imprint of St. Martin's Press LLC Scholarly and
Reference Division and Palgrave Publishers Ltd (formerly Macmillan Press Ltd).

ISBN 0–333–80390–6 hardback
ISBN 0–333–80391–4 paperback

This book is printed on paper suitable for recycling and
made from fully managed and sustained forest sources.

A catalogue record for this book is available from the British Library.

Cataloging-in-Publication data is available from the Library of Congress

10   9   8   7   6   5   4   3   2   1
10   09 08 07 06 05 04 03 02 01

Printed and bound in Great Britain by Creative Print & Design (Wales), Ebbw Vale

Contents

Acknowledgements

The editors and publisher wish to thank the following for permission to use copyright material:

Figure 14 Mark Dovat, © Mark Dovat. Figure 15 Helen Marcus, © Helen Marcus. Figures 1, 2, 3, 4, 5, 8, 9, 11, Ann Ronan Picture Library. Figure 13 Barry Ryan, © Barry Ryan. Figure 10 Tate Picture Library.

The author and publishers are grateful to publishers Faber and Faber Ltd for permission to reproduce extracts from *Collected Poems* by Sylvia Plath and *Lupercal* by Ted Hughes.

Every effort has been made to contact all the copyright-holders, but if any have been inadvertently omitted the publishers will be pleased to make the necessary arrangement at the earliest opportunity.

Notes on Contributors

Catherine Belsey chairs the Centre for Critical and Cultural Theory at Cardiff University. Her books include *Critical Practice* (1980), *The Subject of Tragedy* (1985) and *Desire: Love Stories in Western Culture* (1994).

Martin Coyle is Senior Lecturer in English at Cardiff University where he teaches Shakespeare and Renaissance Drama. He is series editor of the Macmillan – now Palgrave – *New Casebooks* for which he has edited *Hamlet* and *The Merchant of Venice*.

Vincent Gillespie is Reader in English at the University of Oxford and a Fellow of St Anne's College. His publications cover Middle English, the History of the Book in Britain, and modern British drama. He was a consultant to the English Qualifications and Curriculum Authority on the development of the Advanced Extension Award in English and is Vice-Chair of the Council for College and University English.

Heather Glen is Fellow and Director of Studies in English at New Hall, Cambridge, and Lecturer in the Faculty of English, University of Cambridge. She has edited Charlotte Brontë's *The Professor* (Penguin Classics, 1989), and is the editor of *Jane Eyre: New Casebook* (Macmillan – now Palgrave, 1997), and *The Cambridge Companion to the Brontës* (Cambridge University Press, forthcoming). She is currently completing a study of Charlotte Brontë's novels for Oxford University Press.

Thomas Healy is Professor of Renaissance Studies at Birkbeck College, London. He is the author of books on *Richard Crashaw, Christopher Marlowe,* and *New Latitudes: Theory and English Renaissance Literature.* He edited *Literature and the Civil War* with Jonathan Sawday, *The Arnold Anthology of British and Irish Literature in English* with Robert Clark and, most recently, the Longman Critical Reader on Andrew Marvell. He is completing a study entitled *The English Boat: The poetics of sectarianism in early modern England.*

Elisabeth Jay is Associate Head of the School of Humanities at Oxford Brookes University and a member of the Council for College and University English Executive. She has published several books on the subject of religion and literature in the nineteenth century, and on the work of various Victorian women writers, including Charlotte Brontë, Elizabeth Gaskell, and Margaret Oliphant.

Stephen Knight is Professor and Head of English Literature at Cardiff University. He has written widely on medieval and modern literature, including *Geoffrey Chaucer* in the 'Re-reading Literature' series edited by Terry Eagleton (Oxford, 1987). His most recent book on a medieval topic is *Robin Hood: A Complete Study of the English Outlaw* (Oxford, 1994).

Linden Peach is Professor of Modern Literature at Loughborough University and Assistant Secretary of the Council for College and University English. Apart from his work on Toni Morrison, his recent publications include *Angela Carter* (1998) and *Virginia Woolf* (2000). He is currently writing a study of the Irish novel and researching the representation of crime and deviancy in modern literature.

David Punter is Professor of English at the University of Bristol. He is the author of *The Literature of Terror* (1980), *The Hidden Script* (1985) and *Gothic Pathologies* (1998). *Postcolonial Imaginings* and *Writing the Passions* will appear in 2001. David Punter is an ex-President of the British Association of Romantic Studies and was Chair of the Council for College and University English 1995–97. He is a Fellow of the Society of Antiquaries of Scotland.

Rick Rylance is Professor of Modern English Literature and Dean of the School of Arts and Letters at APU, Cambridge. He has worked with and in secondary schools for many years and is presently Chair of the Council for College and University English. He is author of *Victorian Psychology and British Culture 1850–1880* (Oxford, 2000) and other books, and is presently writing the mid-twentieth-century volume of the new *Oxford English Literary History*.

Marion Shaw is Professor of English at Loughborough University. She has published on Victorian fiction and poetry, particularly Tennyson. During recent years her area of interest has extended to the interwar period, and in 1999 she published *The Clear Stream*, a biography of the Yorkshire novelist and social reformer, Winifred Holtby.

Judy Simons is Dean of Humanities and Social Sciences at De Montfort University. Her books include *Fanny Burney* (1988); *Diaries and Journals of Literary Women* (1990), *Rosamond Lehmann* (1992) and *What Katy Read: Feminist Re-readings of 'Classic' Stories for Girls* (1995). Most recently she has edited the Macmillan – now Palgrave – *New Casebook* on Jane Austen's *Mansfield Park* and *Persuasion*. She was Chair of the Council for College and University English 1997–2000 and is a member of its Executive committee.

Roger Webster is Professor of Literary Studies and Director of the School of Media, Critical and Creative Arts at Liverpool John Moores University. He has published on Thomas Hardy, working-class fiction and literary theory, and is currently editing a volume of essays on suburbia.

Peter Widdowson is Professor of Literature at Cheltenham and Gloucester College of Higher Education. He was a founder editor of the journal *Literature and History*, and has published extensively on Thomas Hardy, literary theory and twentieth-century novelists. His most recent book is *Literature* in the 'New Critical Idiom' series (Routledge, 1999).

Nigel Wood is Professor of English and Head of Department at De Montfort University. His books include a critical study of Jonathan Swift (1986) and *Swift: A Critical Reader* (1999). He is the general editor of the series *Theory and Practice*. He is director of the Hockliffe Project which is conducting research into children's books 1780–1840.

Introduction: Why Study the Contexts of Literature?

Rick Rylance and Judy Simons

I

What happens when we pick up a book and begin reading? We peruse the words on the page, and these tell us a story, conjure up images, invite us to participate in an imaginative world that is simultaneously very different from and strangely similar to our own. That world mirrors our desires, appeals to our memories and our fantasies, and recreates familiar experiences in ways that make them fresh and arresting. Literature is undeniably a powerful medium with the capacity to convey equally powerful messages. More than this, it helps shape our personal and collective cultural imagination. Consequently, the formal study of literature becomes an activity which is much more complex than passive absorption; it incorporates an enquiry into the influence of the medium itself, into the ways in which words carry authority beyond their isolated dictionary definitions, into the history of ideas and into the mechanisms whereby we, as readers, absorb and make sense of these intersections.

An interest in the study of the contexts of literature is by no means new. As several essays in this book make clear, from time to time – maybe in all periods – literary critics, and cultural and intellectual historians, have been concerned with investigating and establishing the contexts in which works of literature are produced and understood. Although one common critical position has always been that what matters in reading a literary text is 'the words on the page', there has always been an opposing pressure. Literary works naturally engage with the worlds that surround them and of which they are a part. Readers too, however engrossed by the micro-world bounded by the page, are people whose lives are enmeshed in social, intellectual, cultural and other circumstances to which they both spontaneously and reflectively relate their reading. So reading literature is essentially a dynamic activity. Of itself it encourages readers to make connections between the diverse aspects of their world, including the represented worlds they find in their reading. But literature is a dynamic activity in another sense too. Images of readers in paintings and other visual representations often stress the solitariness of reading as an occupation. It is, for instance, striking how frequently the covers of modern editions and critical works feature women in Edwardian costumes alone with a book. But in fact the reading of literature is an intensely public activity involving frequently impassioned discussion of the issues that arise from these representations. Apart from anything else, this goes some way to explaining the immense popularity of literary studies.

English remains amongst the most popular of subjects chosen by students for study at college in both Britain and the United States. Why should this be so? It is a complicated question. If asked, students might nominate the sheer pleasure of reading as their principal reason for choosing the subject. However, another answer might be that the study of literature allows the opportunity, perhaps uniquely, for discussion of ideas, feelings and values at the intersection of personal and public experience. It enables a centrally important conversation to occur in our culture at exactly that point where the private meets the public, where personal reflection joins general discussion, where the public communication of often intensely private feeling (which is frequently the very business of literature) allows us to maintain an open interest in the way we thrive as human beings in our own particular cultural environments. Not only do the texts of literature invite consideration of their contexts, the very presence of literature in the culture at large demands its appreciation. Literature offers a remarkable perspective on how we function as imaginative and intellectual beings in a society which is itself evolving, and which moreover has an all-consuming interest in re-creating and representing itself in myriad artistic forms. It is exceptional in its exploration of the reverberating effects of language, and of how words interact with their multiple milieux to create meanings that resonate so compellingly with readers. These resonances tell us a good deal about the ways in which we thrive and fail as human beings in particular cultures, both now and in the past.

But what is meant by context? There is still open debate about this issue. Dictionaries define the word variously, but most call attention to two key features. The first is that context is, in one of its root meanings, a matter of language; the second stresses relatedness and interweaving. In *Chambers Twentieth-Century Dictionary*, context is defined as: 'the parts of a discourse or treatise which precede and follow a special passage and may fix its true meaning', and by extension refers to the 'associated surroundings, setting'. The related word 'contexture' refers to 'the process or manner of weaving together' in a structure or a fabric. In the *Oxford English Dictionary*, context is 'the connection of parts of a discourse', especially those preceding or succeeding a given passage which 'determine its meaning'. It, too, records the use of the companion word 'contexture' in the textile industry from the 1600s to refer to the 'action of weaving together' of 'a mass of things'. But it also notes the use of the same word from the same date in relation to language: 'contexture' is 'the weaving together of words, sentences, etc. in connected composition; the structure of a literary composition; a connected passage'.

This primary understanding of context as a matter of relationships within language is emphasised by more specialist definitions in modern dictionaries of critical terms (see, for example, Abrams, Baldick, Fowler, Gray and Hawthorn). Indeed a powerful school of twentieth-century critical opinion has primarily understood context in a way that goes to the heart of a continuing, fundamental debate in literary studies. Should critical attention be primarily aimed at the appreciation – in the widest sense – of textual detail, focused on the particular words to be found in particular works? Or should it enlarge the frame of attention by placing literary works in wider contextual relationships? The answer, of course, is that it should do neither *exclusively*. A criticism which is not in confident possession of a text's detail is unlikely to be convincing when it moves to assessing its relationship to context. By the same token, a commentary which is ill-informed about the contexts in which works are written and received seems wilfully to deny those important parts of literary works which make strong connections with the world that surrounds them.

Yet a powerful body of opinion in the twentieth century has opposed the making of these enlarged connections in critical work. Whilst the extant texts of English literature go back to Anglo-Saxon times, the study of English literature as a recognised academic discipline is relatively new. It was only introduced as a subject thought suitable to be taught in British schools and universities in anything like a modern form in the late nineteenth century. One of the arguments that was made to establish its academic credentials was that – in an early version of an accelerating information-based economy increasingly dependent upon written information – the close study of verbal detail created skilled, discriminating and independent readers. This sort of argument for the subject is still often made, and remains largely true. It was not, by any means, the only justification launched for English, but it was an important one. The discipline, it is often claimed, developed strongly from the point at which it settled, during the first three decades or so of the twentieth century, on a distinctive method and approach based upon the intensive, detailed scrutiny of texts. This approach – as successful in America as in the UK – was variously called 'practical criticism' or 'close reading', and as a method it had many advantages. It was coherent and relatively easy to teach. It was, theoretically, equally comfortable with different kinds of material from different periods (though, in practice, it tended to set aside differences in style and period). And it was exceptionally efficient in terms of teaching resources. It required the text (perhaps from an anthology), the student and the teacher; and this trio – in uninspired versions – invited intensive concentration on the words on the page, rarely lifting the eyes in other directions.

Some leading theorists, indeed, pointedly discouraged wider thinking. Murray Kreiger, a leading member of what became known as the American 'New Criticism' which influentially adapted and consolidated British initiatives, defined 'Contextual Criticism' as the study of 'the tight, compelling, finally closed context' of the words on the page, and this prevents 'our escape to the world of reference and action beyond' (quoted in Abrams, *Glossary*, 224). The assessment practices favoured by this method often – though never entirely – enforced what was, in Kreiger's own metaphor, an imprisoning regimen. In critical practice, most teachers of English will be familiar with an old style of question known as the 'context question' which became a familiar, indeed in many places dominant (though never exclusive), part of examinations in English. In this type of question, candidates would be offered a passage from a larger work, and invited, first, to reflect upon the meaning and significance of individual words and phrases in the local context of their usage in the passage cited, and then, in one way or another, to place the whole extract in the context of the work from which it was taken. The method of assessment at least had the advantage of stocking candidates' minds with detailed memories of what came where in a five-act play by Shakespeare or the 'Prologue' to *The Canterbury Tales*, but too often it was used simply to test whether candidates had got the plot straight and learnt a few archaisms. In some respects, this kind of context paradoxically *disengaged* the words from the page. Expecting candidates to construe exactly the meanings of 'Your wisdom is consumed in confidence' from *Julius Caesar*, or 'a gipoun / al besmotered with his haubergeoun' from *The Canterbury Tales* seems a textual exercise some distance from significant usage, and implies a pedagogy with some muddled priorities.

These methods have, largely, now fallen into disuse, but in highlighting their limitations we should not imply either that detailed textual knowledge is unimportant, or that the continuing argument in criticism between text-centred and context-centred approaches has been settled. The dangers of an over-emphatic methodological outlook, and the shortcomings of a particular assessment method, do not diminish the crucial importance of alert, informed, detailed reading. Without skills of this kind, and the corresponding ability to relate local detail to broader pictures, contextual thinking in a larger framework is merely a short cut to superficial generalisation. The particular, prized skill in contextual work – which will be rewarded at all levels – is the ability to connect the detail to the pattern, the nuance to the generalisation, and the ability to recognise what is exceptional as well as what is typical in the works under consideration.

But the idea of literary context also entails what one recent glossary definition calls the 'other, more open-ended part of criticism [which] involves relating literary works themselves to their relevant psychological, social, and historical contexts' (Fowler, *Dictionary*, 41). For many contemporary critics, the idea of context has come to acquire a sense somewhat opposed to what many perceive as a narrow and confined scrutiny of verbal detail and concentration on the single text. Modern contextual studies open out the perspective and shade more towards the second dictionary definition of context, that associated with 'contexture': the mingling and weaving of different strands. In such approaches, the individual text, or groups of texts, are understood in a wider framework, often specifically in relation to other art forms, or movements of ideas, or broader developments in the society of their times or that of their readers. The splendid, 1200-page *Encyclopedia of Literature and Criticism*, edited by Martin Coyle, Peter Garside, Malcolm Kelsall and John Peck in 1990, provides an excellent, wide-ranging source for contextual ideas. In its section on 'Contexts' it includes essays on literature's relationship to the history of ideas, the Bible, the classics, folk literature, the visual arts, popular culture and science, as well as a chapter on 'Literature and Language'.

But what looms largest in the background of the development of modern contextual criticism is the change in the information economy that has occurred so rapidly over the past two decades. There is, simply put, much more information, and many more resources, available to teachers and students at all levels, and this presents radically different possibilities from those made available by the 'low-spec' publishing practices and printing technologies of even two decades ago. The spectacular, unfathomed – and as yet unclear – impact of the internet and other sorts of electronic data storage and transmission is clearly the headline news in these developments. But we should not underestimate other aspects. There is the impact of 'in-house' reprographic technologies such as photocopying which can transmit good, affordable packages of contextual material for educational use inhibited only by the just claims of copyright holders. At the same time, the depth, sophistication and extent of modern scholarship on the literature of all historical periods has increased enormously. We now know immeasurably more about more things in the subject than we did. We also have more and better editions of literary texts themselves, and a much more alert sense of the impact of editorial practices on the literature we read (as Thomas Healy's essay in this volume amply demonstrates). Cheaper, computer-based printing technologies nowadays, and alterations in the economics of publishing, have led not just to the beneficial supply of cheap editions of often-studied 'classic' texts, but also to the availability of very much more of the writing of the past in general, and this has altered our sense of the relations between literary works. The work of publishers specialising in women's literature is a case in point. The circulation of this material, and scholarly work on it, has, alongside the growth of feminist awareness in literary studies generally, very profoundly corrected older views of literary and cultural history. Its impact is fundamental to the readings of history in this collection by, amongst others, Judy Simons on *Persuasion*, Heather Glen on *Jane Eyre* and Marion Shaw on *Mrs Dalloway*. This general increase in the range of work available seems unlikely to decline in the shift to on-line and other electronic mechanisms. Altogether, these developments constitute in themselves a significant context for the revival of interest in contextual studies in recent critical and educational work.

These infrastructural developments have been accompanied by significant changes of outlook in the overall academic community across a number of disciplines which have advanced contextual studies in all fields. At the core of this is what most commentators agree has been a significant alteration in our sense of truth or value. Social and natural scientists, as well as commentators in the humanities, are aware that an observation cannot be separated from the context in which it is made, and that the stance and values of the observer will influence what is seen. Does a phenomenon occur in the same way in laboratory as 'real world' conditions? Have the biases of a social observer skewed his or her perceptions? Do the values we hold in our culture make us blind to the different beliefs, traditions and assumptions of other cultures? All of these examples invite consideration of the role of contextual factors in judgements and analysis. In the social sphere, this is intimately connected to our awareness of living in an increasingly multicultural and global environment, and of our need to negotiate the frictions between the many cultures, past and present, that compose our world.

Consider, for example, the range of perspectives offered in the essays in this volume: Linden Peach's discussion of Toni Morrison or Catherine Belsey's discussion of Shakespearean drama (to name just two of the many possible case studies here) locate literary works in a pluralistic and multi-faceted world, complicated by the levels and varieties of knowledge available to their writers and readers. They provide alternative approaches to textual analysis which enrich our perceptions not just of the many meanings inherent in literary texts but of our subjective positions as readers of them. Literary critics are acutely aware that the ideas formulated in literary works are highly dependent upon the multiplicity of contexts which shape their elaboration. These are of many different kinds as we shall see. But in the end it comes down to this, one of the strongest arguments for contextual knowledge: we know ourselves by recognising what is different in ourselves from others, and we cannot know this until we try to understand what is different and particular about them. Our understanding is created by the recognition that things were and are different for different people, and to understand them with a due, respectful, tolerant and humane sense of enquiry we need to recognise the essential differences between then and now, this social group and that, you and me. These differences may be huge, but they are rarely absolute. Though I cannot stop being me in order to be you, it is the particular virtue of human interactions that we can articulate our differences and, to a degree, negotiate them. It is the privilege of literature and other art forms that they allow us such open, reflective, exploratory access to the rich, human world of others, and an understanding of the contexts in play – our own, and those of others – is fundamental to this process of enlarged understanding.

This sense of a contextual basis for the understanding of important issues central to our lives as well as our studies is one reason why the growth of contextual work has developed hand in hand with an accelerating interest in interdisciplinary work. As subject domains are extended, scholars and teachers appear more interested in the relationships between phenomena, and less interested in the differences between what are conventionally considered discrete areas of expertise. Such developments are exciting, and hold out the possibility of a substantially enriched cultural conversation in the areas of overlap between literature and history, psychology, philosophy, the visual media and so many other disciplines. The essays in this volume by Elisabeth Jay on *Middlemarch* for instance, or by Roger Webster on Thomas Hardy are rooted in an acceptance of the importance of just such a conversation.

In the last twenty years this position has been most forcefully represented by schools of criticism, broadly categorised as 'new historicism' and/or 'cultural materialism' (though these labels are often as controversial as they are helpful). These critics argue that it is exciting and illuminating to read a literary text in full awareness of its cultural and social determinants as registered in the other 'texts', including the non-verbal, which are contemporary with it and with which it enters into a creative dialogue. New historicist critics insist on recognising how a work of literature is informed by its non-literary sources which might include materials as diverse as popular songs, newspaper articles, medical treatises, paintings, sermons, political tracts and scientific papers. Such materials should not be seen in any traditional sense as inert or useful 'background' against which the literary text is poised, but as active ingredients in the cultural process which gives rise to that work. The work of art then becomes merely one amongst a number of competing discourses which shape and reflect contemporary culture and which intermingle productively with one another. The intriguing consequence of this approach is that the traditional boundaries between historical and literary materials become blurred and the reader is invited to question not just the privileged status of literature but also the nature of historical evidence and 'truth'. We learn about the past, as about the present, through representations. But we cannot assume that some documents provide stable, authoritative norms against which fictional works can be judged. Our sense of the past might now be considered as something that emerges from a set of representations, all intriguingly different from ourselves and maybe from each other. It is a school of thought which has found particular resonance with critics of Renaissance literature, and more recently of eighteenth-century literature, and its influence can be seen in a number of essays in this collection, including those by Martin Coyle on Shakespeare, Thomas Healy on Renaissance poetry, David Punter on Blake, and Nigel Wood on Swift.

This new vision of context is a strongly open and dynamic one which calls attention to change and diversity as much as the particular circumstances which shape the meaning and production of a specific work. It insists, for instance, that the meaning of literary works cannot simply be 'read-off' from period detail or opinions about a culture's general beliefs: literary works often contest norms, or emphasise uncertain debates, as Catherine Belsey stresses in her essay in this collection. It also emphasises the importance of the context of the present in shaping our understanding of the past, and of how works change their meanings over time as the interests of different groups and periods shape the context of their interpretation, again an emphasis in Belsey's essay. Lastly, the function of contextual criticism at the present time is surely to spotlight the relationship between textual detail and the surrounding range of factors which bear upon the creation and understanding of its significance. It is this project that this volume of essays addresses. It is not concerned to fix works in the aspic of a particular view of the past, but recognises multiplicity of approach and the fact that the very business of literature is an open, evolving inquiry. Each piece focuses on a particular text or writer, chosen as representative of the broad range of writing in English since Chaucer, and with an eye to their likely place in the academic curriculum. The essays include explicit suggestions about how contextual approaches to literature might be pursued. Some mention specific sources for discovering contextual material. Our hope is that they begin an exploration of the possibilities of context. They do not provide a closed book of answers.

II

Context, then, is a broad field of activity, and trying to summarise the different aspects it assumes can be difficult. But the following list gives a broad sense of the different things comprised by the idea – though it should always be borne in mind that individual cases require individual initiatives, as several essays in this book demonstrate.

Generally speaking, the idea of context includes significant facts or processes of different kinds which have shaped the writing and understanding of literary works. The most important types include:

- the context of period or era including significant social, historical, political and cultural processes;
- the context of the work in terms of the writer's biography or milieu;
- the context of a specific passage in terms of the whole work from which it is taken;
- the context of the work in terms of other works, including other works by the same author;
- the literary context, including the question of generic factors and period-specific styles;
- the language context, including relevant episodes in the use and development of literary language, the question of demotic, colloquial or dialect styles, and so on;
- the different contexts for a work established by its reception over time, including the recognition that works have different meanings and effects in different periods. This might include an awareness of different critical responses.

This is firmly on the side of a broad understanding of the relationship between literary texts and wider contextual processes (though it continues to acknowledge the importance of 'the context of a specific passage in terms of the whole work from which it is taken'). But clearly the various levels it differentiates have very different orientations and methodological pertinences, and several – such as the second which includes both personal biography and the activities of a whole circle or milieu – contain within them activities which might be further discriminated. The list also makes clear the generous range of activities that might be encompassed by the modern understanding of context.

Certainly it is rare for any student nowadays, whether at secondary level or at university, to read literary texts in isolation. This collection of essays is designed to enhance an understanding of the interpretative process, as the authors seek to identify and explain some of the most familiar contexts in which texts can be read. At the same time the volume also exposes the difficulties and complexities that are inevitably embedded in such an exercise. None of the essays in this collection assumes that a single context is sufficient to 'explain' a work of literature. Nor do any of the essays assume that the texts they discuss have a particular fixed meaning that is there to be teased out by the most perceptive and best-informed of readers. Rather they all start from the presupposition that reading is an enormously subtle and dense activity, and that the more knowledgeable a reader is about the conditions in which a work was produced and has been received, the more subtle and dense that activity becomes. It also becomes correspondingly more intellectually challenging and rewarding. Reading is not a mechanistic occupation nor a passive one. The greater our awareness of the complexities involved, the more inventive and fulfilling reading becomes. Sometimes this is difficult: but a full education should encounter difficulty as the point and pleasure of study, not as a cause of evasion or simplification. The beauty of the study of literature is that there are no eventually 'right' answers, only ones with good reasons.

These points emerge compellingly in Stephen Knight's essay on Chaucer which begins the collection. Knight identifies five of the most pertinent contexts which need to be taken into account in coming to terms with a literary work written in the pre-modern age. In highlighting history, religion, society, literature, and language as key factors in unravelling the meanings inherent in such a work, Knight's essay focuses on the central question of literary period and how texts both reflect and are shaped by the age and the cultural climate in which they were produced. One of the challenges for modern students of literature is precisely that: how to capture the defining characteristics of a particular period and, correspondingly, whether or not it is possible to recover a full apprehension of the impact of the text on its original audience. Furthermore, although the process of textual production: not just the author's act of composition, but the editorial and publication policies (as well as accidents) which can affect the entire process of transmission. Some of these points are taken up in Nigel Wood's piece on Jonathan Swift, which also follows the editorial history of a text, and investigates whether it is possible to put ourselves in the position of the first readers of *Gulliver's Travels*. These essays point out how readers, both past and present, can never take for granted the fact of the text's existence in its current form as being the authoritative version. Modern versions of old texts often remove them in very straightforward ways from the originals. By the same token readers are not static beings either. They too evolve as their lives and cultures change. Reading communities are formed and determined by the versions of the texts that are available to them at a particular point in time. Works often exist in multiple versions, and part of the appreciation of context consists in the understanding of how texts and reading communities interact.

In examining the process of textual production – a process which seems to become ever more fraught the more it is analysed – several of the contributors to this collection consider biography, the study of the writer's life, as one of the many contexts which affect our understanding of authorship. The essays by Roger Webster, Marion Shaw and Rick Rylance on writers as different as Thomas Hardy, Virginia Woolf and Sylvia Plath all take figures whose works have been notoriously reconstructed and re-read, as knowledge of the circumstances of their lives has come to light. They examine the authors' non-fictional prose, their essays, diaries and letters, as significant contextual factors in reading their literary works. Together these pieces demonstrate convincingly the impossibility of isolating a single text from the continuum of a writer's thinking. Intellectual and aesthetic personal history is an important dimension of the biographical approach to literary criticism, and these essays show how knowledge of this history can inform reading without reducing it to psychological speculation. Marion Shaw's essay, for example, discusses how Virginia Woolf's personal interest in the history of literary production and the impact of gender on writing, as articulated in her non-fictional work, *A Room of One's Own,* provides a key to reading *Mrs Dalloway*. In the process Shaw necessarily locates both the fiction and the non-fiction within the intellectual milieu which formed and informed Woolf's writing practice. Roger Webster, approaching Thomas Hardy's novels from another but not totally dissimilar perspective, notes how accounts of Hardy's life, whether produced by the author himself or by others, can influence and even distort a reading of his fiction. He too situates the ideas which underpin Hardy's writing against a background of contemporary thought, Hardy's own training as an architect, and his interest in modern aesthetic and especially visual codes. Rick Rylance's essay deepens this understanding of biographical context by examining the controversy which has surrounded critical debate on Sylvia Plath's poetry. His searching discussion of the letters and essays which Plath wrote during her formative years as a poet helps to place her artistic work within the political debates of that period as well as the development of her own intellectual and social attitudes and ideas.

As these pieces indicate, authors are deeply impressionable beings, alive to the burning issues of their day. Virtually all the essays in this collection treat politics as a seminal influence on literary production. Writers can never isolate themselves from the political issues which shape their cultures, and texts are unavoidably products of the ideologies of their age. As the essays on Blake, Jane Austen, Sylvia Plath and Toni Morrison demonstrate, authors from widely disparate historical periods and cultures respond to and reflect political positions, specific events and topical debates either through explicit intervention or through attitudes and ideas which are embedded in the conceptual basis of their work. David Punter's discussion of Blake for instance, uses the overt concerns with issues of class, race and slavery as expressed in the poems as a means of opening up important critical questions about conscious and unconscious influences on writers. Judy Simons' essay on Jane Austen suggests that a writer who was once thought to be completely distanced from political concerns is, in fact, profoundly responsive to the radical debates and social and political changes of her time. In turn this knowledge influences critical reception of her works. Whilst we might tend to think of sexual politics, the class struggle and racial awareness as questions uppermost in our modern consciousness, they were also central to the thinking of earlier writers, such as Blake and Austen. The politics of gender, for example, is intrinsic to the narrative fabric of *Persuasion* and just as deeply embedded in the conceptual framing of personality and situation as it is in a more apparently openly political novel such as Toni Morrison's *Beloved*.

Genre provides another principal context for both writing and interpretation, as writers' choices are inevitably determined by their sense of a literary inheritance and their appreciation of certain artistic conventions which govern the forms in which they work. The essays in this volume deal with literature written in the three major genres, poetry, prose fiction and drama, and they variously address the special conventions and expectations inherent in each of these. In particular, the essays on dramatists from the Renaissance to the present day focus on the non-verbal elements in dramatic performance, such as gesture, spectacle, costume, scenery, properties, dance or the pause, which affect the theatrical interpretation and consequently the audience's reception of the written text. Martin Coyle and Vincent Gillespie, in their pieces on Shakespeare and Harold Pinter respectively, relate these theatrical and performative elements to the writers' contemporary political as well as aesthetic contexts, and thereby illuminate the relationship between the theatre and the developing culture in which it operates. But novelists too are aware of narrative codes and their own relationship to past and familiar fictions. As Heather Glen points out, *Jane Eyre* is a book that begins with an act of reading. This self-consciousness about the power of imaginative and other literatures impacts on novels as different as Toni Morrison's *Beloved* and Graham Swift's *Waterland* or *Last Orders* which deliberately draw on and make explicit reference to modes of storytelling.

The dimensions of time and history are, of course, crucial to an appreciation of the impact of context, and this is as true for the way people read as the way authors write. A number of pieces in this collection consider the reading history of specific texts and the impact this has had on critical understanding. Catherine Belsey's essay for instance shows how the variant interpretations of Shakespeare from Victorian to modern productions reflect the cultural beliefs of the age in which the productions occur, and moreover how interpretation will be affected by the political orientation or the geographical location of the audience. In this she points to the essential richness as well as the elusive nature of Shakespeare's 'meaning'. For other critics, such as Simons and Webster, this reading history expands to take into account modern film adaptations of classic novels, often one of the most powerful of modern interpretative modes.

In the end, as several of the contributors to this collection point out, a literary work, whether poem, novel or play, can also transcend its many contexts. Whilst this volume emphasises the value of being informed by the extra-textual materials, it is also important that when studying a work of literature we do not forget or lose sight of its creative immediacy and its ability to enlighten and absorb us instantaneously. Virginia Woolf's remarks on *Jane Eyre*, quoted in Heather Glen's essay, remind us of the utterly compelling power that books still exert over their readers. 'We open *Jane Eyre*', observes Woolf, 'and in two pages every doubt is swept clean from our minds. Nor is this exhilaration short-lived. It rushes through the entire volume, without giving us time to think, without letting us lift our eyes from the page.' As students of literature, we are invited and indeed trained to 'lift our eyes from the page'. At the same time, however, as we are engaged in that intricate process of intellectual enquiry and analysis, we should never forget the initial exhilaration which attracted us to the enterprise in the first place, and its rich location in the broad business of human culture.

References

M. H. Abrams, *A Glossary of Literary Terms*, 5th edn (London, Holt, Rinehart and Winston, 1985).

Chris Baldick, *The Concise Oxford Dictionary of Critical Terms* (Oxford, Oxford University Press, 1990).

Martin Coyle, Peter Garside, Malcolm Kelsall and John Peck (eds) *Enclyclopedia of Literature and Criticism* (London, Routledge, 1990).

Roger Fowler (ed.), *A Dictionary of Modern Critical Terms*, rvsd edn (London, Routledge, 1987).

Martin Gray, *A Dictionary of Literary Terms* (Harlow, Longman, 1988).

Jeremy Hawthorn, *A Concise Glossary of Contemporary Literary Theory* (London, Edward Arnold, 1992).

1 Chaucer: The Canterbury Tales

Stephen Knight

Canterbury Pilgrims: from John of Lydgate (1370?–1451?) 'Story of Thebes', written *circa* 1420, designed as an additional 'Canterbury Tale'.

1

History

Chaucer was involved in royal and aristocratic courts, in government business, including diplomacy and the customs service, and he was famous as a writer in his time, so there are more surviving records about his life than about many early authors – far more than about Shakespeare, for example. Apart from the records mentioning Chaucer, his lifetime, from about 1340 to 1400, has been closely studied by historians because it included a series of major events: the plague that devastated Europe in 1348–9, the ongoing 'Hundred Years' War' with France, the serious political uprising of 1381 (usually called the Peasants' Revolt) and, right at the end of Chaucer's life, the political difficulties and final overthrow of Richard II. There were also major social changes in the last half of the fourteenth century: the labour shortages caused by the plague forced up wages for the poor and made it easier for serfs (bound to a particular lord and manor) to escape to paid work and freedom, especially in the towns, and for ordinary people to accumulate money and even power. Social mobility was driven by growth in the economy, again especially in towns, largely caused by the success of the English trade in wool and cloth, especially with the Netherlands, and also the financial gearing-up linked to English military activities in the first half of the long war with France. Chaucer was closely involved in many of these new processes: he was captured in France in 1360, but ransomed by the king; as Controller of Customs from 1374–86 he made sure the king received his proper dues – literally royalties – on exports from the London docks; he was an MP in one of Richard's most turbulent parliaments; and, remarkably, when the Peasants entered London in 1381 they passed through Aldgate, a stone arch with lodgings above it, which were at the time occupied by Chaucer himself.

Cultural change was as deep as socio-economic change, and was to be as long-lasting. The period saw English steadily replacing French as the language of the court and culture: Chaucer's poetry was itself a major force in that development. At the same time the Catholic church was under pressure from reformers within: some criticised the lax and corrupt practices of many men and women in the church, and others argued for change in the pattern of worship, seeking a bible in English, not just in Latin, and for greater involvement of the individual Christian in the practice of worship. At its most extreme this was called the Lollard movement, and a number of Chaucer's friends seem to have been sympathisers (Pearsall, *Life of Chaucer*, 181–3).

But to know so much as we do about Chaucer's world does not automatically enlighten his work. This is partly because literature is never directly related to context, and partly because Chaucer makes that relationship even more elusive than other writers. Unlike Shakespeare in the history plays he did not deal overtly with the political history of his own period; unlike Dickens he did not shape stories to handle the social issues of his own time. But throughout *The Canterbury Tales* Chaucer's imagination transmutes the materials of his context into complex and memorable images, and in order to see how this has operated it is necessary to look at specific aspects and different areas of Chaucer's treatment of his context – or rather, his contexts.

Religion

The power of religion permeated all aspects of thought and culture in the fourteenth century; there was general belief in the whole Christian system, including saints, miracles, the need for regular confession and absolution, and a devout faith in a last judgement when sinners will suffer and the good be located in heaven.

The Canterbury Tales is based on a pilgrimage to the shrine of St Thomas Becket, the murdered archbishop of Canterbury, who stood primarily for the value of religion against the secular world, but from the start the tales also envisage more secular values. The birds and plants awaken in spring to physical, not spiritual, stimuli, and the first plan is for an entirely worldly competition of tale-telling, where the best story-teller will be rewarded with a free dinner when they all return to London. Many of the tales celebrate the sensual delight, both sophisticated and crude, of ordinary physical life in the period, but there is also a recurrent sense of the duties people owe to religion. Major tales come from five members of the church described in the 'General Prologue' (Prioress, Monk, Friar, Clerk, Parson) and two undescribed (Nun's Priest and Second Nun); in addition figures like the Summoner and the Pardoner were in minor clerical orders, and both their tales have a religious focus, albeit a highly negative one.

A quarter of the pilgrims are in the church, and church ideas are implied throughout the texts. In the description of the Prioress we read:

And sikerly she was of grete desport
And ful plesaunt and amyable of port
And peyned hir to countrefete cheere
Of court, and to been holden digne of reverence.
But for to speken of hir conscience,

She was so charitable and so pitous
She wolde wepe, if that she saugh a mous
Kaught in a trappe, if it were deed or bledde.
Of smale houndes hadde she that she fedde
With rosted flessh, or milk and wastel-breed,
But soore wepte she if oon of hem were deed,
Or if men smoote it with a yerde smerte;
And al was consience and tendre herte.
(Chaucer, *The Canterbury Tales*, ed.
Benson, 'General Prologue', lines 137–50)

It seems a charming enough picture of a rather elegant nun who is under-standably sentimental about little dogs. But the language tells a sharper story. Your 'conscience' was a major concept in medieval culture: it was the voice of God speaking inside you which awakened you to your wrong-doing; for it to be reduced to the equivalent of 'tendre herte' (line 150) is a deep criticism of the Prioress's very limited values and her inadequate 'reverence' (line 140). The conflict between religious and secular values, raised at the opening of the 'General Prologue', recurs implicitly through-out the whole *Tales*, and can at times be posed explicitly. 'The Clerk's Tale' seems to be a grotesque account of wife-tormenting, but this is suddenly reversed as the Clerk says that the audience should not be upset by all this apparent cruelty (lines 1142–62): the story is symbolic, and teaches how Christ tests the Christian soul, and how we must suffer all in patience if we hope for heaven. Then the Clerk seems to withdraw this in an ironic conclusion (lines 1163–212), and we are left wondering whether Chaucer is advocating or satirising contemporary Christian faith – or just exploring its complexity.

In much the same ironic way 'The Pardoner's Tale' is in form completely religious: a sermon brilliantly told to make people realise how, according to its text, 'Love of money is the root of all evil'. But it is told by a com-pletely corrupt and selfish Pardoner, just for the sake of making money from ignorant anxious Christians. Both the ideal values and the real cor-ruptions of contemporary religion are realised, just as in the 'General Pro-logue' the limitations are exposed of the romantic Prioress, the hunting Monk and the lecherous Friar, yet at the same time the serious scholar-ship of the Clerk is praised (apparently without irony) and the devotion of the Parson is explored in the longest, most ideal and least physical of all the descriptions. The complex world of religion, and responses to it, is a constant context to the text.

Society

There was a long-standing medieval theory that society was divided into 'Three Orders'. One Order was what we might think of as an upper class: the knights, who owned land, and could fight to defend themselves and the country. They were regarded as basically equal to the second Order, the priests, who operated in the spiritual domain, whose role was that of prayer, worship and providing spiritual service. Both were clearly superior to the third Order, labourers, who were often serfs, bound to a place and a lord, and worked physically and very hard. The tripartite scheme was meant to be mutual: the lords defended all, the priests prayed for all and the labourers worked to feed and clothe all. There were occasional suggestions that this social model was unfair to labourers, either from theorists or from rebels, but it persuaded most people. Jill Mann has explored this approach to people and judgement of them in a major book; the literature is called 'estates' theory because all people were said to have their 'estate' or position in life, and were expected to fulfil it.

As it starts to describe pilgrims, the 'General Prologue' looks to be following the Three Orders model. First comes the land-owning, fighting Knight, with his son, the Squire, and his servant, the Yeoman. (Terry Jones's treatment of this group as satirical is not supported by most medievalists.) Next comes the religious estate, Prioress, Monk and Friar; contemporary criticism of the church is heard as each of them reveals failings which show they are inherently trying to change their estate: the Prioress would like to be a courtly lady; the Monk rides and hunts like a landed knight; the Friar exhibits a vulgar version of the Squire's obsession with love.

But then the 'General Prologue' abandons the Three Orders model, and offers, consciously it would seem, a lengthy list of people who neither own land, nor pray, nor labour. From the Merchant through to the Wife of Bath, thirteen pilgrims are described (though as the five Guildsmen are taken together, nine might be a fairer count). Chaucer appears to have gathered together a group of people who live in ways not imagined in the feudal world, and outside the analysis of the Three Orders. The Clerk does pray, but only for money to support his studying; the Shipman certainly fights, but only at sea to defend his cargo – and so his business; the wealthy Franklin owns land but is below knightly status and is involved with probably paid legal work; the Sergeant of Law, the Merchant, the Physician, the Wife of Bath (who is a weaver, and so a small industrialist) and the Guildsmen are all town-based and have a social coherence that makes them look almost like a fourth Order.

Having thoroughly disrupted the simple progress through the Three Orders, Chaucer then returns to them, in mostly satirical mood. The Parson, as he is the brother to a Plowman, is in fact a sort of labourer; in his powerful fulfilment of his duty, he is the most honoured member of the church, but, with a satirist's touch, Chaucer places him outside the comfortable priestly order. And while his brother is a perfect example of the labouring Christian peasant, the rest in this category are a mixture of brutality (Miller and Summoner), cunning (Manciple and Reeve) and selfishness (all five but especially Pardoner). These are both socially and morally the lower depths of the medieval populace, and with characteristic mock-humility, Chaucer places himself among them (lines 542–4). The orderly beginning of the Prologue, with the Knight and his archetypal family, has descended into a babble of aggression and greed among those who should work, but prefer to steal, connive and argue – and, in his own case, write poetry.

Real social disorder against a background of idealised order is the basic pattern in the course of the whole of *The Canterbury Tales*. The 'General Prologue' realises a conflicted social world and the tales often develop that vision of disharmony. The opening tales are at odds in this way: the Knight's grand, epic story of a love conflict in ancient Athens is answered, and consciously so, by the Miller's vulgar fabliau, with an unseemly tussle over a landlady's body in medieval Oxford. The basic plots are surprisingly similar, but everything else is different: there seems to be no winner in the contest between Knight and Miller, just a literary realisation of differing views, with an implied relation to social conflict in the period: some critics have seen this sequence as an encoded version of the Peasants' Revolt itself (see Knight, *Canterbury Tales*, and Patterson, 'No Man His Resoun Herde').

Similar conflict underlies the squabble between those rival church scavengers, the Friar and the Summoner, and it may well be that the reason the Knight stops 'The Monk's Tale' from droning on any more is because it is the knight's own estate that the hard-riding Monk imitates. Implied social tensions lie beneath 'The Merchant's Tale', where this very rich man without high social status tells a story that wanders in tone and style between the classic nobility of the Knight's epic romance, with gods and high rhetoric, and the direct vulgarity found in a fabliau. The Merchant's claim to a literary and social status that is in traditional terms above his order is one of Chaucer's responses to the social change of the period; another occurs when 'The Franklin's Tale', ostensibly about rivalry in love between nobles, comes down to a direct question of who is the most noble of three men – a lord, a squire, or a professional magician. Both the story and its teller apparently find great difficulty in separating these three figures, when normal hierarchical thinking would very easily set them in order: lord, squire, magician. The story creates the social mobility to which the Franklin aspires, and which was increasingly common in Chaucer's world.

That story does not seem to consider the heroine, Dorigen, as a real candidate for the honour of nobility, as she fades out before the end of the story, but Chaucer does not therefore ignore the question of the social role and developing status of women. The tale and character that most fully represent the range of contemporary social forces, starting with the issue of gender, is that told by the Wife of Bath: a helpful analysis of the context has been made by Finke.

The Wife challenges many of the established systems of authority and control in the period: first as a vigorous, talkative, even aggressive woman who, the 'General Prologue' tells us, wears spurs and has a hat like a shield. She also, in the Prologue to her own Tale, challenges in her opening words the scholarly Christian (and therefore male) tradition of relying for knowledge and judgement on 'authority', what it says in books, rather than 'experience' – living experimentation. The traditional authority of husbands is vividly challenged in her Prologue's account of her much-married life, and the notion of gender resistance is vigorously realised when her tale starts with a knight raping a peasant girl – but he is punished by women. The answer to the question 'what do women want?', an answer he cannot imagine, is 'sovereignty' but the wise fairy who tells him this, and claims him as a husband as her reward, has more to say. In a lengthy and too often overlooked speech she explains emphatically to the knight that nobility is not a matter of birth, but that being judged as truly noble depends on the quality of your behaviour, and that Christ, a poor carpenter's son, is the model of true nobility (lines 1109–64).

This speech is a radical challenge to the traditional social structure, a challenge being heard increasingly in the period, whether from Christian or from revolutionary voices. Chaucer's Wife of Bath is an agent of change in many ways: outside the feudal world of the Three Orders she is a successful small industrialist; she is involved in the newly expanding world of money; she is deeply critical of church corruption, as is clear in her exchange with the friar at the start of her tale. She stands for the value of present experience against inherited bookish tradition (itself dominated by churchmen), and, in the fairy's long speech, she rejects inherited authority when judged against personal merit. The image of a woman fighting back is a lens through which Chaucer envisages much of the dynamic contextual change of his period.

Literature

The Wife's choice of tale is also revealing. Medieval literary tradition and genre are an important part of the context of *The Canterbury Tales* and Chaucer's selection and treatment of genre are major means of encoding contemporary conflicts. The Wife's story is set at the court of King Arthur: some have felt this romance genre was old-fashioned by Chaucer's day, and so represents a typically unfortunate choice by a social climber. The same might be said about the other romance-tellers, the Franklin, also upwardly mobile, and (with deep irony), of Chaucer himself, whose first tale is the disastrous 'Sir Thopas', a brilliant parody of an Arthurian poem in feeble tail-rhyme. But the effect of Chaucer's treatment of the Wife's choice is that, as Mary Carruthers argues, the powerfully masculine genre of romance is in fact subverted, just as in the rapidly changing contemporary world women were at times gaining, or at least sharing, power at court, in business and even in the religious world.

A classic genre-conflict is between the Knight and the Miller where, as has been noted, basically the same story is told, first as classical epic, with its elaboration, rhetoric and idealism, and then as fabliau, with its speedy action, realistic detail and vulgarity. Other tales show genre being subverted not by contrasts between each other but internally. The Franklin tells a 'Breton Lay' which is, as would be expected, about courtly love and magic, but this lay becomes a vehicle for the teller's own social anxiety; 'The Merchant's Tale' combines the splendid and the vulgar, romance and fabliau, in story and in poetry, to suggest that this very rich man is not in fact all he seems – just a merchant, not a lord at all.

In much the same way traditional religious discourses can be undermined to suggest conflicts belonging to the contemporary world. The Pardoner's brilliant sermon against the love of money is told merely to serve his love of money: he can use all the skills and persuasive methods of the church to further his own greed. The same is true of the friar, the sly seducer of the 'General Prologue' who offers an inherently moral 'Look out for the devil' story, but exposes his own unreligious nature by telling it in anger against his clerical enemy and rival money-grubber and seducer, the Summoner. Another mistargeted genre that reveals contextual tensions appears when the Prioress tells a well-known Christian genre, about the Virgin's miraculously intervening on behalf of a little Christian boy murdered by Jews. The language and style of the tale have the calm beauty of Virgin-worship, but some modern commentators have felt that it deliberately suggests the prioress is both sentimentally attached to the 'litel body swete' (line 682) of the boy (just like her own little dogs) and also improperly savage to the Jews:

all of those who simply knew about the murder are executed, but the word 'mercy' is only heard in the last stanza, as the Prioress prays for mercy for herself (lines 687–91).

A similar ironic, socially focused rehandling of a traditional genre is found in 'The Monk's Tale' where this under-religious hunting man with noble aspirations seems to recite an endless list of banal and mostly noble tragedies, until he is stopped by the Knight, who told a truly noble tragedy. In 'The Clerk's Tale' Chaucer seems to be asking us to decide whether this is in fact generically a religious fable or a fully secular, even humanist, account of human oppression, a question seeming to relate to the newly secularised role of people like the Clerk, a scholar rather than a priest. The most striking generic mix and conflict is found in 'The Nun's Priest's Tale', where the very popular and simple genre of the beast fable is massively overloaded with scholarly, theological and literary references and yet we are finally told this is only a story of a cock and hen. Just as the old widow is healthy because of her bare diet, it is implied that readers, and even writers, can be literary gluttons and that even such a multigeneric display as 'The Nun's Priest's Tale' – a medieval equivalent of Joyce's *Ulysses* in learning and reference – may have little to do with simple goodness. 'Is modern sophistication worth anything?' the tale seems to be asking. Its critique of contemporary styles of elaboration may well point towards the Parson's sober and religious conclusion to the whole of *The Canterbury Tales*. It is notable that some tales which are not apparently ironised in any way, whose genres are presented without any sign of being undermined, are the devoutly moral and religious ones, 'The Man of Law's Tale', 'The Physician's Tale', 'The Second Nun's Tale', 'The Parson's Tale' and, perhaps most tellingly of all, Chaucer's own second tale, 'The Tale of Melibee'. Social conflict and religious conflict are created through Chaucer's choice and manipulation of literary genre, but ultimately faith in religion is reasserted.

Language

Language is not only the medium of Chaucer's work but is itself shaped by contextual forces, and also reveals them. The Knight's noble high style and the Miller's blunt but rich colloquial language – and then the Reeve's bleaker, angrier language – all reveal and realise their different social and ethical positions. The contrast between the richly religious language of the 'prohemium' to the Prioress's tale and the simple, even naïve, style of the tale itself suggests a gap between this particular nun and true religious complexity. The Wife of Bath has power over language, both the inherently male language of romance in her tale and the aggressively male language of church thinkers in her prologue – and she even speaks her old husbands' thoughts about her, as if they were ventriloquist's dummies.

But Chaucer's language has contextual depths beyond these pilgrim self-realisations. The vocabulary and even sound of the language itself has implications. Since the Norman conquest of 1066 and its imposition of French as the language of law, rule and prestigious culture – with Latin continuing as the language of the church – English had held low status, and while it was obviously still widely spoken and there were songs and stories and moral tracts in English, there are few signs of a complex literature outside Latin and French. In the fourteenth century this begins to alter as more and more people used English as their first or only language, and especially because, with social and economic developments, more of those people might want to listen to, read or even own reasonably elaborate literary texts.

It is in this context that Chaucer works – apparently consciously – not only to write some major poems in English but also to make English itself a language capable of transmitting the sophistication of European literature. His contemporaries, English and French, saw this as Chaucer's major achievement; through the words he uses, and what he implies through them, he constructs subtleties that relate to and communicate the range of contexts in which he worked.

Any passage of Chaucer will reveal linguistic complexity and reference. Good examples are the Prioress's description (General Prologue lines 118–62), the Wife's attack on friars (lines 857–81), the Miller's description of Alisoun (lines 3233–70), the Pardoner's mock-sermon (especially lines 463–548), the lengthy treatment of the wedding of January and May in 'The Merchant's Tale' (lines 1696–857), the wooing of Dorigen by Aurelius in 'The Franklin's Tale' (lines 901–87), the response to Chauntecleer's peril in 'The Nun's Priest's Tale (lines 3221–401). But both the best-known and in many ways the finest example of Chaucer's linguistic contextual subtlety is the opening lines of *The Canterbury Tales*:

Whan that Aprill with his shoures soote
The droghte of Marche hath perced to the roote
And bathed every veyne in swich licour
Of which vertu engendred is the flour;
Whan Zephirus eek with his sweete breeth
Inspired hath in every holt and heeth

The tendre croppes, and the yonge sonne
Hath in the Ram his half cours yronne,
And smale foweles maken melodye,
That slepen al the nyght with open ye
(So priketh hem nature in hir corages),
Thanne longen folk to goon on pilgrimages,
And palmeres for to seken straunge strondes,
To ferne halwes, kowthe in sondry londes;
And specially from every shires ende
Of Engelond to Caunterbury they wende,
The hooly blisful martir for to seke
That hem hath holpen whan that they were seeke.

(lines 1–18)

One set of implications is carried by the syntax, which has an elaboration
characteristic of material written in Latin or French, but not earlier English,
which tends to be more straightforward. This, though, is a very long,
complex sentence – in part to catch attention and to demonstrate the
author's powers at the start of a major poem. But its length and complexity
also have meaning. There is a deliberately delayed main verb: 'longen folk'
in line 12 provides the main verb and subject, and lines 1–4, 5–8 and 8–11
are all subordinate clauses of time, telling us just when people 'long' to
go on pilgrimage. This long lead-up gives prominence to the waited-for
subject and verb: line 12 is also the first to introduce humans to the
passage: before then it is the earth, flowers and birds which are awakening in spring. The syntactic pattern structures a difference of viewpoint
between the natural creation which awakes in sensual ways, and the
human one which experiences a spiritual awakening.

Or does it? That is how most critics read the passage, and they often
note that just as people here wake to God, so the whole of *The Canterbury
Tales* will end with a sermon in Jerusalem. But that is both too simple an
account of the religious context of Chaucer's world, and also not close
enough a reading of this passage. In line 18 we learn that the pilgrims seek
St Thomas because he has helped them when they were sick (the rhyme
emphasises the point). This is in fact not a religious urge, at all, but simply
gratitude because they too, like the flowers and birds, are again in good
physical shape after the winter and the illnesses associated with it.
Chaucer's delayed last point, about the physical basis for the pilgrim urge,
has been largely ignored (tucked away as it is in subordinate syntax), but
it points directly to the major conflict of the period, between the religious
and the secular – a conflict central to the *Tales* as a whole.

Chaucer's rich vocabulary operates in addition to – and more widely than – complex syntax. The language of the first two lines is fully Anglo-Saxon – 'shoures', 'soote', 'droghte', 'roote' – except for the dramatic verb 'perced'. It is of French origin, and it introduces a flow of exotic language: 'bathed' is original English, but 'veyne' and 'licour' are French, and then exoticism increases with 'vertu' and 'engendred', which while also in fact borrowed from French are still in sound evocative of their Latin origin – and here 'vertu' does not simply mean modern 'virtue' but also has its Latin sense of 'force' or 'virility'. So the sense of rebirth in these lines – or even reimpregnation – has a European cultural dynamic. It is not only the flowers and birds and people who are being invigorated: the language also implies the refertilisation of an old and wintery culture, just that process which Chaucer himself is undertaking through his work.

A wider invigoration of England and English itself is linguistically, poetically, created: in line 5 'Zephirus', the classically named god, has a fully English impact as his 'sweete breeth' lands on 'every holt and heeth' but the verb again carries exotic weight: in Latin 'inspiro' means 'breathe on', and 'so give life to'. Chaucer seems to be suggesting that English is a bleak monosyllabic literary landscape which can, through European subtlety – and his own rich manipulation of language – be made green and sophisticated.

The small birds are the first animals to wake in spring – as in any morning – but they too have cultural reference. They are 'smale', which means 'slender' not just small: the word is English, but has French connotations: ladies in romance are 'smale' in body, arms and fingers. Nature excites the birds' romantic love when it 'priketh' their hearts in blunt English, and this implies physicality – the sexual pun on 'prick' operates in Middle as well as Modern English. But elaboration still exists because it is their 'corages' that are excited, not their 'hearts'. The French word points towards the domain of courtly love, an aristocratic elaboration that Chaucer himself has disseminated in English with his translation of part of *The Romance of the Rose* and his earlier dream poems about love like *The Book of the Duchess*.

It might seem that French and Latin language is in this passage only used for love and such excitements: as the people appear, with their apparently religious feelings, the language of this passage becomes less European in its reference, with no more than a few non-referential French words being used like 'straunge' and 'specially'. When the saint himself is discussed the language has become completely Anglo-Saxon and increasingly monosyllabic: in the final couplet (lines 17–18) there are no words that are not found in Anglo-Saxon, including the originally Greek 'martir'.

But they are not only Anglo-Saxon: they are also plodding, plain lines, expressive of limitation, not spirituality. This alone should have made readers suspicious that the pilgrims being described are not entirely spiritual, but themselves physically motivated: Chaucer's account of true religion, as in the description of the Parson in the 'General Prologue', and even of the Plowman, is always delivered with at least some language of Latin origin and authority, the language of the church (of the Parson, 'diligent' [483], 'pacient' [484], 'vertuous' [515], 'discreet and benynge' [518], and of the Plowman 'pees and parfit charitee' [532]). Indeed, after looking at the way the language of the 'General Prologue' opening works, we might well feel that the sickness of the people is in fact associated with the limited, Anglo-Saxon nature of 'every holt and heeth' before this gentle and linguistically subtle Chaucerian wind started to blow.

This is not only a brilliant opening to a great poem; it is also a major poet's demonstration of how the full implications of rich language can transmit a vivid sense of what the human contexts felt like in a period. Here, as elsewhere, Chaucer's awareness of the implications of language both responds to and also communicates to us the historical, social, cultural and religious experiences of his remarkable – and remarkably realised – period.

Further Reading

The modern standard edition of Chaucer's *Works*, general editor Larry D. Benson (Oxford, Oxford University Press, 1988), contains a wide range of information on the tales and their contexts. Derek Pearsall's *Geoffrey Chaucer* (see below) is the most useful biography of the author in his historical setting. The most helpful general guide, with a good deal of contextual comment, is Helen Cooper, *The Canterbury Tales* (Oxford, Oxford University Press, second edn, 1996), and some context is discussed in Derek Brewer, *An Introduction to Chaucer* (London, Longman, second edn, 1998).

Books on Chaucer that pay particular attention to the contexts of his work include Peggy Knapp, *Chaucer and the Social Contest* (London, Routledge, 1990), S. H. Rigby, *Chaucer in Context* (Manchester, Manchester University Press, 1996), Helen Phillips, *An Introduction to the Canterbury Tales: Reading, Fiction, Context* (London, Macmillan – now Palgrave, 1999), Lillian M. Bisson, *Chaucer and the Late Medieval World* (London, Macmillan – now Palgrave, 1999) and Stephen Knight, *Geoffrey Chaucer* (Oxford, Blackwell, 1994). The religious context can be approached through Dee Dyas, *Images of Faith in English Literature* (London, Longman, 1998); Chaucer's language can be explored more fully through David Burnley, *A Guide to Chaucer's Language* (London, Macmillan – now Palgrave, 1983). There are many books on fourteenth-century history and society, but two that seem especially useful are J. T. Bolton, *The Medieval English Economy* (London, Dent, 1980) and S. H. Rigby, *English Society in the Later Middle Ages* (London, Macmillan – now Palgrave, 1995).

References

Geoffrey Chaucer, *The Works*, ed. L. D. Benson (Oxford, Oxford University Press, 1988).

Mary Carruthers, 'The Wife of Bath and the painting of lions', in *Feminist Readings in Middle English Literature*, ed. R. Evans and L. Johnson (London, Routledge, 1994).

Laurie Finke, '"Alle is for to selle": Breeding capital in the Wife of Bath's Prologue and Tale', in *The Wife of Bath*, ed. Peter G. Beidler (Boston, Bedford, 1996), 171–88.

Terry Jones, *Chaucer's Knight: The Portrait of a Mercenary* (London, Weidenfeld & Nicolson, 1980).

Stephen Knight, '*The Canterbury Tales*' in *Chaucer: Contemporary Essays in Criticism*, ed. V. Allen and A. Axiotis (London, Macmillan – now Palgrave, 1997), 156–68.

Jill Mann, *Chaucer and Medieval Estates Satire* (Cambridge, Cambridge University Press, 1973).

Lee Patterson, '"No Man His Resoun Herde": Peasant Consciousness, Chaucer's Miller, and the Structure of *The Canterbury Tales*', in Allen and Axiotis, *Chaucer* (1997) 169–92.

Derek Pearsall, *The Life of Geoffrey Chaucer* (Blackwell, Oxford, 1992).

2 Shakespeare: Theatrical and Historical Contexts

Martin Coyle

The interior of the Swan theatre, Bankside, 1596; from a drawing by the Dutchman Johannes de Witt.

I

The most obvious context for discussing Shakespeare's plays is the Globe theatre in Southwark, London, where many of the plays were first performed. We need to remember, however, that plays were staged not just outdoors at the Globe and other theatres, but also indoors at court. And the Globe itself was only built in 1599, more or less midway through Shakespeare's career; it would, therefore, be misleading to refer to it as the location of Shakespeare's plays before that date. Nevertheless, we can perhaps use the Globe as a kind of shorthand for the different kind of theatre and staging that existed in the early modern period which, in turn, will provide a basis for thinking about Shakespeare's texts. There are, too, other contexts in which we can consider the plays, contexts which will not only enrich our sense of the texts but also our own critical practice. In the sections that follow I try to illustrate some of these by taking three Shakespeare plays: a tragedy, a history and a comedy. I make no pretence of trying to cover the plays in detail or of giving a full context for each. The intention, rather, is to show how to use contextual material, and how to make a little go a long way. That seems to me one of the secrets of contextual study, and I had better say why.

It would be possible to draw up a long list of different contexts for Shakespeare's plays: social, political, linguistic, biographical, historical, textual and so on. No one would deny that these fields of study are important, and recent critical work has opened them up in a number of exciting new ways. There is, too, much to be gained from a book such as Richard Dutton's excellent *William Shakespeare: A Literary Life*, which gives both an overview of Shakespeare's work as a whole and detailed information about the theatres, acting companies and staging conventions. Indeed, Dutton's book seems to me an ideal starting-place for the study of Shakespeare. As with any work of this kind, however, it is easy to become swamped by the volume of information it offers and, in the process, miss its critical purpose. What Dutton offers is a complex and multilayered sense of the dramatic, intellectual and cultural framework in which Shakespeare was writing. But he is not suggesting that this contextual material provides an easy or direct explanation of the plays.

This was one of the problems with E. M. W. Tillyard's very famous and influential book, *The Elizabethan World Picture* (1943). Tillyard proposed too neat a relationship between the plays and their context, arguing that the Elizabethans shared a common belief in the concept of a cosmic order and that Shakespeare's plays endorsed this belief. According to this Elizabethan system, everything in the universe had its place in a set of correspondences. Thus, just as the sun was the prime light of the heavens, so the king was seen as the prime figure on earth, and the eagle first among the birds. Tillyard argued that underpinning the Elizabethan world picture – the social, political, religious and philosophical thinking of the age – was an awareness of the fallen state of humankind brought about by Adam and Eve. But not just this. The Tudors had come to the throne after the Wars of the Roses (1455–85), and Tillyard suggested, in his book on *Shakespeare's History Plays* (1944), that the bloodshed of that civil war had a profound influence on the Elizabethan psyche so that they came to accept a single set of ideas and values. In particular, they shared an abhorrence of rebellion and disorder.

If Tillyard's thesis is correct, then there is little left for us to dispute. The plays simply express a common set of meanings that they share with everything else in the period; there is a common philosophy and a common set of ideas. Given the rich diversity of the period, however, this seems not a little implausible, to say the least. Indeed, a close look at a map of Elizabethan London, showing the location of the playhouses, offers a very different kind of picture from that drawn by Tillyard. The place of the stage, to borrow the title of a book by Steven Mullaney, in such maps is not immediately obvious. A few theatres are dotted to the north of the city, and there is a cluster outside the city, specifically to the south, across the Thames. These theatres are located near the Bear Garden which was used for bear-baiting. Mullaney speaks of the theatres being sited in an area called the Liberties, outside the control of the City of London, but it is not clear if anything was really outside the control of the authorities. Nor is it clear if the theatres stood in opposition to the law and the church, challenging their moral values, or were part of a hierarchical ordering of the urban landscape. Possibly, though, the theatres stood in a more fluid, ambiguous relationship to the city, with their players able, both literally and symbolically, in terms of moving in and out of the social order, to cross the bridge back into London and the court, and then to retrace their journey. Whatever the merits of Tillyard's reading of the Elizabethan mind – and in some senses it remains both a powerful and persuasive account – it does not easily fit the kind of dynamic, changing, commercial culture the theatres themselves seem to symbolise and to stage. Tillyard offers us a sense of a world in which everyone knew their place and role, but the physical location of London's theatres offers a sense of a more mobile, perhaps even slightly anarchic, society.

There are other visual documents we might read alongside maps to fill out a concrete context for the plays, such as the drawing of the stage of the Swan theatre by Johannes de Witt, or the sketch by Henry Peacham of an early performance of *Titus Andronicus* (they are reprinted in *The*

Riverside Shakespeare, The Norton Shakespeare, and in Russ McDonald's excellent *The Bedford Companion to Shakespeare*). These two drawings are, in fact, key documents for constructing a sense of the spatial and cultural differences between the Elizabethan stage and our own modern theatres. Much has been written about them, especially the de Witt sketch with its depiction of an open stage jutting into the audience; above it is a structure representing the heavens, but also there is a trapdoor giving way to hell below. Of particular note is the absence of scenery and the essentially non-illusionist or non-realistic nature of the stage. It is, as such, a theatre quite unlike most modern playhouses, but one which was flexible enough to stage scenes ranging from battlefields to bedrooms, from the simplicity of the soliloquy to elaborate spectacle using machinery and music.

One straightforward thing to do with such drawings is to think about what it would be like to be there in Shakespeare's London as opposed to sitting watching a modern production. It could be argued, of course, that we no longer have to imagine Shakespeare's Globe, given the building of a replica of the Globe theatre on Bankside in London. Here it is possible to witness a performance in the open air during daylight, stand near the stage or sit in one of the tiered rows. The effect is startling: instead of the plays being closed off by an invisible fourth wall, there is an immediate sense of contact with the public sphere, as if the plays were almost quite literally bringing to light issues of social and political concern. Not that the modern Globe solves all our problems. Indeed, to some critics it seems to raise as many questions about what we are doing with Shakespeare as it provides historical evidence about how the plays were first performed. Isn't the new Globe a kind of theme park? Isn't it more about our commodification of Shakespeare than about Renaissance stage practices? Doesn't it actually demonstrate the impossibility of recovering or recreating the past? Such doubts linger about the new Globe. That, however, may be true of all contexts we bring to bear on the plays, that we can only see the past through the present, and that we need constantly to remind ourselves of its distance from the modern world.

Nevertheless, a visit to the Globe seems a practical way of trying to engage with a culture that is manifestly different from our own. But what if you cannot get there? What other sources are there? There are now a number of Shakespeare websites which offer a variety of visual information (see Further Reading). There are also the volumes in the Texts and Contexts series, including *Hamlet, Macbeth, The First Part of King Henry IV, A Midsummer Night's Dream* and *The Taming of the Shrew* (all listed in the References). These contain reprints of a range of historical materials: extracts from contemporary political works, pamphlets, treatises, official legal and religious documents, which offer a sense of the wider interpretative context. In addition, there are background books, such as the volume on *Elizabethan-Jacobean Drama* by G. Blakemore Evans, from which I quote three passages below in order to try and illustrate how context in the period can illuminate the text and vice versa. The dates I have in mind for the period, it is perhaps worth making clear, are 1576–1623; that is, from the opening of the first regular playhouse, called the Theatre, to the publication of Shakespeare's plays in a single volume, an edition known as the First Folio. We could equally refer to the period 1558–1642, that is from the start of Elizabeth's reign through to the beginning of the English Civil War and the establishment of the Commonwealth under Cromwell. Charles I was executed in 1649, and it has become a commonplace of modern criticism that the tensions and violence we see acted out in Elizabethan and Jacobean drama were a premonition of the Civil War. It could be argued that in all the extracts cited below there is a sense of a country moving almost imperceptibly towards such events; that what we see is a society engaged in a struggle to define itself, but already entangled in a violent clash of values. That may be an exaggeration, but it does provide a framework for thinking about the relationship between the plays and other writings of the period, and one sharply different from the ordered hierarchy envisaged by earlier 'contextual' critics such as Tillyard.

II

My concern, as I noted above, is largely with method, with relating historical and theatrical details to each other and exploring their implications. In essence, the method amounts to no more than taking a small extract and niggling away at its details, always on the look-out for how the context adds to our nuanced understanding of the play. In other words, we are not only searching for links between passages, but also thinking about how the evidence helps us grasp the larger pattern in the text, the larger questions about the social and political order and its tensions. I begin with an account of an Elizabethan performance of *Julius Caesar*:

On September 21st after lunch, about two o'clock, I and my party crossed the water, and there in the house with the thatched roof witnessed an excellent performance of the tragedy of the First Emperor Julius Caesar with a cast of some fifteen people; when the play was over, they danced very marvellously and gracefully together as is their wont, two dressed as men and two as women. . . .

. . . Thus daily at two in the afternoon, London has two, sometimes three plays running in different places, competing with each other, and those

which play best obtain most spectators. . . . The actors are most expen-
sively and elaborately costumed; for it is the English usage for eminent
lords or knights at their decease to bequeath and leave almost the best of
their clothes to their serving men, which it is unseemly for the latter to
wear, so that they offer them then for sale for a small sum to the actors.

(Blakemore Evans, 56–7)

This is an extract from the diary of Thomas Platter, a Swiss traveller who
visited England in 1599 (the original diary is in German). It offers, from the
perspective of a foreign visitor, a series of insights into the Elizabethan
theatre – here most probably the Globe itself, with its 'thatched roof' (*Julius
Caesar* may have been the first play to be staged there). The London
theatres had already become something of a tourist attraction even in
1599. We might be surprised that Platter says nothing about the main
figures in *Julius Caesar* or about the action of the play; he does, however, comment on the excellence of the performance, reminding us that
Shakespeare's was a professional company in competition with other
companies and other theatres.

We can find a similar kind of theatrical awareness in *Julius Caesar* itself
in the speeches immediately after the murder of Caesar (all quotations
from Shakespeare are from the Alexander edition):

Cassius Stoop then, and wash. How many ages hence
Shall this our lofty scene be acted over
In states unborn and accents yet unknown!
Brutus How many times shall Caesar bleed in sport,
That now on Pompey's basis lies along
No worthier than the dust!

(*Julius Caesar*, 3.1.112–17)

Cassius and Brutus both claim that the action on stage is real in contrast
to the 'sport' or acted version which will follow in 'ages hence'. They claim,
that is, a sort of historical authenticity, that what is being watched is actually happening, and that the audience is transported back into ancient
Rome. At the same time, the very words 'lofty scene', 'acted over' 'accents'
and 'sport' – the language of dramatic performance – remind us that what
we are watching is a play. This kind of doubleness may be what Platter
has in mind when he speaks of 'witnessing an excellent performance', as
if he were convinced that he was actually present as a witness at the death
of Caesar, while at the same time being aware of how artfully the whole
has been managed. Platter, then, provides us with a context for thinking

about the play's complex dramatic effect, as something that purports to be real but also fictional, and about how the Elizabethan theatre seems to work both at the level of realism and at the level of symbol.

But Platter also gives us another thread to trace when he refers to the costumes of the actors as expensive and elaborate. A key image running through Mark Antony's funeral oration over the dead Caesar is his reference to Caesar's cloak, something he uses to stir up the emotions of the crowd to take violent revenge against the assassins:

> If you have tears, prepare to shed them now.
> You all do know this mantle. I remember
> The first time ever Caesar put it on;
> 'Twas on a summer's evening, in his tent,
> That day he overcame the Nervii.
> Look! in this place ran Cassius's dagger through;
> See what a rent the envious Casca made.
>
> (3.2.169–75)

It may seem idle to speculate at this distance whether Caesar's cloak was indeed a Roman mantle or an Elizabethan gentleman's cast-off, but the evidence of the *Titus Andronicus* sketch is that in the Roman plays the nobles did wear Roman costumes while lesser figures wore contemporary dress. We cannot, however, be certain, and we might ask what difference it might make to have Caesar robed like an English gentleman or, possibly, even an English king. Or perhaps to have the conspirators in contemporary dress and Caesar alone in Roman costume. The play, we might conclude, is always potentially switching from its fictional historical time to the real time of its audience in 1599, so drawing them both visually and verbally into the debate it stages. That debate is about Caesar's aspirations to be king. The conspirators kill Caesar because they believe he seeks to replace the rule of the senate by monarchical government. In their eyes he aims at absolute power which they equate with tyranny. On stage his death and its causes come to be symbolised in the image of his cloak.

It is, then, perhaps no accident that Platter notices the costumes of the actors, nor that he mentions their connections with the larger political order of 'lords . . . knights . . . serving men'. The details of the passage direct us to the social hierarchy and how it is embedded in the very fabric of everyday life. But it also calls attention to how that hierarchy can as easily be overturned as clothes can be passed from hand to hand. In the image of serving men selling off the best clothes of their deceased lords we have perhaps a glimpse of a different order of things in which money rather than status matters, trade rather than class. It is a glimpse, we might argue, of an emergent modern world of buying and selling, entertainment and leisure, a world that threatens to replace the old hierarchical order of service and rank with one based on commodities and finance. Paradoxically, the imagery of clothing thus seems simultaneously to suggest both servitude and social mobility, a doubleness of meaning that reflects the cultural and historical changes of the late sixteenth century as a dying feudal structure gave way to an emergent capitalist society.

It has to be said, however, that Platter's diary is chiefly interesting for its note about the end of the performance. Tragedy, we have all learnt, excites pity and fear which is then purged; there is a catharsis. Platter, though, remembers not this moment of terror and release, a facing of death which we realise is not our own but will be. Instead, he recalls the graceful dance performed at the end of the play by two men and two men dressed as women. Did he remember it because it was graceful? Because the men were dressed as women? Because it fitted in with his idea of the theatre as entertainment? We don't know. What we perhaps learn is that Elizabethan expectations of theatre seem to have been very different from modern ones, or, at least, less rigid. We expect a play to end on a consistent note with a clear signal to the audience to clap, the lights in the theatre to come on and then to go home.

In Platter's account, however, the end of the play is not the end of the performance or the entertainment; it is not the end of the actors' exhibition of their skills and craft. If Platter's description suggests something of the modern world of entertainment and theatre, it also reminds us that the play belongs to a long-established tradition of popular drama in which the actors play to the crowd, ignoring the boundaries of the fictional world created by the plot. It is a drama that recognises the collective importance of ordinary people rather than the might of kings or emperors. Platter's account, it might be argued, in this contrast between the tragic events of the play and its comic end-dance, glances not just at a rift between high and low drama but at a potential rift in the social structure, a rift between rulers and the ruled which was to open up in 1642 into a civil war not unlike that dramatised in *Julius Caesar*. Platter's description, it thus would seem, tells us more about the political significance of the play than might initially appear to be the case from its lack of discussion of the action and characters. But what we also see here is the manner in which an awareness of, and use of, the theatrical and historical context can add to our sense of the kind of complex statement the play itself might have been making in terms of its society at this particular time. More concretely, what we see is the way in which contextual material can help us grasp the dynamic relationship between the open nature of Shakespeare's theatre and the surrounding political and social debates.

III

In this section I want to look briefly at a history play and then a comedy. Originally my intention had been to take *Richard II* as the history play and link it with Elizabeth's famous remark in which she compared herself to Richard II. There seemed to me to be some potential in the remark for examining the way in which the Queen actually conceived of herself as a kind of performer on a public stage. However, I could not find the speech in which she does that. I mention this point as an illustration of the kind of difficulty contextualising work can run up against. Sometimes the material does not appear immediately to hand or does not fit what you hoped to do. This is partly because working with context does involve some potentially quite complex research moves and searching for appropriate examples. In turn this can often lead to other possibilities and different ideas. In this case I knew that I wanted a speech by Elizabeth and something that might go with a history play. I came across the following:

Let tyrants fear; I have always so behaved myself that, under God, I have placed my chiefest strength and safeguard in the loyal hearts and good will of my subjects. And therefore I am come amongst you, as you see, at this time, not for my recreation and disport, but being resolved, in the midst and heat of the battle, to live or die amongst you all; to lay down for my God, and for my kingdom, and for my people, my honour and my blood, even in the dust. I know I have the body but of a weak and feeble woman, but I have the heart and stomach of a king, and of a king of England too, and think foul scorn that Parma or Spain, or any prince of Europe, should dare to invade the borders of my realm; to which, rather than any dishonour shall grow by me, I myself will take up arms, I myself will be your General, Judge, and Rewarder of every one of your virtues in the field. I know, already for your forwardness, you have deserved rewards and crowns; and we do assure you, in the word of a prince, they shall be duly paid you. In the mean time, my Lieutenant-General shall be in my stead, than whom never prince commanded a more noble or worthy subject; not doubting but by your obedience to my General, by your concord in the camp, and your valour in the field, we shall shortly have a famous victory over those enemies of my God, of my kingdoms, and of my people.

(Blakemore Evans, 183)

This is Queen Elizabeth, at Tilbury in 1588, visiting her troops just after the defeat of the Spanish Armada, but with the Duke of Parma still threatening an invasion from Holland. The Queen travelled to Tilbury by barge and delivered the oration on August 9th (it is recorded in a letter from a Dr Leonel Sharp to the Duke of Buckingham). It seems clear that Elizabeth deliberately 'staged' her approach to her army in order to have maximum impact in the same way that Mark Antony 'stages' his funeral oration over Caesar's body. Indeed, much has been made in recent criticism of the dramatic nature of royal power and the potentially intrinsic relationship between theatre and monarchy. Perhaps the most powerful evidence of this link is the public executions staged to remind the populace of the terrifying punishments the state, in the figure of Elizabeth, had at its command. This connection between the scaffold and the stage forms the basis of Leonard Tennenhouse's book *Power on Display*, which examines the extent to which the stage and state mirror each other in terms of the devices they use to dramatise power and control. In this particular instance, however, the connection seems more obviously to be between the stage and the sea. Elizabeth addresses her army from her barge on the Thames, as if she wishes to associate herself with the force of the sea or with the image of such men as Sir Francis Drake, who had commanded the fleet against the Spanish Armada.

In addition to this idea of the theatrical nature of monarchical power, there are other themes we can draw out of Elizabeth's speech which might prove useful in thinking about Shakespeare's history plays. For one thing, there is the strong focus upon rhetoric, upon the power of language to persuade, win over, move, change, influence. Elizabeth emphasises that she has 'come amongst you, as you see', so suggesting a parallel with Christ appearing to the disciples. Repeatedly she draws attention to herself through the use of 'I' or 'I myself', so that we are made intensely aware of her presence. Similarly, she stresses the position of her listeners as worthy and loyal subjects, praising them, and building the speech into a carefully wrought climax of balanced phrases: 'my God', 'my kingdoms', 'my people'. Throughout, the language works to manoeuvre the moment into a larger hierarchical structure akin to Tillyard's Elizabethan world picture, with Elizabeth as God's commander on earth and her loyal subjects in their proper place. It is not, then, that Tillyard's picture did not exist. What Elizabeth's speech tells us is that, rather than being ingrained in the natural order of Elizabethan thinking, it was part of official state rhetoric designed for political purposes to secure a fixed social order.

We can set Elizabeth's speech against Henry V's address in Shakespeare's play of that name to his troops just before the battle against the

French at Agincourt where the English are completely outnumbered and seem doomed to die:

> This day is call'd the feast of Crispian.
> He that outlives this day, and comes safe home,
> Will stand a tip-toe when this day is nam'd
> And rouse him at the name of Crispian.
> He that shall live this day, and see old age,
> Will yearly on the vigil feast his neighbours,
> And say 'Tomorrow is Saint Crispian'. . . .
> We few, we happy few, we band of brothers;
> For he to-day that sheds his blood with me
> Shall be my brother; be he ne'er so vile
> This day shall gentle his condition;
> And gentlemen in England, now a-bed
> Shall think themselves accurs'd they were not here.
> (King Henry V, 4.3.40–65)

Like Elizabeth, Henry seeks to inspire his men to further heroic effort against the enemy. Like Elizabeth, too, Henry employs repetition of emotive names to move his listeners, and, indeed, the two speeches share a number of other common political tactics: the direct contact with the audience through personal pronouns; the use of religious values to endorse the appeal to patriotism; the identifying of a common enemy threatening England. What is also evident in the two speeches is the construction of a certain kind of identity for speaker and audience which is both gendered and nationalistic. Elizabeth, we see, acknowledges her 'weak and feeble' body as a woman, but then aligns her courage with that of a 'king of England'; Henry, more obviously, plays upon the ideal of Englishness linked to a masculine world of fighting.

Elizabeth's visit to Tilbury was an intervention at a crucial point in the war with Spain; she needed her army to stay loyal and firm in resolve, but she also needed them to obey and remain her subjects. The fictional Henry's emphasis is different: his stress is upon brotherhood, upon a sort of equality achieved through noble action and fighting. It could be suggested that Henry V is here treading on politically sensitive ground: Elizabeth has only money to offer her army, while the play suggests that the proper reward for fighting for England should be a 'gentl[ing]' of one's 'condition', an ennobling of one's status. Henry's promise, in other words, seems to undermine the fixed hierarchy that Elizabeth carefully constructs in her speech. Where she emphasises position and order – she is God's 'General, Judge and

Rewarder', they are her obedient subjects – Henry speaks of the ordinary soldier becoming his 'brother', suggesting a much more mobile social structure based on merit, though one noticeably excluding women.

It might be argued, however, that Henry is simply making a magnanimous gesture, given the situation in the play, with the English totally outnumbered by the French, and that his words are not meant to be taken too literally. In turn this raises the question of how we are to interpret political speeches: do Elizabeth and Henry really mean what they say, or is it just a case of saying what is needed at that moment? Perhaps political speeches are always provisional in this way, and always ambivalent in the promises they make. But they are also always concerned with potential threats to the political order, both from within and from without. Behind both speeches lies the recognition of the obvious importance of keeping troops loyal, whatever the cost, since they are not only the means to defeat external enemies, but also the way of maintaining internal order in the country. In a sense it does not really matter what Henry promises: as long as he controls the army, he can control his kingdom, be it France or England. Power here is more than a theatrical gesture: it is the very real business of armed soldiers who will carry out the king's wishes.

Henry's speech succeeds, as does Mark Antony's when he persuades the crowd to turn against the assassins of Caesar. The power of rhetoric is a theme that runs through the histories and the Roman plays, but it is also something common to this period in which rhetoric was taught and valued in the education system. Indeed, it seems evident that the audience went to the Globe not just to watch but to listen to well-delivered speeches. That, at least, is the implication of Thomas Heywood's advice in his *Apology for Actors* (1612) to 'speak well' and for the speaker 'not to . . . confound his voice in the hollow of his throat, or tear his words hastily betwixt his teeth' (Blakemore Evans, 85). But the audience are also constantly addressed in the plays of the period and implicitly asked what they think. It is in this sense that the history plays, like the tragedies, are interrogative rather than realistic, encouraging debate as much as consent. This ties in with the point made above about costume in *Julius Caesar*, and how Renaissance plays override the limits of theatrical realism, breaking through their fictional worlds to forge connections with the audience and their contemporary society. Henry speaks to his men before the battle, but the language is also calculated to include the audience, momentarily merging past with present only for the last line to remind the audience that 'they were not' there after all, that the male, heroic world of Agincourt is no more. The historical context of the play in this way becomes double; it embraces both England in 1415, in the battle against the French, and England in 1599, when English soldiers were sent by Elizabeth to quell rebellion in Ireland. One context reflects and refracts another as the play shifts between times, touching a number of historical moments, and, of course, eventually erupts in the violence of our own time.

I began this discussion by noting that I could not find Elizabeth's speech about Richard II. What I have offered instead is a series of tentative comparisons between another of her speeches and Henry V's address at Agincourt, trying to open up similarities and differences about the operation of the language in the different domains of the theatrical and the real. At the same time, I have tried to suggest how both speeches lead back to large questions about the political and social order and threats to it. Underlying the analysis is not simply the point that literary texts always engage with contemporary concerns but also the more central point about the way in which texts function, how they embody the conflicts and contradictions of a society caught up in a process of transformation. We cannot, of course, know how Elizabethan audiences responded to the dramatisation of English history. Did they, as Tillyard proposed in his book on the histories, believe in a history shaped by providence directing events towards the founding of the Tudor state, or is that the very notion which the plays question? The evidence seems to be that, while Elizabeth's speech follows orthodox political thinking, Henry's recognises that the old feudal, heroic world has gone, that England is changing and that the new pressures are beginning to make themselves felt. Taken together the two speeches suggest the same kind of rift that was evident in Platter's account of *Julius Caesar*, of a society enmeshed in conflicting discourses as it undergoes transformation and alteration. What the use of contextual material offers, then, is, in part, an opportunity to verify something we have sensed in the text itself, but also, as in this case, where we are comparing two forms of discourse – that in the play and that in a speech by the Queen – the use of contextual material can add considerably to our perception of the fuller implications of what is said.

IV

It may be relatively straightforward to find contextual material for the histories and tragedies, primarily because they deal with recognisably urgent issues of public record. What, though, of the comedies? Comedy can seem the most elusive of the genres to contextualise simply because it deals with the most elusive of subjects: love. On the other hand, there does seem to be a common pattern in the plays. We know that in most comedies the demands of plot lead to disguise, with boy actors playing the parts of girls who disguise themselves as boys, so that the characteristic action of comedy is a confusion of identity and gender roles. This confusion is dependent on the specific historical circumstances and conventions of the Elizabethan stage, with its absence of women actors and use of men or boys to play female roles. It was this which, above all, outraged the Puritans in their opposition to the theatres and which led in turn, both on stage and off, to counter-accusations against the Puritans as not only kill-joys but sexually corrupt hypocrites. But the matter went beyond mere charge and counter-charge. At issue was a struggle about the values society was to adopt as it moved into the seventeenth century. We can see some of this at work in *Twelfth Night*, written around 1601, shortly after *Julius Caesar* and *Henry V*, both of which belong to 1599.

In *Twelfth Night* Malvolio, Olivia's steward and the play's kill-joy, is duped by his fellow servant Maria into believing his mistress Olivia loves him. Maria's plot involves dropping love-letters for Malvolio to find 'wherein, by the colour of his beard, the shape of his leg, the manner of his gait, the expressure of his eye, forehead, and complexion, he shall find himself most feelingly personated' (2.3.146–9). The ruse works, and Malvolio is persuaded to exchange his usual wear for that of a lover, in particular, to wear 'yellow-stockings' which are 'cross-garter'd' (2.5.138). On stage Malvolio is thus made to look a complete fool and is forced to join in the carnival festival world he scorns at the beginning of the play.

Carnival, however, is not necessarily pleasant, and there is something vicious in the way that Malvolio is pushed towards madness by the other characters as they take their revenge upon him for his pomposity. But there seems even more to it than this. Despite his Italian-sounding name, Malvolio clearly does not originate in the fictional romance world of Illyria in which the play is set. He is instead a recognisable type from the contemporary world of the Elizabethan audience. He is a Puritan obsessed with decorum and behaviour, a figure like the Puritan Philip Stubbes who, in his *The Anatomie of Abuses* (1583), attacked both plays and contemporary fashion:

> Then have they netherstocks to these gay hosen, not of cloth (though never so fine), for that is thought too base, but of Jarnsey worsted, crewel, silk, thread, and such like, or else at the least of the finest yarn that can be, and so curiously knit with open seam down the legs, with quirks and clocks about the ankles, and sometime (haply) interlaced with gold or silver threads, as is wonderful to behold . . .
>
> To these their netherstocks, they have corked shoes, pinsnets, and fine pantofles, which bear them up a finger or two from the ground, whereof some be of white leather, . . . black, and . . . red; some of black velvet

. . . raced, carved, cut, and stitched all over with silk and laid on with gold, silver, and such like. Yet, notwithstanding, to what good uses serve these pantofles, except it be to wear in a private house, or in a man's chamber, to keep him warm?

(Blakemore Evans, 132)

Stubbes is writing about what he sees as the extravagance of men's fashionable dress outside the theatre. His diatribe is a mixture of horrified fascination and moral outrage, but he is particularly concerned with the way that laws about dress were being violated. As Blakemore Evans notes (129), in 1565 the government had resurrected the sumptuary laws which laid down who could wear what kind of fabrics. These laws were designed to preserve class distinctions by making visible such things as occupation, social status and gender. Read in this context, Stubbe's satire is more than a protest against the rapidly changing fashions of Elizabethan middle-class society, itself a sign of the buoyant economy and the growth of a new if small sector of the population able to afford lavish clothes, including imported fashions. Rather, Stubbes is attacking those forces in society which were sweeping aside the visible signs of order such as dress and social propriety in favour of a new moral decadence.

In the play, Malvolio's yellow stockings are, then, a symbol not just of his folly but of his social aspirations, as a lover, to become a man of fashion married to Olivia's wealth and status. But the suggestion also seems to be that what drives the Puritans on is envy of the rich, and that Puritanism itself is a kind of disguise hiding a vain self-love. To this extent the play seems deliberately not only to mirror Stubbes's accusations, but to represent them as the suppressed desires of Puritanism. The perceptive reader might, of course, intuitively have grasped that there is some connection between Malvolio and the sexual attitudes encountered in seventeenth-century Puritanism. The use of contextual material, however, not only gives substance to the intuition, but it also enables us to investigate layer upon layer of complication within seventeenth-century attitudes. Significantly, elsewhere Stubbes writes of the abomination of cross-dressing in plays, with boys dressed as women being kissed by men (Blakemore Evans, 11). The charge levied at the plays becomes thus a charge of covert homosexuality, of a vicarious titillating of the audience and an offensive flouting of moral values. The trick against Malvolio seems designed to turn him into the very image of Stubbes's obsessions, a cross-dressed man in love with a woman played by a boy-actor. Indeed, in the play it looks as though Stubbes's worst fears will be fulfilled when Malvolio offers to come to Olivia's bed; here, with a boy playing the part of Olivia, the action totters on the edge of homoeroticism. But it is only a tottering: in the carnival world of comedy all manner of irrational behaviour is allowed to reign for a while before it is checked by the restoration of everyday life at the end of the play.

I am not arguing that *Twelfth Night* was specifically written against Stubbes or that Malvolio is a portrait of Stubbes. I am simply saying that the play includes a ridiculing of Puritan obsessions. For Stubbes the theatre is a site of transgression, a dangerous place where Christian and social traditionalism are being destroyed. It is this wider context that allows us to grasp why the play centres on Malvolio and why, in the end, it is more than just a piece of light-hearted fun. The theatres were part of a changing social structure in which not only old values were under increasing pressure but new political and religious forces were making themselves felt. Malvolio's Puritanism itself may not seem very serious in the play, but outside the Liberties, in the City, it was to be a different story. Ironically, even as Thomas Platter was travelling to the Globe from Switzerland to enjoy a play about the killing of a would-be king and potential tyrant, Calvin and other Protestant reformers in Switzerland were inspiring the Puritan revolution which resulted in the Civil War, the closing of the theatres in 1642, and the execution of the king in 1649.

As I noted above, it is a commonplace of modern criticism that the tensions and violence we see on stage in Shakespeare's plays anticipated the conflicts that were later to erupt into the English Civil War of 1642, and that this provides a framework for contextual criticism in this period. Similarly, I have suggested that the way to work with contextual material is to look closely at the details, but also to bear in mind the larger pattern, the larger issues. It is the case that every extract will disclose a society undergoing a transformation of values and ideas; every extract will be concerned with some kind of conflict or contradiction. In the discussion above I have also suggested that it is important to hold on to the differences between the plays and their contexts so that we do not merge them into a unified world picture or see the latter as somehow 'explaining' the former. Indeed, the purpose of looking at contexts is the very reverse of this. Contextual study is a way of opening up the text to new readings and new meanings with the aim of arriving at a more subtle understanding of the text and of its complex relationship both to its own time and to ours.

Further Reading

Not all the books listed here deal directly with context, but they do offer a range of stimulating material and approaches to the topic.

Catherine Belsey, *The Subject of Tragedy* (London, Methuen, 1985).

Catherine Belsey, *Shakespeare and the Loss of Eden* (Basingstoke, Macmillan – now Palgrave, 1999).

Jonathan Dollimore, *Radical Tragedy* (Brighton, Harvester, 1983).

John Drakakis (ed.), *Alternative Shakespeares* (London, Methuen, 1985).

Andrew Gurr, *The Shakespearean Stage, 1574–1642* (Cambridge, Cambridge University Press, 1980).

Terence Hawkes (ed.), *Alternative Shakespeares: Volume 2* (London, Routledge, 1996).

Peter Hyland, *An Introduction to Shakespeare: The Dramatist in his Context* (Basingstoke, Macmillan – now Palgrave, 1996).

Graham Holderness, *Shakespeare: The Histories* (Basingstoke, Macmillan – now Palgrave, 2000).

David Scott Kastan (ed.), *A Companion to Shakespeare* (Oxford, Blackwell, 1999).

Arthur F. Kinney (ed.), *Renaissance Drama: An Anthology of Plays and Entertainments* (Oxford, Blackwell, 1999).

Kathleen McLuskie, *Renaissance Dramatists: Feminist Readings* (Hemel Hempstead, Harvester Wheatsheaf, 1989).

Michael Neill, *Issues of Death* (Oxford, Clarendon Press, 1997).

Gerald M. Pinciss and Roger Lockyer (ed.), *Shakespeare's World: Background Readings in the English Renaissance* (New York, Continuum, 1995).

Kiernan Ryan (ed.), *Shakespeare: Texts and Contexts* (Basingstoke, Macmillan – now Palgrave, 2000).

David Underdown, *Revel, Riot, and Rebellion: Popular Politics and Culture in England 1603–1660* (Oxford, Clarendon Press, 1985).

Valerie Wayne (ed.), *The Matter of Difference* (Hemel Hempstead, Harvester Wheatsheaf, 1991).

Stanley Wells (ed.), *The Cambridge Companion to Shakespeare Studies* (Cambridge, Cambridge University Press, 1986).

Richard Wilson and Richard Dutton (eds), *New Historicism and Renaissance Drama* (London, Longman, 1992).

Websites

http://daphne.palomar.edu/shakespeare
http://www.library.upenn.edu/etext/furness
http://www.wwnorton.com/nael

References

Peter Alexander (ed.), *William Shakespeare: The Complete Works* (London and Glasgow, Collins, 1953).

William C. Carroll (ed.), *William Shakespeare: 'Macbeth': Texts and Contexts* (Boston, New York, Bedford/St. Martin's – now Palgrave, 1999).

Frances E. Dolan, *William Shakespeare: 'The Taming of the Shrew': Texts and Contexts* (Boston, New York, Bedford/St. Martin's – now Palgrave, 1996).

Richard Dutton, *William Shakespeare: A Literary Life* (Basingstoke and London, Macmillan – now Palgrave, 1989).

G. Blakemore Evans (ed.), *Elizabethan-Jacobean Drama* (London, A. & C. Black, 1988).

G. B. Evans (ed.), *The Riverside Shakespeare* (Boston, Houghton Mifflin, 1974).

Stephen Greenblatt et al. (eds), *The Norton Shakespeare* (New York, Norton, 1997).

Barbara Hodgdon (ed.), *William Shakespeare: 'The First Part of King Henry The Fourth': Texts and Contexts* (Boston, New York, Bedford/St. Martin's – now Palgrave, 1997).

Russ McDonald (ed.), *The Bedford Companion to Shakespeare: An Introduction with Documents* (New York, St. Martin's – now Palgrave, 1996).

Steven Mullaney, *The Place of the Stage: License, Play, and Power in Renaissance England* (Chicago, University of Chicago Press, 1988).

Gail Kern Paster (ed.), *William Shakespeare: 'A Midsummer Night's Dream': Texts and Contexts* (Boston, New York, Bedford/St. Martin's – now Palgrave, 1999).

Leonard Tennenhouse, *Power on Display: The Politics of Shakespeare's Genres* (London, Methuen, 1986).

E. M. W. Tillyard, *The Elizabethan World Picture* (London, Chatto & Windus, 1943).

E. M. W. Tillyard, *Shakespeare's History Plays* (London, Chatto & Windus, 1944).

Susanne L. Wofford (ed.), *William Shakespeare: 'Hamlet': Texts and Contexts* (Boston, New York, Bedford/St. Martin's – now Palgrave, 1994).

3 Shakespeare: Interpretative Contexts

Catherine Belsey

An illustration for Act III, Scene 2 of Hamlet, published in the early twentieth century.

His father is dead and his mother has married his uncle – with what most people would call indecent haste. At midnight on the castle walls an apparition, speaking in the name of the father, demands revenge for murder by the same uncle. In the heat of the moment, horrified to hear his own worst suspicions confirmed, the Prince would readily risk damnation to obey his father's Ghost but, on subsequent reflection, the project – and the possible consequences of the project – are not, after all, so simple. 'To be, or not to be, that is the question' (*Hamlet*, 3.1.55).

But what exactly *is* the question? What is Hamlet asking himself here?

> Whether 'tis nobler in the mind to suffer
> The slings and arrows of outrageous fortune,
> Or to take arms against a sea of troubles,
> And by opposing, end them. To die . . .
>
> (3.1.56–9)

Is it more honourable to 'suffer', to permit luck to do its worst (however appalling) or to fight back, to put an end to the problem (however overwhelming) – and die? Death, after all, is no more than sleep. Who wouldn't choose to be rid of the accumulated miseries of this life, if it weren't for what might happen in the next? But after death there is a price to be paid for the wrong choice. 'Thus conscience does make cowards of us all' (3.1.82), and the question which alternative is nobler remains apparently unanswered.

The Victorians assumed, almost without exception, that in this soliloquy Hamlet was considering suicide as a way out of his difficulties: 'And by opposing end them. To die . . .' But there was always, even in the nineteenth century, an alternative possibility: taking arms, opposition, do not sound like evasion; and suicide is 'noble' elsewhere in Shakespeare only after taking arms and losing, preferably in ancient Rome, where it offered an honourable way to avoid humiliation. What the Ghost is asking for is another murder, which in this case is also regicide, but early modern revengers don't usually get away with either. 'And by opposing end them. To die . . .' Is Hamlet perhaps not thinking of killing himself, after all, but debating an ethical question: whether it is nobler to tolerate a wrong without protest, when righting it may incur not only death, but also damnation?

How are we to decide? The words on the page do not settle the issue. They can be read either way. The words on the *stage*, by contrast, have often settled it in advance, by bringing the speech into line with the actor's or the director's understanding of Hamlet's role in *Hamlet* – in the light, that is to say, of an interpretation of the play as a whole. The individual performance can imply deliberation about either suicide or killing Claudius accordingly.

Readers have understood Shakespeare in different ways at distinct historical moments, in the light of their own cultural perspectives. Victorian criticism largely took for granted the view that revenge was a sacred duty, violence was a reasonable way of solving problems, and Hamlet's primary obligation was to obey his father. The fact that it took him five Acts to get round to killing Claudius made most critics and, indeed, most actors of the period, conclude that there must be something radically wrong with Hamlet himself. They commonly portrayed him as a slight, pale, languid, melancholy, but thoughtful figure, who found the world's demand for action too much to cope with. The part was often played by women, on the grounds that fit male actors might look too muscular to impersonate the poetic Prince. In 1904 A. C. Bradley produced his brilliant reading of the play as the case history of a clinical depressive, pathologically incapable of decisive intervention on behalf of what he knew to be right.

For Bradley, as for Coleridge a hundred years earlier, the plays were primarily character studies. Novelistic 'rounded' protagonists were the origin of everything that occurred on the stage. In effect, Hamlet was the explanation of *Hamlet*. At that time, making sense of the plays was relatively simple, if a bit dull, not least because it had been done so well for so long. You had to analyse the characters to reveal their motives, declared or otherwise, see how they fitted together to make the plot, and elicit from their success or failure a universal moral message (in this instance, 'just do it').

What has changed? In the case of *Hamlet*, two world wars and any number of more localised but no less bloody struggles have called into question the idea that violence is necessarily the best way of righting wrongs. Meanwhile, fathers no longer seem entitled to unquestioning obedience from beyond the grave. Just doing it, when 'it' means killing your uncle, who is also the king, as well as the husband of the mother you love, does not appear quite so straightforward.

More generally, explanations are not now so easily traceable to character. In real life, individuals, we tend to think, are to a degree produced by their culture, and personality is not, therefore, the only source of events, or the sole origin of history. On the contrary, we need history to account for individuality, to explain how our culture makes us to a high degree the people we are. Meanwhile, interpretation, too, is a cultural product. The Victorian *Hamlet* made sense in terms of certain Victorian values. It makes less sense now. Interpreting the text has come to be seen as historically and culturally relative.

Can we then decide the nature of Hamlet's question? Possibly not. Directors may have to: they want to produce a play which will be intelligible to an audience, even if this is not the only possible version of the play Shakespeare wrote. A production is always, self-evidently, one interpretation. But for criticism, what would constitute a decision? What, in other words, are we trying to settle? Hamlet is a fictional figure: he has no independent existence; what he is 'really' thinking is an illusion. Would his author's intentions for him satisfy us, then? In the first instance, however, we have no access to Shakespeare's intentions, but only a text, and the meaning of the text, plural, polysemic, undecidable, is the problem we are trying to resolve. And second, recent Shakespearean criticism has tended to see the plays as theatrical events, the effect of a collaboration between an author and a company, and thus group productions. Shakespeare's intentions were by no means the only determinant of what early modern audiences actually saw. Are we then looking to the original stage performance for an answer, Burbage's Hamlet as the definitive interpretation? But even if we had records of how Burbage played the part, which performance would count as decisive? The first? Or a later version, improved with practice? Three early modern printed texts of *Hamlet*, two quarto publications and a folio, all different, may conjecturally represent distinct performances, with some of Shakespeare's original words modified, deleted or rewritten, as the company discovered over time what would work best on the stage. In the second quarto Hamlet has more soliloquies than he does in the later folio, where he appears correspondingly less hesitant. There was not necessarily one single moment when Shakespeare's company, the Lord Chamberlain's Men, got it 'right'.

We may, then, have to settle for uncertainty, recognising that undecidability is the condition of interpretation, in this as in so many other instances. Is *Julius Caesar*, for example, about the tragic failure of resistance to tyranny, or the naïvety of idealism in the world of realpolitik? It depends on how you play it. Should we see *Antony and Cleopatra* as the greatest love story ever told, a satirical picture of a shared mid-life crisis, or something in-between? And if we cannot settle these questions finally, absolutely, what are the consequences for criticism? If there is no one correct reading, does that mean that any interpretation of Shakespeare is as good as any other, that we are entitled to make sense of the plays in whatever way we choose?

Stage directors must have a free hand: they have no obligations to historical reading. But scholars and critics can, in my view, misread. It is possible to misunderstand through not knowing the full range of meanings of the words. Did some of the Victorian critics, perhaps, confine 'suffer' to 'undergo pain', without recognising the more archaic meaning of 'allow', 'put up with'? Shakespearean vocabulary is extensive and dense. In addition, it is possible to read inattentively: to ignore counter-indications in the text itself. The other figures in the play do not seem to complain that Hamlet is ineffectual or effeminate. On the contrary, Claudius is frightened enough to send him away to be killed; Fortinbras thinks he was likely to have proved most royal (5.2.398). Moreover, there is also a pragmatics of the theatre: plays set up a critical relationship between the events on stage and the audience. Some scholars too easily conflate the opinions of the characters with the values of the play, as if we were invited to take Hamlet's own agonised self-castigation as the only possible assessment of his reluctance to murder his mother's husband, who is also his uncle and the king.

In other words, the text has a degree of autonomy, and can reasonably be invoked to limit the range of readings we should be prepared to take seriously. Plays do not belong exclusively in the heads of their audiences or readers. It does not follow that because we no longer have confident access to a single 'objective' meaning, interpretation is all 'subjective'. If it were so, if the plays had no independent, material existence, we should hardly be able to tell one from another. If meaning was mine to determine, how would I know whether I was reading *Macbeth* or *A Midsummer Night's Dream* – or *Middlemarch*, come to that? Reading is a transaction between an individual and a work. We make sense of texts, but that does not mean we invent them.

I have suggested, however, that distinct cultural moments make alternative *Hamlets*, that different assumptions produce different readings. This acknowledgement releases the possibility of a criticism which takes active control of its own practices. We have recently come to recognise that the sense we make of a text depends to a degree on the questions we ask about it. During the Second World War, E. M. W. Tillyard sensed the imminent danger of democratisation as a result of the mixing of classes that war always creates. Soldiers had seen their officers at close quarters, in some cases with justifiable scepticism, and there was a determination not to return to the extreme inequalities of the nineteen-thirties. The question the conservative Tillyard silently, perhaps unconsciously, asked was, 'How can the Elizabethan golden age be shown to demonstrate the virtues of a hierarchic society?' In *The Elizabethan World Picture* (1943) and *Shakespeare's History Plays* (1944) he argued, brilliantly, fluently, in favour of seeing the culturally sophisticated, early modern world as a profoundly authoritarian society, and Shakespeare, the genius, as its deeply conservative voice.

But just how conservative *are* Shakespeare's histories? Tillyard's case was so persuasive that for more than one generation after the war it seemed to critics on the left, as well as the right, that the plays were deeply reactionary. Are they? The monarchy of Richard II is an unremitting disaster, because the King is not capable of running the country. Henry IV doesn't do much better: filled with guilt, he cannot control a factional nation. And Henry V, the great Christian hero immortalised by Laurence Olivier? He exports the war on shaky legal grounds, and when a common soldier questions his right to require the sacrifice of arms, legs and heads, and the pain of the consequent widows and orphans, the King replies that death is fine as long as your conscience is clear. Anyone bent on promoting hierarchy as an ideal system of government could surely do better than this? To compete with Tillyard's, the alternative case would need to be argued equally patiently, historically and fluently, but even my caricature perhaps indicates that there is room for debate, that the distinct values of another moment in history more than half a century after Tillyard's may lead to a different interpretation.

Racial politics changed too in the course of the twentieth century. Embarrassment about Britain's imperial past and commitment to its multicultural present mean that the time has long gone when it was acceptable to identify Othello as a 'noble savage', or worse. Nor, paradoxically, is it helpful to go along with the Duke's judgement to Brabantio: 'If virtue no delighted beauty lack, / Your son-in-law is far more fair than black' (*Othello*, 1.3.289–90). Liberal colour-blindness like Desdemona's ('I saw Othello's visage in his mind', 1.3.252) does not resolve the question of the relationship between race and power, but merely denies its existence. The play alludes again and again to the hero's blackness, but what exactly does it say about racial difference?

Here too, directors and critics may have distinct projects. A production of *Othello* is inevitably political in our own current context, and necessarily makes a statement about race, beginning with its casting of the protagonist. But the case it puts forward, or that director and cast construct, might not be the same in London as it would be in Washington, DC, where the specific historical disgrace to be acknowledged is not imperialism, but slavery. Similarly, when Janet Suzman produced the play in the old, apartheid South Africa, she was making a defiant gesture in opening up Shakespeare to black performers, whereas in India, where the mission schools had so effectively co-opted Shakespeare on behalf of empire, it might be more genuinely radical not to produce his plays at all.

Critics, by contrast, might be interested in the historical difference between our own perceptions of blackness and those of Shakespeare's early audiences. The play was the product of a society already fascinated by travellers' tales of distant cultures, and beginning to be interested in the mercantile possibilities of colonial conquest. Some of this appears in Othello's stories of cannibals and men with shoulders above their heads, as well as the references to his own captivity and sale into slavery (we should, perhaps, remember that Africans enslaved each other at this time, as well as being victims of the European slave trade). Imperial values developed a mythology of white civilisation and black barbarity, which readily mapped onto an existing system of differences, familiar from Christianity on the one hand and secular love poetry on the other, between what was fair, beautiful and good and all that was dark, ugly and evil (see Hall, *Things of Darkness*).

At the same time, it is noticeable that the most overtly racist statements in *Othello* are made by the least sympathetic characters, Iago, Brabantio and Roderigo, and are consistently prompted by the villain himself. Racial contempt in the play is associated primarily with the wanton and deadly destructiveness of a white Venetian. The hero himself begins to worry about his own blackness only after Iago has ensnared his imagination in delusions of betrayal and loss. This play too is plural, perhaps un-decidable, but on one possible reading, the colour blindness of the virtuous figures is not adequate to counter the incitement to racial hatred which is depicted as truly uncivilised. Surely Iago, not Othello, represents the real 'erring barbarian' here (1.3.355–6).

Meanwhile, it is in the sphere of gender that historical difference most challenges traditional readings of the plays. Here our own cultural posi-tioning makes perceptible features that were barely visible as recently as two generations ago. In the light of Michel Foucault's account of sexual history, and Thomas Laqueur's history of anatomy, most people now agree that the cementing of sexual difference and sexual identities in terms of simple binary oppositions – masculine and feminine, gay and straight – took place as late as the eighteenth century. What once seemed like nature now appears culturally specific in the sphere of sexual- and gender-identifications too. For the early modern period friendship might be as powerful as sexual love. Moreover, homoerotic practices did not nec-essarily point to homosexuality as their point of origin and explanation. Identity was perceived as more fluid, or perhaps more discontinuous; beautiful boys might attract both men and women without impugning the 'normality' of either; cross-dressing could have an effect on behaviour, demonstrating the degree to which gender itself is performative.

In our own postmodern culture this discontinuity and performativity no longer seem so surprising, or so disturbing. Shakespeare's sonnets are love poems to both a fair young man and a dark woman. In the plays intense relationships between men – Antonio and Sebastian, Coriolanus and Aufidius, even Antony and Enobarbus – are taken for granted. Women may be loyal to women (like Paulina to Hermione), even when this conflicts with their commitment to their husbands (like Emilia's to Iago). And girls dressed as boys, but played by boys dressed in the first instance as girls, are central to the plots of no less than five comedies or romances.

Early modern love is anarchic and unpredictable. Who is it that Olivia falls in love with? Malvolio has already whetted her curiosity, however inadvertently, by describing the young 'fellow' who will not leave her door in negative terms that specify the defining traces of a range of identities other than his own:

> Not yet old enough for a man, nor young enough for a boy; as a squash is before 'tis a peascod, or a codling when 'tis almost an apple. 'Tis with him in standing water, between boy and man. He is very well-favour'd, and he speaks very shrewishly. One would think his mother's milk were scarce out of him.
>
> (*Twelfth Night*, 1.5.156–62)

The feminine allusions to Cesario's shrewish (shrill) voice and mother's milk are an instance of dramatic irony, reminding the audience, which now sees a male actor playing a boy, that Orsino's messenger is Viola in disguise. But they also have the effect of constructing for Cesario an identity which is neither this nor that: not boy, not man, reminiscent of femininity but defined by male pronouns.

And when Cesario speaks, the alternative similarly invades the selfsame. Modern productions, where the part is played by a woman, and printed texts, where the speech prefixes specify 'Viola' throughout, obscure the ambiguities of the speeches, which on the Elizabethan stage would have been exchanged between two male actors, both probably boys. But whose voice is it that says, 'Most radiant, exquisite and unmatchable beauty – I pray you tell me if this be the lady of the house, for I never saw her. I would be loath to cast away my speech; for besides that it is excellently well penn'd, I have taken great pains to con it' (1.5.170–4)? The extravagant opening phrase is surely spoken by Orsino's ambassador, possibly pronouncing the Duke's own words, or Viola's words written on his behalf. But then the messenger breaks off, and an adolescent boy cheekily points out that it's all an act, as far as he's concerned, and he doesn't want to waste on the wrong woman the part he's mastered with such an effort.

At the beginning of the scene Olivia is in disguise and in control. But the elusive identity of her insistent visitor fascinates her: 'Whence came you, sir?' (1.5.177); 'Are you a comedian [actor]?' (1.5.182); 'What is your parentage?' (1.5.277). Very rapidly indeed the power changes hands, Olivia reveals her identity, and Viola–Cesario withholds hers–his, thus constructing this mysterious figure as an object of desire for Olivia. Meanwhile, who is it who wants to see Olivia's face (1.5.230)? Cesario, who has a speech to deliver, whether Olivia wants to hear it or not? Or Viola, who is in love with Orsino and wants to assess the competition? And who replies to Olivia's challenge, 'Is't not well done?' with 'Excellently done, if God did all' (1.5.235–6)? A youth whose charm is his impudence, or a woman acknowledging a serious rival? Can we be sure? Isn't the enigmatic Viola–Cesario offered as an object of desire for the audience too?

The same figure can also be exceptionally lyrical, but when Viola–Cesario imagines making a willow cabin at Olivia's gate to write poems of unrequited love, and crying out the loved one's name, what is the word we expect to hear echo repeat? Cesario loyally says 'Olivia', and yet 'Orsino' might come as no surprise, since this speech does not sound like a well-penned formula, but comes as if from the heart. The speaking voice is now Cesario's, now Viola's, now male, now female.

Olivia cannot marry Cesario, since marriage in this period is about procreation. But Viola's twin will do perfectly, without any moralistic rituals of courtship or getting to know each other: he has, after all, the same physical features (5.1.216) with one crucial addition. The depiction of romance in this most romantic of comedies hints at a flexibility of sexual identity and the nature of desirability that seems adventurous even now.

But the surprise is that even now the adventure seems worth undertaking. Why are we still watching or interpreting Shakespeare? Why do Stratford and London, Stratford, Ontario, New York and Washington, amateur theatre companies all over the world, reading groups, schools and, not least, Hollywood, keep on returning to the plays? What sustains the continuing discussions of Shakespeare in academic books and journals? The language is alien and difficult, and the plots are derivative, often, indeed, from fairy tales, that least elevated of genres. Have we all been conned into believing that Shakespeare somehow does us good? There have been other candidates for pre-eminence: Gary Taylor, editor of the works of Thomas Middleton, argues that, but for an accident of history, our national dramatist would have been Middleton himself. Then why in practice is it Shakespeare we single out?

The Victorians would have answered this question by adducing his timeless wisdom and knowledge of human nature. We are no longer sure that any wisdom, however profound, is genuinely timeless, or that there is such a thing as a transcultural, ahistorical human nature. Instead, my own tentative answer would be that Shakespeare's works construct themselves, like Viola–Cesario, as objects of fascination and, indeed, desire, precisely by their undecidability. It is because we cannot resolve the questions they prompt, including the meaning of *Hamlet*, the racial politics of *Othello* and the nature of love in *Twelfth Night*, that we keep returning to the texts in the hope of producing the definitive reading.

With luck, they will go on eluding us. The definitive reading indefinitely deferred, each generation will continue to enter into a relationship with texts that succeed in unsettling any settled account of what they say. Questions, rather than answers, are the basis of our access to Shakespeare now.

Further Reading

Catherine Belsey, *Shakespeare and the Loss of Eden: The Construction of Family Values in Early Modern Culture* (London, Macmillan – now Palgrave, 1999).

Terence Hawkes, *Meaning by Shakespeare* (London, Routledge, 1992).

Ania Loomba, *Gender, Race, Renaissance Drama* (Manchester, Manchester University Press, 1989).

Annabel Patterson, *Shakespeare and the Popular Voice* (Oxford, Blackwell, 1989).

Kiernan Ryan, *Shakespeare* (Hemel Hempstead, Harvester Wheatsheaf, 1995).

Bruce Smith, *Homosexual Desire in Shakespeare's England: A Cultural Poetics* (Chicago, University of Chicago Press, 1991).

References

A. C. Bradley, *Shakespearian Tragedy: Lectures on Hamlet, Othello, King Lear, Macbeth* (1904: London, Penguin, 1991).

Michel Foucault, *The History of Sexuality, Volume One: An Introduction* (London, Penguin, 1979).

Kim Hall, *Things of Darkness: Economies of Race and Gender in Early Modern England* (Ithaca, NY, Cornell University Press, 1995).

Thomas Laqueur, *Making Sex: Body and Gender from the Greeks to Freud* (Cambridge, MA, Harvard University Press, 1990).

William Shakespeare, *The Riverside Shakespeare*, ed. G. Blakemore Evans et al. (Boston, Houghton Mifflin, 1974).

E. M. W. Tillyard, *The Elizabethan World Picture* (London, Chatto & Windus, 1943).

E. M. W. Tillyard, *Shakespeare's History Plays* (London, Chatto & Windus, 1944).

4 Reading Contexts for Renaissance Lyrics

Thomas Healy

Portrait of John Donne (1573–1631).

Addressing his lover in the 'Canonization', John Donne argues:

> And if unfit for tombes and hearse
> Our legend bee, it will be fit for verse;
> And if no peece of Chronicle wee prove
> We'll build in sonnets pretty roomes;
> As well a well wrought urne becomes
> The greatest ashes, as half-acre tombes
>
> > (Donne, *Poems*)

Opposing the public milieux of court, the law and commerce with the private sphere of the lyric, the poem proclaims a desire to be separated from society, one that could be argued as paradigmatic of the Renaissance lyric generally. These poems' very forms, Donne proposes, emphasise their more confined, intimate scope. In contrast to the public issues taken up by genres such as epic or ode, in shorter lyrics the poets appear to focus on private, even apparently confidential, preoccupations.

In a collection of essays arguing the importance of context in literary study, it might appear misconceived to include Renaissance lyrics. Where the prophetic vision of Blake, Jane Austen's ironic comedy of manners, the performed dramas of Shakespeare and Pinter, or the historical vision of Toni Morrison readily engage with social and political environments, the lyric appears to resist external context. It might even be proposed that to single out context is to miss fundamentally the lyric's opposition to it by focusing on the very things the poems announce they reject. A consideration of larger-scale Renaissance works of 'chronicle' verse designed to circulate in published volumes (e.g. Spenser's *Faerie Queene* or Milton's *Paradise Lost*) would suggest themselves as subjects more obviously suited to this volume.

Indeed, recalling that many of the most celebrated writers of Renaissance lyric verse did not publish their poems during their lives only highlights the apparent privacy of this poetry. Wyatt, Donne, Herbert and Marvell did not seek wide public attention for their lyrics. It was often their later admirers or inheritors who arranged publication posthumously. Donne's *Songs and Sonnets*, for instance, was not so called until the 1635 edition of his *Poems*. This was four years after Donne's death and two after the first edition of his poetry in 1633. The poems that make up this supposed 'collection' are in reality miscellaneous verses that the poet wrote throughout his life. Attempts to date them with any precision largely result in critical fantasies.

Thus, tying lyric poems to precise external contexts is acutely problematic. For instance, the mention in 'The Canonization' of the King's face (real or on a coin) would seem to indicate this poem was written after the ascent of James I in 1603 because before that Donne would have written about the Queen's face. 'King', though, could merely generically imply sovereign rather than be a reference to a specific monarch. As economic historians of this period would point out, a large variety of coins from a number of countries circulated in early modern England (see Muldrew, *The Economy of Obligation*). We would be mistaken in assuming that Donne's contemporaries expected to see one figure on the coins in their pocket. It is anachronistic to think the poet imagines the worldly companion he chides would be looking at a recently minted Jacobean coin in the way a modern reader might examine our uniform national coinage. Trying to pinpoint the poem's historical milieu from a reference to a king's stamped face only seems to mire us in ephemeral pursuits. This is not the type of context that deepens our understanding of the poem. Unless we want to reduce these verses to sequences of antiquarian intellectual puzzles, any helpful employment of context with lyric is never going to be a matter of footnotes and references, fascinating as such bits of information may be for some readers.

Yet, in other respects, the Renaissance lyric is illuminated by contextualising it. For all their rhetoric of intimacy, the poets themselves are unwilling to isolate themselves in a private world. Donne's affected impatience about external intrusion into the domain of his passion also reveals that he wants his well-wrought poem to be as important as a great chronicle and to attract public reverence. Indeed, he playfully suggests he wants to be celebrated with the highest honours and proclaimed a saint. This is not withdrawal from the world, it is remaking it on the poet's own terms. Private becomes public; the personal becomes the stage for the general. In fact, what often gives Renaissance lyrics their particular quality is their exploitation of the confusion between the intimate, often secret, arenas on which the genre ostensibly focuses, and the poems as documents to be perused, pried into and made communal by readers.

In considering the contemporary context of the Renaissance lyric, therefore, I want to focus on questions of reception. Who read these poems? Under what conditions were they read? And most significant and most difficult to answer, how were they read? An important area of current Renaissance scholarly work is the 'history of reading'. The pioneering work of Donald McKenzie, Roger Chartier and others has increasingly shown us that while texts are the written products of authors, books and manuscripts emerge from complex cultural contexts, ones that importantly influence how we read an author's text. In fact, the transmission of a text can fundamentally change the way it is understood.

Further, how text and the book – or other media where it is found – are understood is additionally conditioned by readers' own cultural locations. These locations include place, history and language. Place involves whether a text is being read in a classroom, at home or among friends, in environments familiar or foreign. History encompasses the social, political and economic factors of a reader's culture; his or her unique circumstances within them, including gender; and the relations these conditions have with the text's initial historical milieu. Language entails a reader's facility with both the structure and idiom of the text itself, including issues of genre and vocabulary, but also involving sound: the voices we hear speaking a text and our aural experience of its words. Who we are, where we are reading a text, and the purposes for which we are reading it, will help determine a text's significance both individually and collectively.

To explore some aspects of the contexts of reading Renaissance lyrics, I want to examine three well-known poems: John Donne's 'The goodmorrow', Sir Thomas Wyatt's 'Each Man me telleth I change most my device', and Andrew Marvell's 'The Garden'. While all of the questions I propose we should ask about reading – Who? In what conditions? How? – overlap in various ways, I want to focus on a specific question in relation to each of these three poems. The design, as will readily become clear, is not to provide exhaustive sets of answers to these questions but to indicate how thinking about the contexts of reading in the sixteenth and seventeenth centuries may influence our approaches to Renaissance poetry.

As already indicated, Donne's *Songs and Sonnets* was an editorial invention of the second edition of his poems of 1635. It was a strange choice of title as few of the 55 poems placed in this category are either songs or sonnets. Although there is no evidence when Donne (1572–1631) wrote these miscellaneous poems, their secular, often erotic, preoccupations have convinced many critics that they must be the product of the poet's youth, written before he was ordained priest in 1615. After this it is assumed that Donne concentrated on his religious verse. In effect, because an early editor created a category called *Songs and Sonnets*, subsequent readers have been enticed to look for connections among these pieces. A type of history of them is proposed, one that helps reinforce the idea of youthful extravagance that the category's title conveys. These lyrics are packaged so as to appear separate from Donne's divine poems.

Another feature that this categorisation of miscellaneous lyrics promotes is that their sentiments are biographically authentic: that in some fashion or other the 'I' speaking in these poems is 'John Donne' and the 'thou' is the lover of Donne. These lovers are either many (rakish Jack Donne!) or few, but the idea has developed that Donne is exploring human sexuality and the conditions of life associated with loving based on his own experience, and that *Songs and Sonnets* is an attempt to map the conditions of secular love. One result of this is that the reader frequently has the sense of being a voyeur: we are looking over lines the poet has drafted to an intimate other or others, lovers who in some respect are the ideal readers of these poems.

While the poems that we have come to know as *Songs and Sonnets* were not published until after Donne's death, many of them circulated in manuscripts during his life, as well as after it. In fact, editing Donne's poetry is a complete nightmare for modern editors because there are so many variants in these manuscript collections. Many of these manuscripts contain only one or two Donne poems, sometimes attributed, sometimes not, in a type of anthology collection of favourite poems which the manuscript's compiler has copied for his or, rarely, her own enjoyment. Manuscript circulation was often the way contemporaries became acquainted with one another's lyric poetry. Unlike an epic, a lyric of say 50 lines (and many are, of course, shorter) can be easily copied, circulated among different readers, borrowed and copied anew. Many sixteenth- and seventeenth-century writers of lyric were well regarded within literate circles before they came to be printed (see Marotti, *Manuscript, Print, and the English Renaissance Lyric*). Donne was well known as a poet among his contemporaries, even though he published little verse during his lifetime.

In fact, publication in book form did not necessarily mean greater public dissemination of lyrics. A well-regarded poet today can expect a modest 'launch' for a new collection. Review copies are distributed to newspapers and serious book supplements on an international scale; radio and television interviews are arranged; a reading tour of universities and arts centres might be organised. An urbanised public can walk into a bookshop and order a copy; anyone, anywhere, in possession of a credit card and Internet access can get hold of the volume relatively easily. Even so, a book of poems is thought to be doing well if it sells more than a couple of thousand copies in a few years. For Donne's age it was very different. A book was published by a printer with usually just one shop which retailed it – there was no systematic distribution network. A modest print run, say 200 copies, could take many years to sell. In fact, a popular lyric (as opposed to a whole collection) was likely to be disseminated more quickly in manuscript, being passed around and copied by those interested. Sometimes it was attributed to an author, often not. This act of manuscript transmission encouraged an image of civilised exchange for those involved. It promoted a sense of participation in a culture that was conducted by coteries of intellectuals and friends.

Thus, if a sense of intimacy results from Donne's lyric, it is not by our sharing in a poem designed for one lover. It is most unlikely 'The goodmorrow' was conceived as having an ideal reader in the figure addressed in the poem. Donne is using a poetic drama to consider experience and language based around a narrative his readers are unlikely to have imagined was authentic in the sense of being based on real events that happened to Donne.

Although Donne knew some of the best-educated women of his day, he almost certainly envisages 'male' readership. By this I don't mean to imply that Donne is necessarily writing to specific men and excluding women. He wrote verse letters addressed to a number of women, all of elevated rank, as well as to men, who tend to be more his friends and intimates. Rather, he carefully deploys language and ideas in the lyrics which make up *Songs and Sonnets* so that these poems' ostensible purposes of address – for example, a persuasion to have sex, an expression of sadness at parting, a condemnation of unfaithfulness, a celebration of intimacy – are nothing more than a pretext through which Donne displays ingenious, simultaneously playful and serious, and carefully many-sided sentiments. In placing a poetic self centrally in these poems, Donne is not being egomaniacal because the poetry's 'I's are a variety of masks or personae. Donne frequently takes delight in exposing the foibles of this poetic self (e.g. 'The Flea'). Indeed, revelling in the generation of meaning is what consistently characterises this poetry. Seeming to argue in one direction, Donne exposes his language's instability, its refusal to be tied to one perspective, one meaning. The poems are vehicles to explore questions that Donne's intellectual and social circle found interesting, a central one of which was the relation between language and experience.

Pleasure in a play of meanings is what these cliques of male, educated readers found enticing. Raised in social environments where 'truth' was frequently publicly claimed to be singular (especially in relation to religion), they delighted in the opportunities of verbal multiplicity. As the educational process these initial readers underwent was effectively wholly based on the acquisition of language skills, both in writing and speaking, they were particularly alert to nuance, cleverness of argument and word-play based on both sound and etymology (especially on Latin derivation).

To turn, then, to 'The good-morrow' and its easy, conversational, opening: 'I wonder by my troth, what thou and I / Did, till we lov'd?'.

Donne establishes a personal, intimate address towards another. His question is rhetorical, however. That is, he does not expect this silent other to answer; he provides the response. And what a response it is. Donne's poem proceeds to mark off a discourse of perfect mutuality with his beloved. It affirms the completeness of love, its transforming qualities, and it concludes in an apparent attempt to demonstrate how the unity which true love brings can defeat death.

In another respect, though, it is painfully aware that death cannot be conquered. The last verse sets up conditions to achieve a perfect equilibrium through love only to alert the reader to its impossibility – thus enforcing the realisation that it is death that dominates the future (the good morrow). It is worthwhile comparing this poem with Donne's *Holy Sonnet* 10, 'Death be not Proud', where the constant repetition of death only serves to reinforce its actuality while the poet is rhetorically trying to 'prove' how death can die.

It is instructive to examine 'The good-morrow''s last verse at some length:

My face in thine eye, thine in mine appeares,
And true plaine hearts doe in the faces rest,
Where can we finde two better hemispheares
Without sharpe North, without declining West?
What ever dyes, was not mixt equally;
If our two loves be one, or, thou and I
Love so alike, that none doe slacken, none can die.

In this stanza, Donne draws on a number of commonplace ideas of his time. First, the belief that the circle was the perfect unified form. Thus, having imagined the lovers projected as hemispheric maps, he concludes they are in reality one 'globe' or whole, only portrayed as the world would be in a book with one hemisphere 'facing' the other on the opposite page. Second, Donne employs the dominant Renaissance medical belief that humans are composed of different elements or humours and that bodily conditions can be fathomed by understanding how these humours combine. An uncorrupted body would be balanced in all its 'parts', a harmonious whole. Such a body, though, was considered impossible for humanity removed from divine grace at Adam's fall and subsequently corrupted.

That Donne recalls his lovers' bodies present corruption is most notable in his witty use of 'die'. This was a commonplace at the time for sexual orgasms or 'little deaths': a euphemism based on the idea that the body spent some of its finite supply of energy in orgasms. Thus, if the lovers reach orgasm, the expected result of their wholeness and oneness, they will ironically be proving their lack of perfect mutuality. They will 'slacken': the visible sign of the penis's 'death' after orgasm. In effect, Donne has playfully created a dilemma with his assertions about wholeness. To be perfect the lovers should be either in a permanent orgiastic relation or, rather, they should not be sexually involved since sex is a recollection of human appetite and, thus, corruption. The problem, though, is that to mix equally the lovers require orgasms to blend their fluids together. What this dilemma reinforces, as Donne is well aware, is that sex is about change; it indicates our mortality (and thus our death), not our permanence.

Another question that arises concerns the sex of the lover the poem is addressing. Based on mutuality and mirroring one another, there is a case for suggesting that the gaze the lover returns is a male one. Since 'slackening' is something that is the particular preserve of the penis, the assertion that 'none do slacken' instead of one slackening might be thought to indicate two men. I offer this possibility not to suggest that Donne was bi-sexual or gay but to indicate how these poems are not designed to work as vehicles for biographical display. In a poem which registers the way language is trying to evade humanity's condition (death's inevitability) precisely at the moment it is trying to celebrate human potentials in love, or which gestures towards incorporeal ideals of perfect mutuality ('good morrow to our waking soules') while grounding the lovers' exchanges in the bodily, it is appropriate that Donne further exploits this lyric's controlled confusion by making even the sex of the lovers debatable.

Announcing a security, intimacy, and privacy in the 'pretty room' of his lyric, Donne's 'The good-morrow' claims a victory over the larger world. The lovers 'watch not one another out of feare; / For, love, all love of other sights controules'. Yet fear is what actually seems to dominate this poem, an anxiety that tomorrow will confirm the change and decay that is the human lot. Experience will overwhelm attempts rhetorically to construct a static environment. Donne relishes precisely this insecurity that language both generates and reveals about our desires. Addressed to an educated audience which appreciates its cleverness, this is accomplished, witty, yet serious verse. It is not a sentimental, even mawkish, adolescent lyric written in a passionate outburst to an actual lover.

Now consider the following verses: are they the same poem or two different poems?

Eche man me telleth I chaunge moost my devise
And on my faith me thinck it goode reason
To chaunge propose like after the season

Ffor in every cas to kepe still oon gyse
Ys mytt for them that would be taken wyse
And I ame not of such maner condition
But treted after a dyvers fasshion
And therupon my dyvernes doeth rise
But you that blame this dyvernes moost
Chaunge you no more but still after oon rate
Trete ye me well and kepe ye in the same state
And while with me doeth dwell this weried goost
My word nor I shall not be variable
But alwaies oon your owne boeth ferme and stable

Each man me telleth I change most my device,
And, on my faith, me think it good reason
To change purpose like after the season.
For in every case to keep still one guise
Is meet for them that would be taken wise.
And I am not of such manner condition;
But treated after a diverse fashion,
And, thereupon, my diverseness does rise.
But you that blame this diverseness most,
Change you no more, but still after one rate,
Treat you me well, and keep you in the same state.
And while with me does dwell this wearied ghost,
My word nor I shall not be variable,
But always one, you own both firm and stable.

The first of these sonnets by Sir Thomas Wyatt (1503–42) represents the lyric as found in the British Library Egerton Manuscript 2711, our source for the poem. The second version is a modern edition of the same sonnet. For the modern reader the second version seems preferable. It is punctuated and a number of words that had unfamiliar spellings have been regularised to modern convention, so it is not as difficult to construe. For the reader coping with unfamiliar expressions and words (for example 'device' meaning both 'appearance' and referring to a heraldic symbol representing the speaker) the modern editorial work is welcome and enables a better appreciation of Wyatt's poem.

Or does it? It allows Wyatt's sonnet to appear easier to read but it also transforms it. Regularising features of language and imposing modern punctuation also limit drastically the ways the sonnet can be read. It was common for manuscripts to present poems without punctuation. Renaissance punctuation was largely controlled by rhetorical rather than grammatical conventions: that is, punctuation suggested how long to pause when speaking or reading the poem, allowing particular emphasis on how words or lines were heard. Removed from the dictates of standardised grammar, rhetorical punctuation could be readily varied. In presenting a poem without punctuation it was to a large extent up to the reader to organise his or her own pauses and phrasings, and, thus, the different ways lines might combine.

The same is true for spelling. In the sixteenth century there was no such thing as Received Pronunciation or what we might call 'Queen's English'. The varieties of English spoken at court (which had only recently stopped using French as its daily language) were as varied as a class of students containing mother-tongue English speakers from Surrey, Glasgow, Dublin, Melbourne, Alabama, Toronto, Delhi, Jamaica, and Cape Town. Writers often used spelling rhetorically, too, emphasising plays of meaning by spelling words to correspond with how they wanted them sounded: for example Wyatt's 'oon' which the modern version renders one. This is an accurate modernisation but it prevents the possible similarity between 'oon' and 'owne' with which the poet appears to be engaging.

To get a sense of the idea of transmission Wyatt may have had in mind, take the first version and read it aloud. Think how these unpunctuated lines might combine. In lines 2 to 6, for instance, is the poet making a self-mocking comment on himself that he is not wise enough to remain steadfast? Is he ironically suggesting that those that would be taken to be wise are acting unnaturally – not allowing change as the seasons do? Is he merely building up to chide his lover with treating him differently all the time and, thus, making it impossible for him to keep to one intention? In fact, whom Wyatt is addressing is not at all clear: lover, friend, ally, or someone who is all of these?

Wyatt's sonnet is about change and appearance. If he is chided for difference, he is also noting the dangers of remaining fixed in a singular behaviour or policy. As a member of a court where an individual's sexual involvements were usually a part of his or her wider political allegiances, Wyatt is only too aware of the consequences of presenting a stable identity instead of assuming different appearances. Wyatt was a lover of Ann Boleyn before Henry VIII (and perhaps after) and this placed him in a dangerous position. Factionalism was the condition of Wyatt's political world, one where groups rose to influence and then fell from favour with startling regularity. The consequences were frequently deadly. The line 'And while with me doth dwell this wearied ghost' indicates the transient, insubstantial condition of this pair, one in which an unvaried regard of one another may be very brief. Wyatt is encouraging his readers to question the quality of the wisdom displayed by those that would be 'taken wyse' in keeping to a fixed self-presentation. Like Donne, Wyatt is drawing on contrasts between ideas of change and those of permanence. His sonnet is conscious of the multiplicity of implications that these conditions bring. What should be noticed, though, is that the unpunctuated lines and the word-play achieved through irregular spellings increase the possible combinations of meanings.

Read the poem again, or have another person read it. Notice how, even after an initial familiarity, the lines can be rephrased so that new emphasis gives new meaning. Wyatt's sonnet in its unpunctuated form is highlighting how appearances change. The poem can be witnessed as his 'devise', the form that symbolically represents him to others. In one respect, this lyric appears as a stable fourteen lines, fixed within the rhythmic rules of what becomes known as the English sonnet – three quatrains with a concluding couplet. In another respect, Wyatt's lines and their possible meanings are open to varying combinations according to acts of reading.

To modernise the sonnet to accepted manners for presenting verse today is, therefore, to abandon many of the qualities the poet is exploiting to convey the difficulties, indeed the dangers, of fixing identity. While recognising plays of meaning, modern editorial convention ultimately seeks to clarify and limit signification by controlling the way lines are displayed. In effect, modern editorial practice is largely based upon the assumption that there is a correct way of reading a text. It assumes the author must have had a singular view about how the verses are to be read, even if interpretations of their meaning are varied. Modern editors usually contend that different versions in print or manuscript reflect errors of transcription, ones that the modern editor seeks to correct by trying to return the text's presentation to its 'authorial' intent. In fact, most Renaissance lyrics envisaged that there can be many readings, that there is not an ideal or right way to order, or punctuate, their lines. Their forms of presentation match the sentiments of multiplicity, instability, and transformation that the poetry itself so frequently considers. In a very real sense, the intention is that the poem changes each time it is read. In an era when silent reading was unimagined, speaking and hearing (in one's own voice or as an audience) the lyric brings the experience of this poetry closer to our understanding of performance. The text is there to be performed by the reader not as static repetition but open to constant amendment. If we make a comparison with music, we could say Renaissance readers experienced their lyrics much more as we would think about hearing jazz – where improvisation is paramount – rather than the fixed scores of the classical tradition. Wyatt's sonnet indicates how the context of transmission has huge implications for our understanding of the poem.

In July 1798, William Wordsworth famously revisited Tintern Abbey and heard some of the 'still, sad music of humanity' which, he proposed, a mature experience of nature encourages:

> And I have felt
> A presence that disturbs me with the joy
> Of elevated thoughts; a sense sublime
> Of something far more deeply interfused,
> Whose dwelling is the light of setting suns,
> And the round ocean, and the living air
> And the blue sky, and in the mind of man
> A motion and a spirit, that impels
> All thinking things, all objects and all thought,
> And rolls through all things.
>> (Wordsworth, 'Lines Composed a Few Miles
>> above Tintern Abbey')

About a century and a half earlier, Andrew Marvell (1621–78), apparently speaking from retired seclusion in a garden, appeared to anticipate the Romantic poets' belief in nature as a creative force:

> Mean while the Mind, from pleasure less,
> Withdraws into its happiness:
> The Mind, that Ocean where each kind
> Does streight its own resemblance find;
> Yet it creates, transcending these,
> Far other Worlds, and other Seas;
> Annihilating all that's made
> To a green Thought in a green Shade.
>
> Here at the Fountains sliding foot,
> Or at some Fruit-trees mossy root,
> Casting the Bodies Vest aside,
> My soul into the boughs does glide:
> There like a Bird it sits, and sings,
> Then whets, and combs its silver Wings;
> And, till prepar'd for longer flight,
> Waves in its Plumes, the various Light.
>> (Marvell, *Poems and Letters*)

Marvell's 'The Garden' offers a more enclosed, cultivated view of Nature than Wordsworth's; one that is placed overtly in a pastoral tradition that recalls both Adam and Eve and episodes from the Latin poet Ovid's *Metamorphoses*. But, despite the witty tone of 'The Garden' in contrast to the serious sublime of 'Tintern Abbey', both poems seem to recognise the transcendent power of nature.

Or is it, rather, that the still powerful influence of Romanticism distorts Marvell's representation of the garden for modern readers? Does it cause them to witness a proto-Romanticised celebration of Nature in this earlier work and, thus, applaud it for its anticipatory insight? Wordsworth's 'I' may be a poetic mask, but it is an idealised representation of the actual Wordsworth. The scene he depicts may also be a construct, but this is to pursue a vision of authenticity, to speak what he experiences as the truth of Nature in an actual place. In contrast, Marvell's narrator is a figure whose pronouncements the poem exposes sceptically as well as seriously. Consider the concluding stanza:

How well the skilful Gardner drew
Of flow'rs and herbes this Dial new;
Where from above the milder Sun
Does through a fragrant Zodiack run;
And, as it works, th' industrious Bee
Computes its time as well as we.
How could such sweet and wholsome Hours
Be reckon'd but with herbs and flow'rs!

It is possible to read this in a celebratory tone. The skilful gardener is God, the maker of all things. The narrator has realigned himself with nature so that time is now properly measured according to the progress of seasons and the stars. However, it is just as persuasive to read this as an exposure of this garden's extreme artificiality. The skilful gardener is just that, a worker who has created a sundial and display of the zodiac out of flowers. This is to rearrange and tame nature so that it now corresponds to mankind's ordering of time. To propose that the bee flying from hour to hour in a floral arrangement has been won over to this artifice is to reveal the curious, distorted logic of the narrator.

Far from using pastoral to come to a new understanding of nature and the self, Marvell is wittily displaying the fatuous artificiality of wealthy garden owners attempting to recreate the conditions of Paradise. During the English Civil War (1640–60), Royalist poetry often celebrated retirement to country estates as the only civilised course open to them during a time of barbarism. Their Republican opponents, of whom Marvell was one, often characterised Royalists as lethargic, people of idleness and debauchery. Similarly, after the Restoration, the creation of classically inspired gardens was part of a landscape movement whose ambitious realisations were aided by the great wealth now pouring into the country. The narrator of 'The Garden' may belong to this class: not the voice of Andrew Marvell, but the voice of indolence. What Marvell is cleverly exposing is that this poetic voice has failed to recognise the fabricated artifice of the garden he has created, one maintained by the labours of skilful gardeners. Nectarines, peaches, melons and grapes, which the narrator relishes, were being grown in Marvell's England, but with a great deal of careful attention in greenhouses. The 'green Thought in a green Shade' could imply vacant thought. The mind's creative power for this narrator is the vehicle for empty fantasy: ostensibly transcending all, but in actuality destroying nature to replace it with a man-made construct. Rather than Wordsworthian recollections in tranquillity, these are recollections in idleness.

However, 'The Garden' is not a simple exposure of the futile attempt by mankind (or a section of it) to recapture a lost Paradise. Marvell is able to combine his sceptical irony with a sense that this garden is also a place of genuine attractiveness. For all its artifice, all its suggestion that the narrator's refusal of the world does not reflect well on him, there is also a sense that the garden is a place of refuge. The lines cited above, where the poet imagines his disembodied soul sitting on a branch with silver wings, well illustrates how this poem unsettlingly combines a double perspective. In one sense, this soul preening its silver wings further exemplifies the luxurious self-involved quality of the narrator. In another respect it recalls the wings of the holy dove or spirit that are silver-white as a sign of their purity. There is a possibility that this garden might indeed be a place where the solitary narrator finds an Edenic environment that prepares him for the heavenly.

How, then, do we read a lyric that seems both to ridicule its narrator and to laud his garden? This poem presents a vision of nature that is playfully elegant, mocking and celebratory, ironic and serious. 'The Garden' is typical of Marvell's lyrics in bringing attention to questions about perception, both what is perceived and who is doing the perceiving. Marvell is obsessed with the idea of mirroring, where what is reflected may appear distorted. He is fascinated by what we see of the self and others when we gaze. As Paul Hammond notes, 'Marvell seems fascinated by the epistemological problem of how we identify something, how we recognise similarity and difference, and how a recognition of the other may serve to produce self-knowledge in the observer' (Hammond, 'Marvell's Sexuality', 186). What is clear is that a different aesthetic is operating here from Wordsworth's. Wordsworth accepts a more direct didactic power to his poetry. In 'Tintern Abbey' he can teach himself, the 'friend' his lines address, and his readers through language. Marvell is much less certain about the persuasive power of poetry. Just as he adopts a wide variety of different narrative voices in his poems, so he appears to anticipate a variety of different individuals reading him.

Unlike Donne or Wyatt, whose poetry we know circulated during their lives, there is much less evidence about Marvell. He was known as a skilful user of words, working in the Protectorate Latin Secretariat during the 1650s and producing controversial prose works (though usually anonymously) during the Restoration. A few poems were published and, as he moved in literary and intellectual circles throughout his life, friends and patrons were presumably reading his verse. It is more difficult to establish which poems they were reading and when they were reading them. Even an ostensibly public, occasional poem such as 'An Horatian Ode upon Cromwell's Return from Ireland' was not in circulation – there is nothing to suggest that Cromwell or anyone else saw it during Marvell's lifetime. He was also remarkably elusive in stating his views unequivocally: even in the letters he wrote as an MP to his constituents in Hull he never admits how he voted on issues.

At the start of this piece I suggested that a particular quality of Renaissance lyrics is how they exploit the private and the public: that the personal voices they adopt, with their pleas seemingly made to intimate addressees, are actually directed at readers outside their poetic enclosures. Yet by envisaging coterie readers, the familiar, even confidential, qualities of these lyrics are nonetheless retained. While promoting varieties of readings, even of opposing implications, these poems anticipate a context of being read in circles conversant with their methods, appreciative of their norms, and where circulating these lyrics helped enforce a sense of shared, educated culture.

Marvell's verse lies at the conclusion of a tradition of Renaissance lyric in which circulation in manuscript was more commonplace than circulation in print. His age saw an explosion in the dissemination of print and reading. More people of increasingly diversified social strata were participating in literate culture. Who was reading a text might be less confidently predicted as the reading public became increasingly factionalised, no longer sharing norms about how to read texts, no longer necessarily sharing in the same educational experiences. In most respects the following generations of poets present their work in ways that anticipate a wider, more anonymous reading public, knowing that the printed book (or journal) will be the media which transmits their texts. The relations between public and private readings alter.

'That Ocean where each kind / Does streight its own resemblance find': if Marvell's narrative voices in his lyrics usually possess a narcissistic quality, so, too, the poet seems to foresee, will the lyrics' readers. This will render the poetry open to manipulation, to the creation of meaning, generating 'Far other worlds, and other Seas' than ever the lyrics' originator anticipated. At the same time, the danger is that this fertility of meaning may also outrun its source, annihilate what is there, and cause the poem to become merely a reflection of the narcissistic reader.

This is a different scenario from those envisaged by Wyatt or Donne when they invite those perusing their lines to 'read differently'. It imagines readings of potentially much wider power either to build or to destroy. Whether Marvell sees such reading opportunities as preferable is impossible to know. His poems remain characteristically elusive about supplying answers. In a sense they are paradigmatic about the difficulties we face when thinking about context and the Renaissance lyric.

References

Roger Chartier, *The Order of Books: Readers, Authors, and Libraries in Europe between the Fourteenth and Eighteenth Centuries*, trans. Lydia G. Cochrane (Cambridge, Polity Press, 1994).

John Donne, *The Poems of John Donne*, two vols, ed. Herbert J. C. Geierson (Oxford, Oxford University Press, 1912).

Paul Hammond, 'Marvell's Sexuality' in Thomas Healy (ed.), *Andrew Marvell*, Longman Critical Reader (London and New York, Addison-Wesley Longman, 1998).

D. F. McKenzie, *Bibliography and the Sociology of Texts* (London, British Library, 1986).

Arthur F. Marotti, *Manuscript, Print, and the English Renaissance Lyric* (Ithaca, NY and London, Cornell University Press, 1995).

Andrew Marvell, *The Poems and Letters of Andrew Marvell*, two vols, 3rd edn, ed. H. M. Margoliouth, revised Pierre Legouis and E. E. Duncan Jones (Oxford, Clarendon Press, 1971).

Craig Muldrew, *The Economy of Obligation: The Culture of Credit and Social Relations in Early Modern England* (Basingstoke, Macmillan – now Palgrave, 1998).

William Wordsworth, 'Lines Composed a Few Miles above Tintern Abbey, on Revisiting the Banks of the Wye during a Tour, July 13, 1798', in Robert Clark and Thomas Healy (eds), *The Arnold Anthology of British and Irish Literature in English* (London, Edward Arnold, 1997).

5 Jonathan Swift: *Gulliver's Travels*

Nigel Wood

Gulliver, having been shipwrecked, regains consciousness and finds himself a prisoner of the Lilliputians. Chromolithograph from an edition of *Gulliver's Travels* published in London and New York in 1911.

One of the motives, if not the major motive, for understanding a literary work's context is that we may come to know more about the text itself as opposed to our responses to it. Ideally, knowledge of how the original audience came to a work such as *Gulliver's Travels* is a prerequisite for differentiating meanings that have only recently become visible from those that were probable at the time. This is especially significant where satirical works are in question and *Gulliver's Travels* has, perhaps, suffered from its own popularity in this regard: motivated by a rage against specific political and ethical prejudices and endemic human complacency, it has been 'universalised' in its comments until it is supposed to speak of no one particular culture or set of individuals.

Gulliver has often been considered a popular classic (even if in a censored version) and this does not aid the process of contextualisation; we think we know about the text due to the mediation of images on paperbacks or film-posters, to say nothing of the intervention of film or cartoon-book. These representations may be inaccurate, but they are also inevitable. Literary works exist through time (sometimes unevenly) because they are regarded as possessing 'timeless' material, but this must also be at the cost of their specific history. Thus, Defoe's tale of individual human fortitude in *Robinson Crusoe* might seem fatally reduced if, in returning the novel to its immediate circumstances for both writer and reader, we discover that the narrative espoused such individualism as part of an early eighteenth-century debate about political rights and the aims of capitalistic expansion. We might feel inclined to ignore the fact that Elizabethan audiences are likely to have sided with the chauvinistic gentiles in Shakespeare's *The Merchant of Venice* against the unfortunate Jewish outsider, Shylock. Instinctively, we would prefer to find the qualities we favour in the writing of the past derived from 'portable' meanings that point to recurrent human truths, not the more limited versions that could only have been available to the initial reading public.

Satire is often designed to work immediately upon the world, to accomplish something at the time rather than to stand as a monument for the future. With this in mind, we may be more inclined to see *Gulliver's Travels* as an event, full of details that indicate the precise stages of its composition, and, once it emerges into the public domain, the cause of a variety of reading experiences and commentary. In Swift's case, such reactions provided him with the opportunity to explore further modifications to the text for later editions and other readerships, so talk of the 'aim' of the book (in the singular) is itself a short cut. This essay is an attempt to recapture the initial relationships between Swift and his readers, and, in so doing, to question some of the most fondly-regarded 'truths' about the work.

Swift thought deeply about *Gulliver's Travels* well before its publication in 1726. In 1714, together with his London friends, the writers Alexander Pope, John Gay and John Arbuthnot (amongst others) who formed the Scriblerus Club, he composed the *Memoirs* of a fictional travelling dunce, Martin Scriblerus. Scriblerus applies himself so assiduously to his studies that he looks on the world according to his textbooks only, and the co-authors present his self-importance and blinkered vision across a variety of travels and apparently serious items of advice on education and other schemes of self-improvement. Towards the close of the *Memoirs*, there is a section wherein 'Martin' provides us with details of his 'Travels', that accurately prefigure those of Gulliver twelve years later. He proceeds from an 'ancient Pygmean Empire' to a 'land of the Giants, now the most humane people in the world' to 'a whole kingdom of philosophers' to, finally, with no hint of how this emerges, the discovery on his fourth voyage of 'a vein of melancholy, proceeding almost to a disgust of his species' and 'a mortal detestation to the whole flagitious race of Ministers' (Swift et al., *Memoirs*, 165). It would be tempting to regard Scriblerus as an ironic persona in all of this, and when we turn to *Gulliver's Travels*, we may simply regard Gulliver himself as an item in Swift's satire, not to be associated with the author himself, who allows the reader to see this misanthropy as an inevitable consequence of a narrow education. Perhaps . . . but this is where serious critical divisions have opened up in estimates of the *Travels*: is Gulliver just a pawn in Swift's complex satirical game, an empty persona that the author coolly manipulates to score a variety of ironic points at 'his' expense, or is the naïve and finally embittered Gulliver actually a key to the depths of Swift's psyche – always allowing for the possibility that both effects could simultaneously be the case?

There are at least three preliminary considerations that students of Swift's work are typically encouraged to bear in mind: that Swift was (1) a Church of Ireland Anglican; (2) from 1714 onwards, and his enforced return to his own people in Ireland, an exile from the wider world that he found corrupt yet still curiously appealing; and (3) a tragic figure, facing, imaginatively and spiritually, a deep split between his sense of the public and private spheres. Passed over for several Church posts that would have kept him in England and near the seat of power and influence, he seemed to have no alternative but to return to Ireland. With the death of Queen Anne in August 1714, this became inevitable. The political friends in high places (in the main associated with the Tory party) whom he had sought to cultivate throughout his protracted stay in England were, at a stroke, rendered powerless. The incoming Hanoverian regime favoured the Whigs who, in turn, were little likely to favour one who, in February 1714, had published an acerbic commentary on their political ethics: *The Public Spirit of the Whigs*. The timing could not have been more disastrous, and the 1714 meetings with fellow Scriblerians turned out to be a last flowering of conviviality. What was to await him in Ireland was a severe interrogation of his own identity: if being Irish (as Swift frequently saw it) defined the Catholic majority as well as the Protestant elite, then how could he, proud of his Anglo-Irish credentials, regard himself as such? The more we consult details of Swift's life when interpreting the *Travels*, the less likely are we to regard Gulliver simply as ridiculous. Swift's own experience tallies with Gulliver's wrong-headed choice of proud isolation.

There are, however, several recurrent satiric patterns in the *Travels* throughout its four voyages, consisting largely of the questioning and over-turning of established patterns. An innocent confidence in British civilisa-tion is a structural feature of Books I and III. In Lilliput, Gulliver's physical superiority over the diminutive inhabitants is easily translated into an effect of greater moral awareness and a similar tactic is deployed in the encounters with the distracted abstract thinkers and scientists on the flying island of Laputa and at the Academy of Lagado, where, by contrast, even Gulliver appears in touch with common humanity. This is safe satire, as the first-person narrative encourages the reader in these passages to side with the satirist, whose perspective is mainly (though certainly not con-sistently) that of Gulliver. Just when we might have thought of the *Travels* as simply a dig at the political manoeuvring of courts and governments, the move to Book II is deliberately disconcerting. Here, where Gulliver is the 'Lilliputian' amongst the Brobdingnagian giants, the reversal of per-spective extends the range of the satire: the human traveller is here not some scientist providing a report on the manners and customs of a 'savage' tribe, but rather someone under the microscope her/himself. When he is set ashore amongst the Houynhnhnms, that eminently ratio-nal and untroubled race of horses, the golden mean for 'civilised' Euro-peans does not exist: to be humanly normal, Gulliver discovers, is to resemble the enslaved and bestial Yahoos much more than his hosts. Any confidence in common humanity that had been reasserted after Book III is here questioned root and branch.

The last scenario of the book has proved a particularly challenging gesture to generations of readers. Swift leaves Gulliver preferring the scents and sounds of his stable to the company of his wife and family, inveighing against human pride – and thereby implicating himself in that very vice, shut out from any charitable impulses whatsoever. If the book had ended at that point, interpretation would have been relatively straightforward: Gulliver is ludicrous, and his extreme love of the Houyhnhnm lifestyle translates here to simple fixation. Swift, however, has Gulliver address the reader directly in one last chapter, and the distance between Gulliver's accents and Swift's narrows. This commences with an assurance that all that he has written has been a 'faithful History . . . wherein [he has] not been so studious of Ornament as of Truth'. He might have gained his audience's attention much more easily with 'strange improbable Tales', yet we are presented with 'plain Matter of Fact in the simplest Manner and Style' (*Gulliver's Travels*, 299). This is puzzling because it is quite clear that the *Travels* is a work of narrative fantasy, yet it does not quite follow that Swift is here indicating just the truth of plain facts. Here there is no pretence that a place such as Lilliput exists, so about what is Swift (through Gulliver) so concerned? The answer lies in the relation between these travels and those of many others who wrote of their experiences to catch the popular imagination. Whereas Defoe strove to adopt the style of colourless reportage in his *Robinson Crusoe*, Swift's Truth lies neither in exotic tropical ideals nor in scientific definitions. Compared to how Gulliver travels (and what he learns about himself and about mankind), the traveller's tale offers the reader a vicarious escape from mortal reality:

> having since gone over most Parts of the Globe, and been able to contradict many fabulous Accounts from my own Observation; it hath given me a great Disgust against this Part of Reading, and some Indignation to see the Credulity of Mankind so impudently abused. Therefore since my Acquaintance were pleased to think my poor Endeavours might not be unacceptable to my Country; I imposed on myself as a Maxim, never to be swerved from, that I would *strictly adhere to Truth*; . . .
>
> [Swift's original emphasis] (*Gulliver's Travels*: 300)

Satiric meaning is always to a degree implicit and potentially variable, as it demands a certain perceptiveness from the reader. Here, the insistence on Gulliver's veracity is at the same time an admission that the common run of readers are gullible, unable, indeed, to tell truth from its superficial appearance in fashionable travellers' tales. This is one of the most persistent threads in the work: 'Richard Sympson', in the prefatory, 'The *Publisher* to the *Reader*', praises Gulliver's almost proverbial 'Veracity': 'The Style is very plain and simple; and the only Fault I find is, that the Author, after the Manner of Travellers, is a little too circumstantial. There is an Air of Truth apparent throughout the whole' (*Gulliver's Travels*, xl). To some degree, the reader here observes a rather 'safe' joke: that Gulliver's constant insistence that he is a truth-teller in effect casts doubt on that very quality. He protests too much.

Satire often unsettles the reader not only because it expresses unpalatable truths but also because it requires a sharpness of response and an alertness to the wider issues about which a satirist cares deeply. There are, indeed, several passages where Gulliver depicts too much 'truth', where the overall effect is to disgust and repel the reader, such as in his microscopic descriptions of the Brobdingnagian Maids of Honour (Book II, Ch. V). Expecting an uncritical travelogue, the reader rapidly has to reassess her/his bearings. Yet we are not much nearer to tracing Swift's motives in this. His immediate historical and personal circumstances in the 1720s provoked powerful reactions that could not always be accommodated to easy prose summaries. What we do feel, almost before understanding the full reason why, is a frustration and restlessness embedded in the experience of reading the work. With that last chapter and several suddenly distasteful passages in mind, *Gulliver's Travels* increases the feeling that ready solutions and destinations cannot be located. Gulliver is rarely 'at home', and finally, even when apparently residing at his own house at Redriff, is estranged from its comforts. This alienation is a case of mood as well as the described events of the narrative. We find several uncomfortable difficulties in tracing a consistent (or 'intended') tone that seems to match the sense of dislocation that both Gulliver is portrayed as enduring and, we might conclude, Swift is actually creating in a complex ironic symbolism. I would stress here, 'complex' irony: simple irony establishes a pattern whereby any statement would appear to mean its very opposite, whereas Swift's meaning in the *Travels* is elusive if we are searching for it in succinct statements. Much of the meaning emerges from this mood (or satiric mode) of reading.

Consider the gradual way in which Gulliver is led to accept his Houyhnhnm master's judgement at the start of Book IV, that he (and, of course, the reader) resembles far more a Yahoo than a creature capable of reason. The initial disgust at the bestial Yahoos is supplanted by a horror that it all depends on one's yardstick as to whether humans have the potential to be either animals or angels. These passages do not just inform us about the Yahoos, as they also affect us in a precise way when we read them for the first time. Any overall concept of unitary form ('I am reading a novel of ideas' or '. . . a parody of a Traveller's Tale') would reduce the difficulties we actually encounter in constructing *Gulliver's Travels* passage by passage. What is more, its irony would be simplified – which, overall, damages the text and removes its immediate history. Swift communicates exactly that sense of losing one's bearings by rendering the attentive reader grasping at straws. Most exercises in contextual readings of literature start with a writer's biography and the pertinent historical records of the date of writing, yet there are often deeper intentions that only fully emerge from a reader's experience. Consideration of these has far-reaching consequences for the task of contextualising literary works. No longer might we be content with consulting a calendar of political or military events and looking back to the novel or play we are considering in order to ask the question, 'How does this literary work fit a pattern of grand history?'.

What is far more relevant is the need to recognise how certain texts were read and thus, in this case, how *Gulliver's Travels* offered itself initially to the interpretative strategies available at the time; in short, the range of ways in which texts make sense to certain people. It is also crucial to reflect upon the fact that at no time do readers form a completely consistent body of people. There may be several, crucially opposed, ways of constructing sense in narratives at any one time. 1726 may appear now as a rather distant point in the past, but it was a vivid and living complexity to Swift and his first readers. The route to this knowledge involves an alertness to the material as well as intellectual histories possible at the time. By 'material' I mean the physical appearance of the book in the first audiences' hands, how it was disseminated in print (its publishing and early critical history) and how it formed, or interacted with, a market. These details can actually disclose important information about the initial impact the work had in its own time and form a valuable supplement to the more usual sources by which we ascertain an author's intention, such as her/his letters, the comments of friends and publishers during the work's composition, or what political views we take the writer to manifest in other works. When writers contemplate the publication of their thoughts in print a complex process of negotiation takes place. First thoughts may be significantly modified by the need to attract a publisher (or, in 1726 parlance, a 'bookseller'), by the assessment of a likely readership once the likely publisher is known and, even after a first edition, the need to revise or self-censor one's own work to overcome, as the writer might see it, that audience's prejudices or lack of critical perception.

It is in this sense that a close analysis of the early history of Swift's writing of *Gulliver* is a contribution to the interpretation of its irony. There are significant shades of meaning and motivation that we cannot expect to survive long after the moment of publication. Irony invites reactions and, in provoking them, could be said to produce a set of readings not always envisaged at first by the author. Swift was acutely aware of how *Gulliver* engaged with both Irish and English cultural expectations. By the 'Second Edition' of late 1727 (actually preceded by at least four subtly different versions), the inclusion of four 'Verses Explanatory and

Commendatory; never before printed' by Alexander Pope testifies to his recognition of the book's popular acclaim. The poems are miniature exercises in mock-heroic 'commendation', especially the pastoral idyll, 'The Lamentation of Glumdalclitch for the Loss of Grildrig', which hides from view the gross difference of size between Gulliver ('Grildrig') and his Brobdingnagian carer. As with some Hollywood 'spin-off', Swift and his publisher, Benjamin Motte, were, within a year, feeding the public's immense appetite for 'Gulliveriana', that is, jokes that could add to the experience of a 1726 reading.

Even thus far, I have already taken a short cut in referring to the work that Benjamin Motte published in November 1726. What has come to be called *Gulliver's Travels* only starts to appear with this name on the title-page as late as 1772, in the reprint of Faulkner's 1735 edition of *Swift's Works*: 'Works of the Reverend Dr. Jonathan Swift, Dean of St. Patrick's, Dublin, containing the Travels of Lemuel Gulliver . . .'. The hint that it would universally be called at some point in time, *Gulliver's Travels*, was, to be sure, carried in the extracts, as 'The Travels of Capt. Gulliver', printed in *Parker's Penny Post* (No. 246, 28 Nov. 1726, onwards) and *The Penny London Post* (No. 252, 25 Nov. 1726, onwards), but this was, in Swift's lifetime and well beyond, the unofficial title, and not introduced for a single entire printing of the work until the 1808 *Walkers British Classics* volume, entitled: *Gulliver's Travels into several Remote Nations of the World*. The consistency with which Swift's work was first known (with very minor variation) as *Travels Into Several Remote Nations Of The World. In Four Parts, By Lemuel Gulliver, First a Surgeon, and then a captain of Several Ships* (the designation of the first octavo edition, published on 28 October 1726) probably indicates an authorial as well as editorial preference. From the first, Motte included the two line plans from Book III and the maps that illustrate each journey's destination. In all of the first three editions that stem from Motte's editorial control (Oct.–Dec. 1726) there appears a portrait of Gulliver at the head of the book. The price, 8s. 6d., was also high for a work we may now call just a satiric comedy. The book imitated the genre of the travelogue not only in its text, but also in its physical appearance. The deliberately bland reportage promised by the title, free of any grand gesture towards a cult of personality, is matched by the rudimentary cartography and rough line-drawings of the amateur.

There is no point pursuing the line that the book actually duped many people. John Arbuthnot's letter to Swift (Swift, *Correspondence*, 3, 182), passing on a story from Lord Scarborough ('who is no inventor of Storys') that he had met a 'Master of a ship' who was 'very well acquainted with Gulliver' and could testify to his residing in Wapping and not Rotherhithe, is an exception to a more discerning rule. On the other hand, the appearance of the book in its first readers' hands was a preliminary exercise in misinformation. As with the vast majority of Swift's published work, it did not carry any sign of Swift's authorship. The fact that Swift did eventually become known as the author (certainly by 1735 and Faulkner's edition of his *Works*) only allowed most readers to regard it alongside his earlier work well after its first edition. We, therefore, have to imagine a set of readers who could not identify, with any accuracy, quite where the book was coming from – not only in biographical terms, but also in its themes and satiric targets.

Gulliver's Travels remains a popular classic, but it was, from the first, the talk of the town. As Swift's friend and fellow Scriblerian, John Gay, reported as early in its critical life as 17 November 1726 (just three weeks after its first two-volume edition had appeared), the 'whole impression' had sold in a week, and 'from the Cabinet-council to the Nursery' it was 'universally read' (Gay, *Letters*, 60). Samuel Johnson noted that 'the price of the first edition was raised before the second could be made' (Johnson, *Lives*, 3, 38), a tall order indeed for the eighteenth-century book trade. The publisher, Benjamin Motte, rushed out three octavo editions in 1726, followed by duodecimo and octavo editions in 1727, all more affordable and portable. In short order, alongside the serialisations, there were abridgements, painstaking summaries and keys to the satire, including Abel Boyer's chapter-by-chapter analyses and decoding as early as November–December of 1726 in his *Political State of Great Britain*. Translations appeared as quickly; January 1727, saw the first French, Dutch and German versions, although the first serious continental notice came with the Abbé Desfontaines' translation, liberally 'correcting' some of Swift's obvious errors of taste – and providing one of the first attempts to censor the original.

This immense popularity was undeniable, and many relished the strain of fantasy that accompanied travels into 'foreign' parts. For academic study, it should not be surprising if we now focus on what we take to be Swift's more universal comments on the human condition. Gulliver's eventual tragi-comic alienation is an item that a reader can identify in any number of different historical contexts. On the other hand, the path from composition to the printing of the text was not always a smooth evolution from a prior design. It is likely that, if the evidence of his letters to friends is a reliable guide, he started composing parts of Books II and IV (exactly the passages where Gulliver's physical and moral frailties are accentuated and dramatised) before I and III, the books most often interpreted as direct satires on contemporary politics and science. Coinciding with the most intensive period of composition (1722–5), Swift was involved in the campaign to halt the debasing of the Irish coinage by the English. His *Drapier's Letters* confront the economic imperialism of this move in the very midst of his composition of the *Travels*. It is surprisingly evident (to many) that he moved on *from* abstract commentary on the human condition *to* more concrete and thinly mediated satiric material. It is therefore telling that the Lindalinian episode from chapter 3, Book III of *Gulliver*, that allegorises English colonialist repression of the Irish, through the lowering of a floating island over the city to deprive it of sun and water, should be missing from the Motte editions and not even make it into Faulkner's edition as late as 1735. When we include it in all recent editions of the text, we obscure the traces of possible political censorship with which Swift had to live on a daily basis. With the withdrawing of the threat of devaluation as late as the autumn of 1725, it is probable that Swift (or probably Swift and Motte) felt that the ironic filter was at its thinnest in this passage – and, legally speaking, the satire was thereby at its most vulnerable. The only authority for its inclusion in our modern editions is its appearance in Charles Ford's manuscript of the first edition, a check-list of Swift's intended alterations to the first copy, transcribed when he visited Dublin from 1726 to 1727, now to be found in the Forster collection of the Victoria and Albert museum. In other words, the Swift who prepared the final text of the *Travels* had not travelled far from the Scriblerian who back in 1714 had devised a plotline of gathering melancholy and political scepticism; indeed, he might have been more aggressive to particular characters or contemporary institutions if the possibility of legal proceedings against him had not given him pause.

To summarise: these facts about the work's earliest appearances in print are like broken shards that an archaeologist pieces together. They are all that is left of that struggle to be published and heard that were pressing realities to Swift at the point of publication. The genesis of the work undoubtedly brought into focus his abiding fear of Man's slavery to his instincts and the startling realisation that, minus the superficies of clothing, we are more apt to be classed with Yahoos than credited with Houyhnhnm rationality. These are fears that appeal to us today and about which we can readily supply contemporary examples. The link to his sense of Irish exile is not as easily traced, but he had, after all, been prosecuted in 1720 by Ireland's Lord Chancellor Midleton for his authorship of *A Proposal for the Universal Use of Irish Manufacture*, a scabrous assault on English economic imperialism, where the same difficulties in assigning a common human nature to the desperately impoverished Irish as well as the Whitehall English are explored in terms next taken up in narrative form in Book

IV of the *Travels*: 'Whoever travels this Country, and observes the *Face* of Nature, or the *Faces*, and Habits, and Dwellings of the *Natives*, will hardly think himself in a Land where either *Law, Religion*, or common *Humanity* is professed' (Swift, *Irish Pamphlets*, 54–5). Travelling from one location to another, as Gulliver is made to do, introduces many questions about the traveller's powers of independent judgement: how long before we 'go native' and blend in with our surroundings? What truths are universal, and which the result merely of nationalistic prejudice and habit? If our information about the humane and ethically sound is derived just from our homeland, then have we experienced enough to encounter anything alien with a clear focus?

John Richetti's rich and incisive study *of Popular Fiction Before Richardson: Narrative Patterns: 1700–1739* locates the ingredients that made accounts of voyages and travels so meaningful. Emerging from an earlier literary and devotional tradition, where travels had to be 'travails' or feats of endurance during which one made one's soul, new secular possibilities were excitingly available as well:

> The stories in question partake of the modern ethos of travel; they glitter with the attractions of exotic locale and action and frequently give us heroes who are capable of 'daemonic' and free-wheeling exploits. But this diversity of scene and event is often balanced by a narrative voice which tries to see in the random and the coincidental the mysterious workings of Providence.
>
> (Richetti, 62)

If you are a pilgrim, you are at least consoled by progress towards your goal. However much certain tales of travel (sometimes termed the 'picaresque') gesture towards change and variety, there is usually a homecoming where the travellers are relocated in a familiar society. If, on the other hand, your aim in travelling is to colonise or record scientifically, then the necessary education of travel is of rather lower priority.

There is a detail added to the book in 1727, in Gulliver's letter to 'His Cousin Sympson', that provides a hint about Travellers' Tales, and their relevance to Swift's more pervasive fears about political optimism. Gulliver envisages the hiring of some University students to help him edit, order and correct the style of his scattered notes, 'as my Cousin *Dampier* did by my Advice, in his Book called, *A Voyage round the World*' (*Gulliver's Travels*, xxxv). Capt. William Dampier (1652–1715) would have been an obvious instance of the romantic traveller. His two most famous accounts of his voyages, *A New Voyage round the World* (1697–9) and *A Voyage to*

New Holland (1703, 1709), were standard examples of an unvarnished sea-faring life. In dedicating his *New Voyage* to Charles Montagu, the President of the Royal Society, there is a transparent desire to pass off his derring-do as factual and so as an addition to knowledge. The Royal Society's aim was to foster the gathering of facts about the world according to what we would now call a scientific methodology of experimental testing and deductive reasoning (Swift's target in the encounter with the Academy at Lagado in Book III). The accounts of their *Philosophical Transactions* were stocked with templates for the recording and classifying of alien vegetation and animal life; in fact, there were at least twelve in the first two years of publication (1665–7). These were collected together as *General Heads for a Natural History of a Countrey* in 1692. Swift had read Dampier's work – or at least had it in his library – and was aware of a certain notoriety that surrounded his name. Granted command of his first ship, the *St. George*, by the First Lord of the Admiralty, the Earl of Orford, in 1700, we next hear of Dampier convicted of cruelty to his Lieutenant in 1702, fined all of his pay and deemed not fit to command a King's ship. Thereafter, and coming nearer to the image more familiar to Swift and his readers, he pursues a seafaring life with 'privateers', or as the *Dictionary of National Biography* unsparingly terms them, 'buccaneers'. What starts as a commercial quest for the country's good descends into private greed. We should remember that Gulliver is forcibly set ashore in Houyhnhnmland by a Dampier-figure, in command of mercenaries versed in 'trade' amongst the South Seas, including a voyage to Campeachy (a route Dampier commemorated in his account of such a journey in *Voyages and Descriptions* [1699] – compare *Gulliver's Travels*, 223–4).

Dampier, like Gulliver, is vigilant in demanding credit from his reader:

> I have not so much of the Vanity of a Traveller, as to be fond of telling Stories, especially of this Kind; nor can I think this plain Piece of mine, deserves a place among your more Curious Collections . . . [He still has, though] a hearty Zeal for the Promoting of useful Knowledge, and of any thing that may never so remotely tend to my Country's Advantage.
>
> (Dampier, 'Dedication' to *A New Voyage*, 1, 17)

The slightest acquaintance with the non-textual Dampier (though perhaps also with hindsight) would allow us to see through this formulaic phrasing. Dampier's 'truth' does not seem to be heavily selective, as he apparently chooses 'to be more particular than might be needful, with respect to the intelligent Reader' (Dampier, 'Preface', 1, 19). It is a delightful find to come across Dampier's literal-mindedness:

. . . the Log of Wood lying out at some distance from Sides of the Boats described at Guam, and parallel to their Keel, which for distinctions sake I have called the little Boat, might more clearly and properly have been called the side log, or some such Name; for though fashioned at the Bottom and ends Boat-wise, yet is not hollow at top, but solid throughout.

(Dampier, 1, 22–3)

Quite . . . The insistence on absolute realism is touching, given what happened in a later escapade. After a failed attack on the Manila galleon and the holing of his ship in 1704, Dampier faced mutiny from half of his command, roughly 34 hands, under the control of one William Funnell. This breakaway crew set sail for home and Funnell, indeed, beat Dampier not only to a home port but to a published account of the voyage and his former Captain's dubious methods of command. Enraged by this, Dampier rushed out *a Vindication in Answer to the Chimerical Relation of William Funnel* (1707), full of circumstantial bluster and compass bearings. But the whistle had been blown on his 'realism' and Dampier's character had been badly mauled. In the same year, Dampier suffered further ignominy: the appearance of *Answers to Capt. Dampier's Vindication, by John Welbe (Midshipman)*, a cogent point-by-point validation of Funnell's version. Dampier is not idly chosen as Gulliver's 'cousin'. The references to his example, some direct, most parodic, produce a precise set of associations, as Dampier's 'truth' is, if anything, not literal enough. Compared to the deliberately shocking inclusion of faeces and body odour in Gulliver's account, Dampier's gripping yarns of the high seas seem rather cosmetic. Swift instead produces an unyielding 'truth' of a human condition that can neither be forgotten nor left behind.

Where the traveller's tale seemed to promise a sense of progress and cultural superiority Swift's parody undermines this habit of reading and, by extension, this instinctive certainty. In this project, Dampier was almost a gift to Swift: his factual reporting seemed to inspire trust (if not imaginative engagement), and yet the fuller truth that emerges from the consideration of this level of biographical detail undermines this fatally. No wonder that *Gulliver's Travels* has so often been edited to suit a younger or excessively polite readership, as the comic narrative ingredients and initial romance of remote lands seem so innocent. The work's comedy and romance can only be maintained if large stretches of the writing are excised or ignored. Travellers seemed so free of context to the early eighteenth-century mind, yet Swift confessed to Pope on 29 September 1725, in a letter that dwelt on the finishing stages of correcting the Travels, that 'the chief end' he proposed to himself in all his labours was to 'vex the world rather than divert it'. He, at the same time, recognised the risk involved in the publication process, how he hoped to find a printer 'brave enough to venture his ears' and how he feared that this 'design' might involve a risk to his own 'person or fortune' (Swift, *Correspondence*, 3, 103). He realised the complexity of negotiating with the world where anything radical needed to be said.

What drew Swift in the Travels to such ironic strategies? The doubt as to whether anything is seriously expressed in the book creates a meaning all of its own. There is humour in the tale, of course, and the entrapment of an unwary reader, but, as long as we remain aware of the full writing process and its constraints, his satire may also be seen as projecting a strain of confessional desperation, enacted as we read. No single reading strategy seems to explain all the varieties of tone and narrative reversals we find in the work. Certainly, the genre of the Traveller's Tale, so voraciously devoured by the popular market, produced the optimistic (and unthinking) conclusion that exposure to exotic foreign lands might demonstrate European superiority and resourcefulness, and that travel inevitably broadened the mind. This was a sentiment that Swift could not and would not share. Swift's last experiences of the mainland were of waiting interminably in the autumn of 1727 for the Holyhead ferry to fill with passengers so that the crossing to Dublin would be profitable. Even then, adverse winds meant a delay of, in total, near to three weeks. *The Holyhead Journal* that Swift compiled is an exercise in anomie and isolation: 'I am afraid of joining with the other passengers for fear of getting acquaintance, with the Irish' (Swift, *Prose Works*, 5, 204). For the purposes of self-assertion, he forgot his Irishness, just as Gulliver prefers to disown his own humanity.

Further Reading

Swift's 'Irishness' (taken to be a trait of his writing as well as a description of his national identity) has provoked some emotional and deeply contested readings in the last decade. S. J. Connolly's 'Swift and Protestant Ireland: Images and Reality', in *Locating Swift: Essays from Dublin on the 250th Anniversary of the Death of Jonathan Swift, 1667–1745*, ed. Aileen Douglas, Patrick Kelly and Ian Campbell Ross (Dublin and Portland, OR, Four Courts Press, 1998), 28–46, has supplied some carefully researched material about Swift's family history as well as his contemporary religious context. It forms a valuable supplement to the best work on the topic, Robert Mahony's *Jonathan Swift: The Irish Identity* (New Haven, CT and London, Yale University Press, 1995), which dissects Swift's Irish reputation and relates the changing critical estimates of his work to non-literary factors. Ian Higgins's *Swift's Irish Politics: A Study in Disaffection* (Cambridge, Cambridge University Press, 1994) contains some excellent passages on his difficulties in finding a comfortable political affiliation, and is especially good on *Gulliver's Travels*.

During the 1980s and 90s critical estimates of Swift's irony changed direction radically to assess the reader's role in its creation and full effect. Richard H. Rodino, in his '"Splendide Mendax": Authors, Characters, and Readers in Gulliver's Travels', *PMLA*, 106 (1991), 1054–70, has related what we know of Swift's first reading public to more modern critical theoretical concerns. Michael Seidel's wide-ranging 'Gulliver's Travels and the Contracts of Fiction', in *The Cambridge Companion to the Eighteenth-Century Novel*, ed. John Richetti (Cambridge, Cambridge University Press, 1996), 72–89, looks at the wider issues of how people at the time actually regarded fiction and also how they might have been able to read it.

The most stimulating piece on Swift's writing, to my mind, is still Edward Said's essay, 'Swift's Tory Anarchy', in his *The World, the Text and the Critic* (Cambridge, MA, Harvard University Press; London, Faber and Faber, 1983), 54–71. It provides a timely reassessment of Swift's satire by focusing less on its targets and more on how it reflects the writer's literary personality.

References

William Dampier, *Dampier's Voyages*, ed. John Masefield, 2 vols (London, E. Grant Richards, 1906).

Samuel Johnson, *Lives of the English Poets* [1779–81], ed. G. Birkbeck Hill (Oxford, Clarendon Press, 1905; repr. 1967).

John Gay, *The Letters of John Gay*, ed. C. F. Burgess (Oxford, Oxford University Press, 1966).

John Richetti, *Popular Fiction Before Richardson: Narrative Patterns: 1700–1739* (Oxford, Oxford University Press, 1969).

Jonathan Swift, *The Prose Works of Jonathan Swift*, ed. Herbert Davis et al., 14 vols (Oxford, Oxford University Press, 1939–68).

——, *The Correspondence of Jonathan Swift*, ed. Harold Williams, 5 vols (Oxford, Oxford University Press, 1963–5).

——, *Gulliver's Travels*, ed. Paul Turner (Oxford, Oxford University Press, 1971).

——, *Swift's Irish Pamphlets*, ed. Joseph McMinn (Gerrards Cross, Colin Smythe, 1991).

Jonathan Swift et al., *The Memoirs of the Life of Martinus Scriblerus*, ed. Charles Kerby-Miller (New Haven, CT, Yale University Press, 1950).

6 William Blake

David Punter

A reproduction of 'The Chimney Sweeper' from *Songs of Innocence and of Experience*, by permission of the Provost and Scholars of King's College, Cambridge, and of the Blake Trust.

William Blake was born in 1757 and died in 1827. Apart from one brief period he spent all his life in London, where he worked as an engraver. He was also an artist and, of course, a poet, now probably one of the most famous poets in the English language. This fame, however, took a long time to come; he was little known in his own lifetime and those few who saw or read his work regarded him as at best eccentric, at worst mad.

One reason for this is the visionary nature of his work, both verbal and visual; he often said that he was not concerned with the depiction of the 'natural world', but wanted instead to portray the world of the imagination. Yet here we come across a significant apparent paradox in Blake: for although his work – and perhaps especially the series of long poems known collectively as the 'Prophetic Books' – appears at first glance to bear little relation to historical circumstance and to concern itself rather with the interactions of various quasi-mythological characters, detailed research by twentieth-century Blake scholars has shown that in fact Blake was deeply responsive to the events of his times (the American Revolution, the French Revolution, economic and political change in Britain), although his interest was always in bringing these events into alignment with his own ideas about how the cosmos worked at a deeper level.

A typical poem of this kind would be *America, A Prophecy*, completed in 1793 and recounting, albeit in a far from transparent form, some of the events of the American Revolution. Here are five lines from it:

> The Guardian Prince of Albion burns in his nightly tent;
> Sullen fires across the Atlantic glow to America's shore,
> Piercing the souls of warlike men, who rise in silent night,
> Washington, Franklin, Paine and Warren, Gates, Hancock and Greene
> Meet on the coast glowing with blood from Albion's fiery Prince.
>
> (Blake, *Complete Poems*, 191)

In order to understand this passage we have to move between two different contexts. First is the 'mythological' context which can provide us with the key to the figure of 'Albion's fiery Prince': Blake uses the figure of Albion, in accordance with older myths, as a representation of Britain in general, and thus here the Prince represents the British State that wants to hold on to its American colonies. America, on the other hand, is represented by a group of seven figures with real historical names, and in order to grasp the full significance of Blake's argument we would need to look to the historical and political contexts and to know at least something about not only eminent American statesmen like Benjamin Franklin but also about lesser-known figures like Horatio Gates and Nathaniel Greene, both of whom were American generals whose names would have been well known at the time.

The sense of context in Blake, then, is complex: we need both to grasp the inner dynamics of his poetry, the manifold meanings of figures like Albion, Los, Urizen, Urthona and many others, while at the same time keeping in mind that Blake sees the cosmic and psychological interactions of these figures as *working themselves out through* the actual events of history, frequently as they were unfolding around him. And at the same time we need to keep in mind the particularities of his own social situation, especially his status as a Londoner who knew the rest of the world only from what he heard and read. Although one of his most famous lines speaks of 'dark Satanic mills' and this has often been taken as a definitive comment on industrialisation, Blake probably saw very little indeed of such processes, which affected other areas of Britain far more than they did London.

However, in order to simplify matters a little, here I want to look in detail at the question of Blake's contexts not in the Prophetic Books but rather in two poems that occur in his best known work, the *Songs of Innocence and of Experience*. The *Songs of Innocence* are usually said to have been published in 1789, and the two sets of *Songs* together in 1794 (the *Songs of Experience* never appeared separately), but the question of 'publication' is also vexed in Blake. In fact, he hardly published anything in the sense we now mean. In the case of the *Songs* – and this is also true of many of his later works – he engraved the poems by hand, which means that no two copies are exactly the same; and one reason why he did this was because the poems cannot really be considered merely as verbal constructions. Each sheet of the *Songs* contains poetic text, but surrounding and in some cases intertwined with the words are pictures, designs, patterns – to call them 'illustrations' would be too simple, for it is clear in some cases that the full 'meaning' cannot be discovered without looking at how the visual material supplements, comments on, even changes the feeling of the poetry.

Some of the poems in the *Songs* are paired, and this is the case with the two poems I shall examine, which are both called 'The Chimney Sweeper'. Here is the one in *Songs of Innocence* :

When my mother died I was very young,
And my father sold me while yet my tongue
Could scarcely cry 'weep' 'weep', 'weep' 'weep'!
So your chimneys I sweep, and in soot I sleep.

There's little Tom Dacre, who cried when his head,
That curled like a lamb's back, was shaved; so I said,
'Hush Tom, never mind it, for when your head's bare,
You know that the soot cannot spoil your white hair.'

And so he was quiet, and that very night,
As Tom was asleeping he had such a sight –
That thousands of sweepers, Dick, Joe, Ned, and Jack,
Were all of them locked up in coffins of black;

And by came an angel, who had a bright key,
And he opened the coffins and set them all free;
Then down a green plain leaping, laughing they run,
And wash in a river and shine in the sun.

Then naked and white, all their bags left behind,
They rise upon clouds and sport in the wind.
And the angel told Tom, if he'd be a good boy,
He'd have God for his father and never want joy.

And so Tom awoke, and we rose in the dark,
And got with our bags and our brushes to work.
Though the morning was cold, Tom was happy and warm;
So if all do their duty, they need not fear harm.
            (Blake, *Complete Poems*, 68–98; see also *Songs*, 40)

How might we situate this poem in its various contexts? The first context, I would say, is the volume, the series of poems, in which it appears: *Songs of Innocence*. What might 'innocence' mean here? Does it refer to a prized quality or virtue, or to a helpless unknowingness of what is going on, of the painful realities of exploitation? More to the point, perhaps, would be to ask *where* the 'innocence' is situated, to whom it belongs. The narrator, of course, may perfectly well be innocent in the virtuous sense, in that he may believe the happy, consolatory outcome of the poem; he may, like Tom, be able to put up with his work and his condition of near-slavery ('my father sold me') because he is buoyed up by a vision of an afterlife of freedom. But this would not imply that the poet is similarly innocent, nor that the reader is enjoined to be so – we may take a very different view of the sweeps' situation.

And this would necessarily bring us to a consideration of the historical context of the poem. The critic W. H. Stevenson comments as follows:

In 1788, Jonas Hanway brought to Parliament the plight of these children. They were often 'apprenticed' (i.e. sold) at the age of about seven;

they were brutally and unscrupulously used by their masters, not clothed, fed or washed; when sweeping, they were in constant danger of suffocation or burning, besides the cancer of the scrotum caused by the soot which was literally never washed from their bodies; they were encouraged to steal, and were often turned out in the streets by their masters to 'cry the streets' on the chance of employment, or for mere begging; their dirt and their reputation for stealing made them social outcasts.

(Blake, Complete Poems, 68)

Almost every aspect Stevenson mentions is relevant to the poem; to take just one example, the practice of' 'crying the streets' (a resonant phrase in itself) immediately illuminates the brilliant way in which Blake has turned the cry of 'sweep!' into the sound of weeping, modulating the child-like articulation into a 'cry' for pity – and this very complexity, of course, will have a further effect on just how we see the concept of 'innocence' at work in the poem.

The poem also, very obviously, has a religious context. Tom Dacre's dream is in many ways cast in the conventional terms of a Christian 'paradise', reminding us – or at least reminding Blake's contemporary readers, such as they were – of hymns like 'There is a Green Hill Far Away', and through that route necessarily taking the reader back to biblical 'origins'. But here again, to contextualise in this way is only to tell part of the story, because we have to place alongside this cultural heritage Blake's own specific modifications of key words. The crucial example here is 'angel'. A reading of Blake's later work shows that his attitude towards angels was profoundly hostile; he saw them as emblems of self-righteousness, always full of pious good advice but really more concerned with being at all times 'holier than thou' than with the saving of souls. This, therefore, will have an effect on how we might read this angel's promise that Tom will have 'God for his father', and here the theological and the social come together in a resonant way because after all it is precisely the fact that he has been 'sold' by his father that has caused the narrator's – and presumably also Tom's – current plight.

The mention of hymns might also lead us to enquire into what we might call the literary contexts of the poem. The eighteenth century, we need to keep in mind, had been an age of intensely formal poetry. From the earlier part of the century, it is the name of Alexander Pope that springs most readily to mind: his use of the couplet, his insistence on rhyme and on rhythmic symmetry, his employment and modification of classical models. Obviously what we see here in Blake is very different. Where Pope sought to communicate with an educated and sophisticated elite, acting on the premise that poetry and indeed culture in general were on the verge of extinction at the hands of waiting barbarians, we find no such restriction of audience in Blake: his vocabulary could hardly be simpler, even the names of the sweeps (Tom, 'Dick, Joe, Ned, and Jack') are the most commonplace imaginable. He does use rhyme, but again in a very simple and obvious way, almost entirely involving common monosyllabic words, and his sentences approximate very closely to the patterns of the spoken language.

The use of simple language; an emphasis on the concerns of childhood; an implicit repudiation of classical and Augustan poetic models: in all of these ways we can see Blake figuring in another context, namely the beginnings of that powerful literary movement called 'romanticism' which originated in the late eighteenth and early nineteenth centuries and which, some would say, is still in certain respects with us today. Wordsworth in particular, we may remember, spoke of using language 'near to the language of men' and, although we may reasonably doubt that poetry can ever do exactly that, there is no doubt that the period saw a huge change in the theory of poetic language and in poetry's relation to its audience (see Wordsworth and Coleridge, *Lyrical Ballads*, 251).

Yet Blake's situation with regard to romanticism is interestingly oblique. For Wordsworth's poetry he cared not at all. In his *Poems* of 1815, Wordsworth speaks of the 'influence of natural objects in calling forth and strengthening the imagination in boyhood and early youth'. Blake owned a copy of this book, and in the margin he wrote in response: 'Natural Objects always did & now do weaken, deaden & obliterate Imagination in Me. Wordsworth must know that what he Writes Valuable is Not to be found in Nature' (Blake, *Complete Writings*, 783). It is certainly unlikely that Wordsworth knew, or could have believed, any such thing; but what is revealed by this little interchange is that romanticism itself had various different strands, and that while Blake's valuation of the imagination may in a sense be regarded as romantic, his scorn for 'nature' in all its forms – a very urban scorn, we might reasonably think – places him very far away from the romantic mainstream.

An urban scorn; and/or, perhaps, a class-based scorn. For Wordsworth or for Coleridge, well-educated men of means, perhaps nature could indeed offer stimulus or solace; indeed, we might well see the romantic period as the origin of the tourism and heritage industries. For Blake on the other hand, an artisan working in a declining trade, only sporadically able to find commissions, frequently let down by those who employed him, such concerns may have appeared merely frivolous when put alongside, for example, what he was constantly seeing of the social evils of London and what he was hearing about the vicissitudes of struggles for freedom overseas.

We have looked at something of the historical, religious and literary contexts of the poem, but there remains one more important context, namely the context of the very page itself on which the poem appears in its original forms. The words are surrounded, as often in Blake, by representations of foliage, but at the bottom of the page there is a picture: what it shows is the 'angel' unlocking the coffins and the young sweeps dancing for joy. The question would be, what does this add to our understanding of the poem? But perhaps this is a question that cannot properly be answered until we have had a brief look at the poem's companion-piece in *Songs of Experience*:

A little black thing among the snow
Crying 'weep', 'weep', in notes of woe!
Where are thy father and mother, say?
'They are both gone up to the church to pray.

'Because I was happy upon the heath
And smiled among the winter's snow,
They clothed me in the clothes of death
And taught me to sing the notes of woe.

'And because I am happy and dance and sing,
They think they have done me no injury –
And are gone to praise God and his priest and king,
Who make up a Heaven of our misery.'
(Blake, *Complete Poems*, 218–19)

As with the previous poem, the best place to start here is by looking at the immediate context, namely the poem's location in a group of poems under the heading 'experience'. What does Blake mean by experience here, and how does he situate the narrator and the reader? We notice immediately that the young sweep's plight is more evidently terrible in this poem: there is the snow, there is the more obvious misery evidenced in the 'notes of woe' and reinforced as the final word of the poem. Yet a question remains as to whether or in what sense experience, as we might expect from the conventional usage of the term, brings a higher level of wisdom or understanding.

What the sweep appears to be saying about his parents is that they have sold him into effective slavery *because* he 'was happy upon the heath /

And smiled among the winter's snow'; but just as Blake appeared to be inviting us to question the naïveties of the 'innocent' 'Chimney Sweeper', again here we might want to question whether the sweep's interpretation is to go unchallenged. In this case, we might think that 'experience' verges either on extreme cynicism (on the part of the parents) or paranoia (on the part of the sweep), and we might further suggest that the poem deliberately offers no single solution to the dilemma in which this puts the reader – in other words, we are being forced to see that the situation is not a straightforward one, that there will be different views of it, and that rather than residing in the comparative certainties of innocence we shall have to work to find our own interpretation of what is going on.

As with the first poem, this interpretation will depend crucially on the role of the Christian religion. The sweep's parents, he says, have 'gone up to the church to pray', suggesting that at least in his opinion the church is more concerned with the niceties of worship than with the relief of suffering. Indeed, the poem goes further; in coupling 'God and his priest and king' it strongly suggests that the church, its priests and even its conception of the deity are all inseparably linked with the exercise of monarchical state power. Whether or not we would regard this as a subversive thought today, there is no doubt that it was in Blake's time; the very phrasing of the line precisely recalls slogans that were current both in revolutionary France and also among radical groups in London.

The more, then, we look at this poem 'in context' the more we may see it not merely as a representation of a plight of suffering but as an active intervention in a political debate. We begin to see the situation of the sweep as less an individual one than one affecting an entire society, in which the church has resigned its duty of care and decisively sided with the ruling classes. 'Dear mother, dear mother, the church is cold', Blake puts it in another of the *Songs of Experience*, 'The Little Vagabond': 'But the ale-house is healthy and pleasant and warm' (Blake, *Complete Poems*, 218). This is by no means an advocacy of strong drink, but rather an invitation to reflect why the contemporary church, despite its protestations, finds it impossible to provide an environment that is 'warm', in any sense of that term.

Yet the church itself is also a symbol: for the 'coldness' spoken of here, which is also the snow amid which the sweep cries, connotes also a broader chill that, in Blake's view, is affecting the very structure of human relationship in the world around him, replacing love by mere charity. 'Pity would be no more', says the cynical narrator of a further song of 'experience', 'The Human Abstract':

If we did not make somebody poor;
And mercy no more could be,
If all were as happy as we
      (Blake, *Complete Poems*, 216)

What Blake is ironically mourning here is the death of a society – however illusory or laden with nostalgia such a view might be – in which people were bound together by ties of real love and friendship and its replacement by one based on the model of the machine; and it is in this respect rather than in any 'realistic' portrayal of features of the 'industrial revolution' that we can see Blake responding to the social and economic contexts of his time.

Perhaps, though, there are also other ways. One of the features we are bound to notice when we place the two 'Chimney Sweeper' poems together is the patterning of 'white' and 'black'. The 'innocent' song is dominated by white: Tom Dacre's white hair is compared to a 'lamb's back', and although the coffins, naturally, are black it is 'naked and white' that the children finally come to 'sport in the wind'. The 'experienced' poem is, in a sense, dominated or at least surrounded by white too, in the form of the snow – a very different white, we may think, from the white of innocence and purity offered to us, whether reliably or not, in the realm of innocence. But within this whiteness, the chimney sweep stands out: he is a 'little black thing', and we are entitled to wonder how much weight is being placed on the word 'black'.

We do know that Blake was concerned with issues of race and slavery, devoting one of the *Songs of Innocence*, 'The Little Black Boy', to a consideration of the place of black people within conventional Christianity (the lines in *America* immediately following the ones quoted above are also about slavery). Whether or not he had such matters consciously in mind here would be difficult to demonstrate, but certainly there is a connection, becoming more apparent as historians revisit the history of empire and slavery, between the industrial revolution and the apparent needs of the empire on which it was built and in whose service it operated. Here, perhaps, is where issues of context become most complex and problematic; for although it may be at least theoretically possible to reconstruct how a writer consciously reacted to his or her environment, the question remains as how unconscious influence might have worked. A final note on the 'experienced' poem: the page carries a picture of a boy with a bag of soot in the snow, an entirely realistic scene. What then *would* the relationship be between this and the very different picture accompanying the 'innocent' poem?

And what, indeed, *is* the 'context of Blake'? To assess this we would have to go back through time, to look at the changes that have affected, indeed structured, the reception of the works of a singular poet. Unknown in his lifetime, Blake only really entered the literary canon in the mid-nineteenth century when the *Songs* became anthologised as a result of the somewhat ambiguous Victorian interest in children. His longer poems were ignored until later in the nineteenth century when they became subject to the interests of mystics, cabbalists and neo-Platonists, all of whom believed that Blake's 'anti-system' could be interpreted or adapted to suit their worldview. Subsequent movements in the twentieth century have seen Blake as an archetypal myth-maker, as a profound historical commentator or as a political radical (see Frye, Erdman, Thompson). This last view, while it undoubtedly exposes and promotes a Blake that is now visible for all to see, sits particularly oddly with the alternative and more traditional view of Blake as the archetypal bluff, bulldog-like Englishman, the writer of those verses which have come down to us as the poem 'Jerusalem'.

Blake's works, then, have changed over time, as do the works of every writer and artist; context gives way to contextualisation as each generation seeks a new framework within which to situate his or her achievement. During the 1960s, a period in which Blake's texts were particularly prominent (lines like 'The road of excess leads to the palace of wisdom' and 'The tygers of wrath are wiser than the horses of instruction', from the *Proverbs of Hell*, becoming among the most often used graffiti of the period), he was seen as a radical harbinger of change, a major indicter of capitalist mechanisation. During the 1970s and 1980s, with the rise of feminism, agonies were expended over his curious anxiety about the 'Female Will'. In the 1990s much is made of his status as an early exponent of mixed media, the unique position of his works in relation to the evolution of print technology, his resistance to the processes of mechanical reproduction.

Perhaps a key word that remains useful in considering Blake and his contexts is the word 'location'. Where was Blake located, what seemed 'local' to his poetry and his art? The answer must be twofold. On the one hand his location is clearly and vibrantly London; to discover more about this, the ideal starting point is Peter Ackroyd's recent biography (see Ackroyd, *Blake*). It is an unusual biography in that it contains no new information; the archive of information on Blake is very small, compared to that available on other well-known poets of his time, and it is highly unlikely that it will ever grow any larger. The virtue of Ackroyd's book is that it provides precisely a more accurate 'contextualisation', a deeper knowledge of the London that Blake inhabited. On the other hand his location is within a complex and largely suppressed tradition which has almost nothing to do with 'high literature' but is instead composed of theological dispute, political tract, Dissenting criticism, biblical textuality: an education of a kind that is hard for us to re-envisage today.

Blake's work, we might say, has an immediate, pressing, urgent context in terms of his apparent wish to make known to his own society the truth as he saw it of what was happening around him; and at the same time it has no stable context in that it offers itself for continual remaking – as, of course, his own poems were continually remade, the major Prophetic Books never really achieving a form that any other writer might consider to be 'final'. For Blake finality itself was a problem; the notion that one might come at a final version of what one had to say would be as difficult to understand as the corollary, which would be that what one was saying had a distinct beginning, a definite origin.

Perhaps, for any literary work, there is no origin, no finality. Origin and finality for Blake would be the work of Urizen, the god of reason; the work of Los, the god of the imagination, would be quite different from that, it would be the work of ceaseless making and remaking, in the process of which it might be possible to remake context as much as it would be text.

Certainly we see no sign of a 'final Blake', and this is entirely as it should be; similarly, we see no sign of Blake being explained by any recourse to origins. What we might perhaps see instead is the weeping of the sweep, the crying of the abused child, the terror of the dark and the hypocrisy of the 'white'; do these images – among the many, many others in Blake – constitute a 'context', or might they suggest to us instead a set of questions about what is local, what is universal, and how over the ages we respond – or do not – to the attempt of the artist to 're-present' the plea of innocence, the distress of the vulnerable?

Further Reading

Nelson Hilton, *Literal Imagination: Blake's Vision of Words* (Berkeley, CA, University of California Press, 1983).

Zachary Leader, *Reading Blake's Songs* (London, Routledge & Kegan Paul, 1981).

W. J. T. Mitchell, *Blake's Composite Art: A Study of the Illuminated Poetry* (Princeton, NJ, Princeton University Press, 1978).

David Punter, 'William Blake', in *Romanticism*, ed. David Punter and Nelson Hilton, Vol. 306 of *Annotated Bibliography of English Studies* (CD-Rom) (Lisse, Swets and Zeitlinger, 1997).

David Punter (ed.), *William Blake: Contemporary Critical Essays* (London, Macmillan – now Palgrave, 1996).

Joseph Viscomi, *Blake and the Idea of the Book* (Princeton, NJ, Princeton University Press, 1993).

References

Peter Ackroyd, *Blake* (London, Sinclair-Stevenson, 1995).

William Blake, *Complete Poems*, ed. W. H. Stevenson (2nd edn, London and New York, Longman, 1989).

William Blake, *Complete Writings*, ed. Geoffrey Keynes (London, Oxford University Press, 1966).

William Blake, *Songs of Innocence and of Experience* (new edn, Oxford, Oxford University Press, 1970).

David V. Erdman, *Blake: Prophet Against Empire*, 2nd edn (Princeton, NJ, Princeton University Press, 1969).

Northrop Frye, *Fearful Symmetry: A Study of William Blake* (Princeton, NJ, Princeton University Press, 1947).

E. P. Thompson, *Witness Against the Beast: William Blake and the Moral Law* (Cambridge, Cambridge University Press, 1993).

William Wordsworth and S. T. Coleridge, *Lyrical Ballads*, ed. R. L. Brett and A. R. Jones (London, Methuen, 1968).

7 Jane Austen: *Persuasion*

Judy Simons

Anne Elliot complimented by her cousin. © Jane Austen Memorial Trust.

Nearly two centuries after their author's death, Jane Austen's novels have become runaway best sellers. Recent television and cinema adaptations of Austen's work have generated an extraordinary boom in paperback sales of the fiction as starstruck fans of Darcy (or Colin Firth?) and Colonel Brandon (or Alan Rickman?) rush to buy the book of the film. More than ever – and far more than in Jane Austen's own lifetime – students and general readers alike are turning eagerly to Austen's work with expectations of . . . What precisely? Men in tight trousers? Smouldering glances and repressed passion? Vistas of stately homes with armies of servants to match?

In their books about the making of *Pride and Prejudice* and *Emma* for British television, the producer and script editor who worked on both films make much of their attempts at historical accuracy. The choice of location, the costumes and make-up, the food, the music and the dance sequences of the TV versions are all designed to reproduce a Regency England that will convince viewers of its authenticity. Andrew Davies, who wrote the screenplay for *Emma* (as well as for *Pride and Prejudice*), has stressed that 'we should not forget that the French Revolution is still very recent history to those of Mr Woodhouse's generation' and that his script is intended to convey 'the fears and evasions of the aristocracy and gentry, living in such close proximity to the great unwashed' (Davies, *The Making of 'Emma'*, 13).

How far this social and historical consciousness emerges in the final production of *Emma* is debatable. What is accepted, however, by everyone involved in the making of this and other films of Austen texts is that narrative and characters cannot be isolated from their mode of production nor from the period in which they are written. It is equally important to appreciate – as a viewing of Davies's *Emma* immediately shows – that period reproduction on its own cannot express the full significance of the written text nor render the linguistic subtleties and the cultural tensions which at once rely on and transcend the awareness of a writer's contemporaries. Social history should not be reduced to nostalgia; at the same time, it is merely one sort of context, which as the different adaptations of the novels demonstrate, is itself a story, and consequently open to multiple interpretations.

I have begun this essay with the filmed versions of Jane Austen's works precisely because their visual impact has had such an influence on the way in which many people approach Austen nowadays. By making an obvious feature of the extra-textual elements in the books and the importance of the non-literary dimensions, the films create an important late twentieth-century context which helps to determine ways in which we find meaning in a work of literature. Screen adaptations of the novels bring vividly to life a world of social formality, with its rituals of evening parties, balls, and the codes governing communication between unmarried men and women. Yet for the most part this re-creation of a particular social environment merely serves to perpetuate the distance that exists between Jane Austen's time and our own. If anything it endorses a commonly held view that Jane Austen's vision is a narrow one, that her 'world' consists only of, as she herself observed, '3 or 4 families in a country village' (Le Faye, *Jane Austen's Letters*, 275), and that consequently it bears little relation to the society we inhabit today. As one newspaper reviewer remarked about a new TV serial, 'Good news, the best. None of this is written by Jane Austen, so it doesn't have a single aristocrat in it. And as yet, no dancing' (*Sunday Times*: 2.2.97). In at least one journalist's mind, the surface of Austen's writing has become confused with its substance.

Such a comment illustrates just how fragile is the subtle interplay between 'context' and 'text' and how a misreading of one affects the other. Dancing, which offered one of the few respectable opportunities for personal contact between the sexes, has a symbolic as well as a narrative function in Austen's fiction. Wentworth's question to his partner in chapter 8 of *Persuasion* as to whether Miss Elliot never dances has a clear inference, and the response – '"Oh! no, never; she has quite given up dancing. She had rather play. She is never tired of playing"' – conveys to him more meaningfully than anything Anne's marginal status. For Anne the dispiriting conclusion is that she is lost to him forever and it is hardly surprising that 'her eyes would sometimes fill with tears as she sat at the instrument' (64). In such a heavily codified society, dancing is no mere innocent recreation but erotically charged and redolent with connotations. In order to interpret accurately the fine gradations of feeling in this and other Austen novels, we need to comprehend something of the operation of these codes and how they governed the experience of women in Georgian England.

It is an irony Jane Austen would have appreciated that in an often-quoted letter to her sister, Cassandra, she herself provided the basis for subsequent critiques of her work. When she compared her writing to painting in miniature, 'the little bit (two Inches wide) of ivory on which I work with so fine a brush . . .' (Le Faye, *Letters*, 323), she drew attention to the restricted canvas which presents readers with its own intellectual and emotional challenge. For many years this served to focus critical scrutiny on textual minutiae and details of novelistic technique. More recently, however, scholars have argued that in order to understand the dense texture of Austen's novels, we need a mature understanding of the complex cultural forces that inform her work. For if we mistake surface for substance and take the characters' parochialism as a simple reflection of the author's own supposedly narrow interests, we overlook the astonishing scope of Austen's fiction together with the imaginative and intellectual rewards that the act of reading can bring.

Persuasion, Austen's last completed work, is a perfect illustration of the sophisticated nature of this challenge. The deceptively simple story of frustrated and then requited love operates within a highly intricate frame of referents. These referents create an implicit dialogue between sets of cultural values, contemporary ideas and moral debates, as well as a whole range of diverse literatures, which are alluded to and which would have been instinctively absorbed by nineteenth-century readers. Of course, we are never going to be able to put ourselves in the position of those original readers. Nor would we wish to. We have other perspectives at our disposal, not least our grasp of Jane Austen's twentieth-century status as a 'classic' novelist and her consequent critical reputation. Nonetheless we can recover something of these debates.

The first paragraph of *Persuasion* immediately raises some of the key questions about reception, context and interpretation.

> Sir Walter Elliot, of Kellynch Hall, in Somersetshire, was a man who, for his own amusement, never took up any book but the Baronetage; there he found occupation for an idle hour, and consolation in a distressed one; there his faculties were roused into admiration and respect, by contemplating the limited remnant of the earliest patents; there any unwelcome sensations, arising from domestic affairs, changed naturally into pity and contempt. As he turned over the almost endless creations of the last century – and there if every other leaf were powerless, he could read his own history with an interest which never failed – this was the page at which the favourite volume always opened:
>
> "ELLIOT OF KELLYNCH-HALL
>
> "Walter Elliot, born March 1, 1760, married, July 15, 1784, Elizabeth, daughter of James Stevenson, Esq. of South Park, in the county of Gloucestershire; by which lady (who died 1800) he has issue Elizabeth, born June 1, 1785; Anne, born August 9, 1787; a still-born son, Nov. 5, 1789; Mary, born Nov. 29, 1791."
>
> (5)

Persuasion is a work that mounts an enquiry into the condition of England at a precise moment in its history. It is therefore appropriate that its opening sentences should introduce the subject of history and should highlight the discomfort felt by Sir Walter, a representative of the old aristocracy, at the dawn of a new century. Unlike other Austen novels, *Persuasion* is set in an exact year, 1814, the year before Jane Austen began writing it and the year before the Battle of Waterloo. It is highly significant that Austen is writing in retrospect, with conscious knowledge of military events denied to her characters, as much of the novel debates ideas about uncertainty and human ignorance as to what the future might hold. The list of dates and names in this first paragraph helps to locate that historical specificity. The quotation from the *Baronetage* – probably Debrett's *Baronetage of England*, which was published in two volumes in 1808 – calls attention to the line of Elliot women and the lack of a male heir for Kellynch Hall. In a novel that is deeply concerned with issues of gender and power, and with the concept of inheritance (in a variety of forms), the signals provided in these opening sentences are crucial. The reference to 'the limited remnant of the earliest patents' for instance, is a reminder that the rank of baronet, which was only created in 1611 and on which Sir Walter places such reliance, is itself a social fabrication and one which is fast disappearing. The impression of a defunct world of privilege is thus definitively established.

In order, then, to probe the multiple ironies of this passage and the force of its attack on Sir Walter, we need some understanding of English history, the early nineteenth-century class structure, the prevailing laws of progeniture and the political circumstances of the Napoleonic wars. It is also helpful to know something of the biographical context to *Persuasion*, the author's family, her own reading and the novel's composition. We need a familiarity with the whole text before it is possible to appreciate the full implications of the opening. It could be argued that it is also useful, although not essential, to have read other novels by Jane Austen. As will become apparent later, an acquaintance with the literary milieu of the late eighteenth and early nineteenth century is indispensable – and in this light the fact that the *only* book that Sir Walter reads is the Baronetage becomes a significant pointer to his refusal to engage with the world of ideas. But how much of this can a modern reader reasonably be expected to absorb? And will this additional knowledge in the end really affect the ways in which the text communicates effectively with its new readers?

An explanation of the social contexts of *Persuasion* could occupy a complete critical study. Although the story focuses on that favourite Austen material of just '3 or 4 families', those families, their histories and their values reflect a major shift in the balance of power in Regency England. As the action develops, a distinct split materialises between the moribund value system of the aristocracy, with its emphasis on inherited status (represented at its most extreme by Sir Walter and Elizabeth Elliot) and the liberal attitudes of the sailors, Wentworth, Harville and Admiral Croft, who embody individualism and reflect an emergent enterprise culture. This sense of a cultural and moral division, which surfaces with increasing intensity during the novel, and which provides the basis of a number of recent interpretations of *Persuasion*, needs to be grounded in its historical moment. In particular the choice of the navy as a vehicle to epitomise the invigorating future is illuminated by an understanding of its particular resonance.

In chapter 3, Mr Shepherd notes that 'This peace will be turning all our rich Navy Officers ashore. They will all be wanting a home. . . . Many a noble fortune has been made during the war' (17). The text's exploration of personal and domestic fracture is set against a climate of national insecurity. In 1814 England had been at war with France for over twenty years and, as Austen knew only too well, the peace to which Mr Shepherd refers was transitory, to be broken again when Napoleon escaped from Elba in March 1815, a date which falls just after the novel's conclusion. The penultimate sentence of the book contains an oblique reference to this when the author, with knowing hindsight, comments that 'the dread of a future war' is all that could disturb Anne's present happiness. For readers whose country had been saved from invasion by the courage of its officers, the navy affords a tangible symbol of national glory.

Furthermore, the navy functioned as the arm of British expansion overseas. Sailors were daring, personally brave and had access to other cultures and worlds of experience that were beyond the imaginative reach of the majority of English men and women. This point is made forcefully in the scene in chapter 8 when Wentworth is describing his exploits to the Musgroves. The number of foreign territories named – Gibraltar, the West Indies, the Mediterranean, Lisbon, the East Indies, Bermuda, Bahama – not only underlines the insularity of the local community of Uppercross, for whom it is an adventure to travel as far as Bath or Lyme Regis, but implicitly celebrates British supremacy abroad. *Persuasion* examines the notion of national identity and English regionalism, in part through the use of different locations within the novel but also by its sense of distant lands, and its tacit acceptance of expansionist policy. A similar point is made in *Mansfield Park* with Sir Thomas Bertram's voyage to his plantations in Antigua, a voyage which has both a straightforward narrative function (it gets Sir Thomas conveniently out of the way) and a central thematic role in the novel's investigation of power, ownership and place.

But in addition to its national standing, its centrality to the defence of the nation and its role in territorial expansion, the navy carries important social connotations. In *Persuasion* the community of sailors represents a progressive approach to modern society which sits in direct opposition to the aristocratic privilege of Sir Walter. I once invited a class of students to explain just how Wentworth had made his fortune. One student suggested that he was a pirate. Although in one sense her remark illustrates the extent of the knowledge gulf that this collection of essays addresses, in an odd way she was right. The navy's system of financial reward in the form of prize money for the capture of enemy vessels enabled intrepid and skilled seamen to amass huge fortunes. Wentworth and Admiral Croft have accumulated personal wealth in a pre-industrial age in one of the few professions which offered commercial profit and career advancement to individuals who could prove their worth. They illustrate the increasing sway of a meritocracy, as encouraged by the navy, and they pose an inherent threat to the hierarchical system on which the Elliots and their like have so long relied. An entertaining and erudite insight into British naval life during the period 1790–1815 is provided by Patrick O'Brian's series of novels, beginning with *Master and Commander*. In their graphic realisation of the emblematic status of Austen's naval heroes, these offer a complement to *Persuasion*'s domestic world, and contextualise some of the many histories that inform Austen's novel.

An increasing tendency among modern biographers is to use an author's works to read her life as well as the other way around. *Persuasion*, with its suppressed personal agendas, forms an ideal vehicle for this sort of detective work, and this biographical context should be acknowledged, whilst also questioned. Does it help our reading of the text to know that two of Austen's brothers were sailors, both of whom reached the rank of Admiral? Austen's immediate family was neither wealthy nor from the land-owning class. Her father was a clergyman, a respectable occupation for an educated gentleman but hardly lucrative. In this light, the successful careers of Frank and Charles Austen, as with Wentworth and Croft, can be seen as models of the social mobility facilitated by the navy. Personal qualities could flourish and be rewarded in this most modern of career structures, and it is easy to empathise with Jane Austen's partiality for naval officers in both *Persuasion* and *Mansfield Park*. A knowledge of Austen's family circumstances does not necessarily explain her published work but it can augment its multiple nuances. Much has been made, for instance, of Austen's personal ill-health during the writing of *Persuasion*. Its relevance becomes apparent in evaluating the conditions surrounding the novel's composition and publication as well as exploring the text's fascination with health and sickness.

Consider, for example, the scenes in Bath, a spa where the sick converged to take the curative waters. The choice of Bath as a fictional setting carries important reverberations in *Persuasion*'s analysis of English life. The city, which in the 1770s had become synonymous with elegance and fashion, featured frequently in popular novels of the time. In this context, it is useful to have read Austen's early work, *Northanger Abbey*, written in 1799 but first published in a joint edition together with *Persuasion* in 1817. By the early nineteenth century Bath had become notorious as a marriage market, part of its role in *Northanger Abbey* and, with a poignant twist, in *Persuasion*. In *Emma* (1816), the bumptious Mrs Elton has the nerve to recommend a visit to Bath to the heroine, Emma, as her last chance to find a husband. Whereas in *Northanger Abbey* the young Catherine Morland approaches the glamorous city of Bath in a spirit of eager anticipation, by the time it features in *Persuasion*, almost twenty years later, the once sophisticated centre has become an urban wasteland, a symbol of disease and aridity. Anne Elliot thinks with distaste of 'the white glare of Bath' and in chapter 14 as she approaches the city, her heart sinks as she compares its cold formality unfavourably with 'the bustles of Uppercross and the seclusion of Kellynch'. *Northanger Abbey* comically satirises the fashionable mores of Bath and its inhabitants. *Persuasion* mercilessly exposes the stylish superficiality as essentially life-denying.

Modern critics have discussed extensively the significance of Bath's topography in *Persuasion* and how the city's architecture perpetuates the social divisions which form such a central theme of the book. As one of the most penetrating of these critics, John Wiltshire, observes, 'Bath is a city of enclosures, Squares and Circuses of geometric design explicitly sequestering the gentry who were to inhabit them from any natural wildness or irregularity' (Wiltshire, *Austen and the Body*, 191). Social demarcation is intrinsic to the town plan, protecting the civilised world from what lies just beyond the stylish boundaries and thus from any direct confrontation with lower class life. In *Persuasion* the addresses for the fictitious homes of the Elliots, Mrs Smith and Lady Dalrymple are real enough and nineteenth-century readers would be alive to the precisely calibrated economic and social value of each street name. Sir Walter is proud to have secured rented accommodation in Camden-place, a prestige spot, but also relatively newly built and, as one of Austen's biographers has commented, 'ever so slightly vulgar' in 1814 (Honan, *Jane Austen: her Life*, 181). Because of the situation of Camden-place, on the north side of the city and away from the centre, Sir Walter can remain in blissful ignorance of what happens in Westgate Buildings, the home of Mrs Smith.

Those who are familiar with the spatial arrangement of Bath would also know the layout of the main streets and crescents, the position of the Pump Rooms and the Assembly Rooms. All these appear in *Persuasion* to effect.

Anne makes feverish mental calculations as to which way to walk on the off-chance of bumping into Captain Wentworth. The distance between Union Street in the city centre and Camden-place works to her advantage, as it makes Charles reluctant to accompany her home and thus provides an opportunity for Anne and Wentworth to be alone. And the gravel walk to which they retire, passing the gardens behind The Circus, is one of the few places in Bath which offers privacy while still officially a public space. This knowledge adds spice for the cognoscenti, but its real value lies in its bearing on the novel's enquiry into solitude, communication and the correlation between language and gesture.

After all, why cannot Anne just tell Wentworth that her feelings for him have not changed? Why does he not speak directly to her instead of writing? The answers to these questions are embedded in the traditions and practices which Austen's society took for granted and which relate to a complicated history of the institution of marriage and gender relations in a society where courtship was governed by rigid behavioural codes. Setting the narrative climax in Bath, a location replete with fictional and social nuances, is a brilliantly ironic stroke. It reinforces both the insistence on and the critique of restrictive systems which suffuse this novel and which can seem so alienating to modern readers. It is worth drawing attention to some of the most telling of these, as frequently the details of architecture, costume and behavioural mannerisms are taken for little more than period devices, the stage dressing on which the camera lingers in certain screen adaptations of Austen. Such minutiae, however, have an important thematic function. When located in the deliberately formal setting of Bath with its narcissistic observance of social ritual, they acquire a further resonance, as the city itself seems determined to keep the lovers apart.

For instance much of the action of Jane Austen's novels is organised around social occasions, visits, parties and balls. This should not be taken to indicate that Austen's concerns are frivolous or that she is blind to the larger political movements that affect the population at large. As the preceding section of this essay demonstrates, Jane Austen's writing reflects and records those movements as they shape individual lives in ostensibly unassuming circumstances. *Persuasion*, in common with the rest of Austen's fiction, recognises, however, that the fabric of ordinary lives consists of daily trivia and the subtleties that govern the most intimate human dealings. It is interesting to note that recent trends in historical scholarship have also shifted towards a concentration on these quotidian experiences as a means of deconstructing 'official' views of history. Some of the most trenchant of these adopt a female perspective, and draw on personal writings, diaries and letters to uncover the covert, alternative histories which are buried beneath the surface of authorised accounts of the period. Such previously neglected source materials, which form the basis for example of Amanda Vickery's excellent *The Gentleman's Daughter* (1998), tell a different story, and one which validates Anne Elliot's impassioned outburst to Captain Harville in chapter 23 about women's historical exclusion from public articulacy.

In its focus on the tension between private feeling and public notice, *Persuasion* forms the fictional corollary to modern investigative scholarship of which Vickery's work is a model. The portraits of the women characters in *Persuasion* are so balanced as to reflect variant ideologies of contemporary femininity. This subsumes and extends beyond simplistic arguments about women's rights. The radicalism which permeated political thought during this period also infiltrated views on family life and domestic management. Conduct books, which advised on correct behaviour for young women, who were legally subject to their fathers and husbands, generally advocated a conservative and passive femininity. Early feminist tracts, such as Mary Wollstonecraft's *A Vindication of The Rights of Women* (1792), vigorously challenged the precepts underlying such advice. *Persuasion* forms an intervention in this controversy by exploring divergent models of womanhood, including the highly unorthodox Mrs Croft, who has no time for ladylike affectation, and has accompanied her husband on numerous voyages overseas. Wentworth is initially disapproving. 'I hate to hear of women on board', he sniffs in chapter 8. Mrs Croft's response, 'I hate to hear you talking . . . as if women were all fine ladies, instead of rational creatures'(63), is a key pointer in the novel's investigation of female behaviour. The figure of Anne Elliot, her shift from a passive character to one who initiates and takes control, acquires added meaning when read in the light of the topical debates on women's roles.

The context for a work of art encompasses far more than historical events or a knowledge of period customs and manners. History is after all merely another fiction, a narrative interpretation of events from a particular viewpoint. As Anne Elliot powerfully reminds Captain Harville in that pivotal conversation, arguments should never resort to quoting 'examples in books. Men have had every advantage of us in telling their own story. Education has been theirs in so much higher a degree; the pen has been in their hands. I will not allow books to prove anything' (206).

Austen is being deliberately disingenuous here, for, paradoxically, given the strength of Anne's declaration, *Persuasion* is littered with references to the power of books, and indeed is itself a book that is out to prove a case. Some knowledge of aesthetic theory and of Jane Austen's own reading can be invaluable in de-coding the clues to other literatures that comprise the novel's intellectual substance. *Persuasion* has frequently been cited as a novel that releases Jane Austen's romanticism. But the allusions to both classical and popular authors in *Persuasion* coalesce to promote not a single literary agenda but a sophisticated response to the surrounding intellectual and literary environment. A study of these contexts is crucial in recognising how and why critical assessments of Austen have undergone dramatic change during the twentieth century. Whereas early critics considered Jane Austen to be little more than an inspired but sheltered amateur, modern scholars now accept that she was an erudite and incisive analyst, steeped in and responsive to the contemporary professional climate of authorship.

Certainly *Persuasion* is a work that celebrates passion as a revitalising force, and gives credence to the inner life of individual emotions. It charts a standard literary opposition of country and city, prioritising the values of rural life and the natural landscape against the artifice of Bath. The description in chapter 11 of the dramatic scenery around Lyme Regis with its 'green chasms between romantic rocks' (86) typifies the spirit of the romantic age, and indeed Jane Austen's own creative period almost exactly maps on to that of the great romantic writers, Wordsworth, Coleridge, Scott and Byron. Byron's poems, *The Giaour* and *The Bride of Abydos*, to which Captain Benwick refers in chapter 11, were published in 1813, making them a particularly fashionable read in the year in which *Persuasion* is set. These and other writings have a key place in the referential scheme of the novel but Byron in particular, the arch iconoclast, is mentioned for sardonic effect. To categorise Austen simply as a romantic writer is to overlook the tension between classical and romantic thought that the text negotiates.

The point is made most tellingly in the depiction of Captain Benwick, a portrait which satirises the stereotypic contemporary reader who slavishly follows the latest literary trends. As Charles Musgrove comments, 'Give him a book and he will read all day long' (118). Benwick, introduced as a man distraught with grief, is rather a man who follows the vogue for maudlin posing but whose melancholy is exposed as relatively shallow. Supposedly inconsolable after the death of his beloved fiancée, his penchant for poetry that feeds his misery arouses both Anne's suspicions and the reader's sense of the potential for emotional indulgence generated by sentimental and romantic literature. Some understanding of contemporary aesthetics, the lineage of sensibility and Austen's own preferences in reading can thus usefully illuminate the novel's discursive framework in relation to these current artistic debates.

Like all Jane Austen's novels, *Persuasion* is heavily allusive. The entire plot of the novel engages in a dialogue with past fictional conventions, and Austen's disruption of common literary prototypes is a fundamental ingredient in the ironic structure of the narrative. It is difficult for readers who are not immersed in the reading habits of that generation to appreciate fully the atypical choice of Anne Elliot and Captain Wentworth as romantic lovers. Conventional heroines, such as those in the novels of Fanny Burney or Charlotte Smith (two of Austen's predecessors), were seventeen or eighteen years old. As that introductory extract from the *Baronetage* reveals, Mary Musgrove marries Charles when she is just nineteen. At twenty-seven, Anne does not fit comfortably into the category of romantic stereotype and the initial references to her 'loss of bloom' endorse the impression of sexual decline. In its choice of ageing lovers, *Persuasion* self-consciously subverts popular fictional norms. For not only are Wentworth and Anne capable of intense passion, they also transpose the customary motif whereby lively and naïve heroines were inevitably chastened and educated by mature heroes. In *Persuasion* it is the dashing Captain Wentworth who learns from Anne's sagacity. Similarly Lady Russell, who represents the older generation, learns from the younger woman whom she treats as a daughter. The advice that Lady Russell gives the youthful Anne Elliot when she is first courted by Wentworth is that traditionally given by literary parents to their impulsive children. *Persuasion*'s critique of this model both explodes the conventional formula of romance storytelling and makes its own narrative design work as a participant in the contest between competing fictional genres and traditions.

It is fitting that a novel so concerned with the act of reading as *Persuasion* should have been exposed to such diverse interpretations by succeeding generations of readers. This essay has drawn attention to several determining contexts for *Persuasion*. These are, however, by no means the only factors to be taken into account in reading this complex work. In addition to the social, political, ideological and biographical factors mentioned here, readers need to be alert to the linguistic contexts, the semantic changes and the proprieties of speech, which so affect meaning and interpretation in Austen's writing, and which have been examined and explained by modern critics such as Norman Page. We also need to appreciate the special circumstances that surrounded the publication and production of *Persuasion*, a novel which appeared in a joint volume with *Northanger Abbey* after Jane Austen's death. *Persuasion* is the only one of Austen's works for which we have evidence of significant redrafting in extant earlier versions of its final chapters. These, taken with the fact that we know the original title of the book was not *Persuasion* but *The Elliots*, tell us much about the thinking behind the novel and the method of artistic composition. In this essay, Jane Austen's own intellectual heritage is referred to only in passing, but it covers an enormous field and is worthy of further intensive study. What this present essay seeks to do is to locate this single novel within a continuum of artistic practice that is in constant dialogue with the currents of thought and social developments of the age in which it was written. It is only by appreciating this fundamental premise and attempting to explore some of those influences, that the book will yield its rewards.

Further Reading

Two editions of Jane Austen, *Persuasion* (London, 1817) are recommended. The Penguin Classics edition, edited and with an introduction by Gillian Beer, is the edition referred to throughout this essay. Another useful modern edition, which has excellent notes and valuable contextual appendices is that edited by Linda Bree (Broadview Press, 1999).

Inevitably, given her classic status, Jane Austen has been the subject of voluminous critical work. A good introduction to Austen in her historical context is Roger Sales' *Jane Austen and Representations of Regency England* (London and New York, Routledge, 1994). Isobel Armstrong's *Jane Austen: Mansfield Park: Penguin Critical Studies* (London, Penguin, 1988) includes contextual material which is seminal to a reading of Jane Austen's work in general. It provides a model for examining ways in which Austen's writing engages in a dialogue with the intellectual and political forces of her day. In this it builds on Marilyn Butler's pioneering critical study, *Jane Austen and the War of Ideas* (Oxford, Oxford University Press, revd edn, 1985).

Mary Lascelles' *Jane Austen and her Art* (Oxford, Oxford University Press, 1937) was one of the first modern studies to challenge the view of Jane Austen as inspired amateur. Lascelles showed how up to date Austen's writing really was. This has been developed in the recent emphasis on Jane Austen's professionalism, as foregrounded in certain biographies of Austen, such as Jan Fergus's *Jane Austen: A Literary Life* (London, Macmillan – now Palgrave, 1991). The allusive nature of Jane Austen's fiction is further developed in Jocelyn Harris's accessible *Jane Austen's Art of Memory* (Cambridge, Cambridge University Press, 1989).

Feminist critiques of Jane Austen's novels have also been a determining factor in her reassessment for modern readers. Among the most important of these is Claudia Johnson's *Jane Austen: Women, Politics and the Novel* (Chicago, Chicago University Press, 1988) which argues that gender itself is profoundly implicated in political debates. A useful complement to this work is Janet Todd's *Sensibility: An Introduction* (London, Methuen, 1986) which gives a historical overview of one of the most significant literary and cultural phenomena to affect Jane Austen's writing. Among the many collections of essays which deal with feminist and other contextual approaches to *Persuasion*, I would single out Margaret Kirkham, *Jane Austen: Feminism and Fiction* (Brighton, Harvester, 1984) and Judy Simons, *Mansfield Park and Persuasion: Contemporary Critical Essays* in the *New Casebook* series (London, Macmillan – now Palgrave, 1998).

References

Jane Austen, *Persuasion* (1818). The page references given here are to the edition edited by Gillian Beer (London, Penguin Books, 1998).

Andrew Davies, quoted in Sue Birtwistle and Susie Conklin, *The Making of Jane Austen's 'Emma'* (London, Penguin Books, 1996).

Deirdre Le Faye (ed.), *Jane Austen's Letters* (Oxford, Oxford University Press, 1995).

Park Honan, *Jane Austen: her Life* (London, Weidenfeld & Nicolson, 1987, revised edn 1997).

Patrick O'Brian, *Master & Commander* (London, Collins, 1970) is the first of a series of novels about navy life in the Napoleonic period. Taken together they offer a superb alternative portrait of the sort of experience that provides the backdrop to *Persuasion*.

Norman Page, *The Language of Jane Austen* (Oxford, Basil Blackwell, 1972).

Amanda Vickery, *The Gentleman's Daughter* (New Haven, CT, Yale University Press, 1998).

John Wiltshire, *Jane Austen and the Body* (Cambridge, Cambridge University Press, 1992).

8 Charlotte Brontë: *Jane Eyre*

Heather Glen

The visit of the mad woman after the marriage between Jane Eyre and Mr Rochester is interrupted. After the watercolour by the Victorian illustrator Fred Walker.

In the opening chapter of *Jane Eyre* there is an image of a girl reading, sitting alone 'in retirement', and turning the pages of a book. It is an image with which the reader can immediately identify: he (or more usually she), too, is bending over a book. And it is an image which reflects upon reading in complex and suggestive ways. It speaks, first and foremost, of enjoyment. 'With Bewick on my knee, I was then happy: happy at least in my way', says Jane. The book over which she pores commands her 'eager attention': like those stories of 'love and adventure' which the maid Bessie tells to the children, it is a 'profoundly interesting' one. For this child whom others berate and harass, reading is a means of entry into private, subjective space. It is a space not of learning, but of wonder. 'The words in these introductory pages connected themselves with the succeeding vignettes', she says, as she quotes Bewick's description of the Arctic regions, and goes on to offer her 'half-comprehended' but 'strangely impressive' 'notions' of what she reads (*Jane Eyre*, 8–9). But if it provides an escape from a loveless, oppressive reality, reading leads, in these opening pages of *Jane Eyre*, not merely out of Jane's actual world, but also into it. Her cousin (throwing it at her) is shortly to use this book as an instrument of violence. And books become weapons for Jane, too, in a rather different sense. 'Wicked and cruel boy!' she cries when he hurls Bewick at her. 'You are like a murderer – you are like a slave-driver – you are like the Roman emperors!' For, as she tells the reader, she 'had read Goldsmith's History of Rome, and . . . had drawn parallels in silence, which I never thought thus to have declared aloud' (11). Here, as in that earlier scene of pleasurable private absorption, reading means liberation: the child is not told how to read, but 'form[s] an idea of [her] own' (8).

Jane Eyre is a novel which questions particularly sharply that which the study of 'English' as an academic subject has come to involve. For this is a novel which seems to disarm criticism, which generations of readers have quite unreflectingly enjoyed. Indeed, its very first critic – the publisher to whom the unknown author submitted it – was, he confesses, unable to put it down. 'The story quickly took me captive', he recalls; and he tells how he missed engagements and meals to finish it the same day (George Smith, quoted in Barker, *The Brontës*, 527). 'We open *Jane Eyre*; and in two pages every doubt is swept clean from our minds', wrote Virginia Woolf in 1916. 'Nor is this exhilaration short-lived. It rushes us through the entire volume, without giving us time to think, without letting us lift our eyes from the page' (Woolf, *Common Reader*, 197). *Jane Eyre* has been, as Angela Carter puts it, 'angry, sexy . . . a perennial bestseller' for 150 years (Carter, *Expletives Deleted*, 161). But it is not merely that this is perhaps the most genuinely popular of all the texts on the syllabus. The novel's own images of reading as a space of private, subjective freedom, both empowering and subversive, appear quite sharply opposed to that public academic context in which the teacher knows more than the student and the student is a 'candidate' to be tested on the 'knowledge' s/he has acquired. If pupils are to be required to show understanding not merely of the contexts in which literary texts are written, but also of those within which they are understood, this academic context, of prescription and regulation, bears a strangely ironic relation to that long, well-attested history of passionate reader-response.

The injunction to understand not merely the text but its context may seem, in the case of *Jane Eyre*, a particularly deadening one. For if this is a novel which generations of readers have quite unreflectingly enjoyed, it is one which, it seems, few readers need assistance to understand. As Jane's intimate addresses to her singular 'reader' suggest, this is the most private of first-person narratives. It seems to speak not of large public issues, but of urgent personal experience: the weakness and defenceless-ness of childhood, a desire for 'Liberty, Excitement, Enjoyment' (89), a pas-sionate longing for love. The requirement to understand context in the case of such a work as this may seem like an effort to claim for the academy that which students see as speaking quite straightforwardly of their own most immediate concerns.

Yet the impulse to know more about *Jane Eyre*'s context has not, as it happens, been entirely an academic one. That image of the child Jane reading is an image not merely of subversive pleasure, but of an encounter with worlds unknown. That feeling, which generations of varying readers have shared, that this is a novel which speaks most directly and intimately to them, has been accompanied, always, by a fascination with the other-ness of its author's life. From the moment of the novel's publication, inter-est in 'Currer Bell' was intense: Mrs Gaskell's *Life of Charlotte Brontë*, published four years after her death, was to make the 'Brontë story' at least as compelling as their works. Even before the opening of the Brontë Museum in 1895, visitors streamed to Haworth Parsonage; since then, mil-lions of *Jane Eyre*'s readers have made the 'Brontë pilgrimage'. It is easy to mock Brontë tourism. But it might also, I think, be seen as expressive of something too often missing from more sophisticated critical analyses – that leap of the historical imagination which finds in the records of the past not simply a reflection of self, or of present-day concerns, but some-thing tantalisingly inscrutable, and which leads to the urge to find out more about the world from which they came.

What do we need to know in order to understand *Jane Eyre*? It might be helpful to think of our reading of the novel as like an encounter with a person from a culture different from ours. We will misunderstand such a person, even if we seem to share a language, if we assume that the meanings of the words they use, or their ways of making sense of their world, are exactly the same as our own. But in order to understand them, we do not need to have an exhaustive knowledge of the structures and customs of the culture from which they come. What is required is, rather, a respect for and an openness to difference, and a willingness to ask and find out about that which it seems we need to know. Our enquiries will of course be prompted by that which interests us most. Just so, in reading a text like *Jane Eyre*, we need to be aware that its meanings and its ways of configuring its world may be rather different from ours. But we do not need a great deal of knowledge to have such an awareness as this. Rather, we should simply read carefully, attentive to what seems strange in the text, and allow that strangeness to lead us toward the context we need to understand. For a novel such as *Jane Eyre* tells us a good deal more, more explicitly, about its relevant contexts than another person would. It is not merely that it offers a distinctive representation of a distinctive social world. Its very medium – language – is a historically freighted one. It draws our attention to its contexts in distinctively literary ways – sometimes, indeed, by emphasising terms which the novel itself indicates are problematic or strange.

'I had drawn parallels in silence', Jane recalls of her youthful reading. And at a later point in her narrative she echoes these early words. 'Millions are condemned', she says, 'to a stiller doom than mine, and millions are in silent revolt against their lot.' She goes on to make a passionate plea on behalf of womankind:

> Women are supposed to be very calm generally: but women feel just as men feel; they need exercise for their faculties and a field for their efforts as much as their brothers do; they suffer from too rigid a restraint, too absolute a stagnation, precisely as men would suffer; and it is narrow minded to say that they ought to confine themselves to making puddings and knitting stockings, to playing on the piano and embroidering bags. It is thoughtless to condemn them, or laugh at them, if they seek to do more or learn more than custom has pronounced necessary for their sex.
>
> (p. 115)

Here, Jane connects her own most intimate yearnings to that which 'millions' 'feel'. And here she speaks directly of a context which might help us to understand that which 'millions' of readers have found inspiring in *Jane Eyre*.

For the 'custom' to which Jane here refers was a powerful and pre-
scriptive one. Women in early nineteenth-century England were 'supposed
to be' quite different from men; destined by God and by nature not for an
active life in the world, but for the domestic sphere. Advice books of the
period reiterate this belief. 'Woman . . . must not be on the look-out for
excitement of any kind', one such book declares. 'She . . . must find her
pleasures as well as her occupation in the sphere which is assigned to her.
St Paul knew what was best for [her] when he advised her to be domestic. He knew that home was her safest place; home her appropriate station'
(Sandford, 169). For women were seen as 'relative creatures', designed to
be dependent on men; 'all independence is unfeminine', one typical writer
maintains (*Woman: as she is, and as she should be*, I, 37). They were not
'supposed' to have desires of their own, but to minister to others' needs.
It is against such 'pronouncements' as these that Jane is protesting when
she says that 'women feel just as men feel', and insists that 'they need
exercise for their faculties . . . as much as their brothers do'.

That which she here proclaims is writ large in her narrative. For in *Jane
Eyre* the girl who once 'possessed herself of a volume' which her cousin
considered his becomes an accomplished woman whom others respect
and admire. She who thrilled to Bessie's stories and longed for 'incident,
life, fire, feeling' (122) insists upon her right to 'a full and delightful life'
(265). She who rebelled against authority claims equality with her
employer and resists the call to end her days as 'helpmeet' to a mission-
ary (428). She gains an education, she earns her own living, she struggles,
she survives: above all, she refuses to compromise herself. 'I am not an
angel', she says to Rochester. 'I will be myself' (272). '*I* care for myself',
she says (334); 'I married him' (473) And if that final address to the reader
describes a conventional feminine fate, the form of the sentence in which
Jane describes it is quite at odds with what convention saw as the femininity of her time. 'A book more unfeminine, both in its excellences and
its defects, it would be hard to find in the annals of female authorship',
wrote one contemporary reviewer, indeed, in the *Christian Remembrancer*
(quoted in Allott, *The Brontës*, 89). Yet this is what has excited 'millions'
of the novel's readers, not merely in its own time, but since. As the American poet Adrienne Rich puts it, 'The wind that blows through this novel
is the wind of sexual equality' (Rich, *Selected Prose*, 105).

Yet to reconstruct this context is not to explain *Jane Eyre*. For if 'millions'
have thrilled to Jane's as a story of a woman's self-assertion, millions more,
perhaps, have been yet more powerfully moved by a rather different *Jane
Eyre*. To them, the novel is a Cinderella fable, in which she who was 'less
than a servant' becomes the lady of the house; in which the orphan

child finds kinsfolk and she who was unloved finds love. This, as present-day feminists have not been slow to point out, is not exactly a story of self-sufficiency. If Jane returns to Rochester as an 'independent woman', her wealth is the result of a fortunate legacy. She has, it is true, supported herself as a teacher. But this 'exercise for [her] faculties', this 'field for [her] efforts', cannot, it seems, really satisfy her. 'And yet, reader', she says, with confessional intimacy,

> after a day passed in honourable exertion amonst my scholars, an evening spent in drawing or reading contentedly alone, I used to rush into strange dreams at night . . . and then the sense of . . . loving him, being loved by him – the hope of passing a lifetime at his side, would be renewed, with all its first force and fire.

> (386)

On hearing a 'mysterious summons' from him whom she calls her 'Master', she readily abandons this 'free and honest' life. She who urged that 'women . . . need exercise for their faculties, and a field for their efforts' finds contentment now in domestic retirement. That rebellious, solitary reader, drawing 'parallels in silence' is by her story's close a very different figure: 'never did I weary of reading to him' (475).

Indeed, it is simply as a love story that *Jane Eyre* has won much of its enduring popularity. Yet this aspect of the novel has always, as it happens, been a controversial one. Jane's passionate longing for love has, predictably, proved disquieting to those who have tried to read this as an inspirational narrative of feminine independence. But it was also, differently, disturbing to those other early readers who saw such a longing as this as an offence against 'propriety'. 'That men and women should marry we had all of us acknowledged as one of the laws of humanity', wrote Mrs Oliphant, one of the novel's first reviewers. 'But up to the present generation most young women had been brought up in the belief that their own feelings on this subject should be religiously kept to themselves' (quoted in Allott, *The Brontës*, 391). Of all the feminine faults which the advice book writers strove to correct, one of the most deplored is woman's yearning for love. 'The desire of being beloved . . . who shall record the endless variety of suffering it entails upon woman?' lamented Sarah Ellis, one of the most famous of such writers. 'The world has no wealth to offer, that she would possess alone' (Ellis, *Women of England*, 305). 'This species of feeling is a mere *ignis fatuus*, leading often into all kinds of bogs and morasses', another declared. 'We may find in the events of a single day many channels in which our feelings may flow and with propriety, without need of this especial one which is called love' (Lamb, *Can Women Regenerate Society?* 87, 94). Indeed, such sentiments are echoed by the governess Jane Eyre. 'It is madness', she says, as she struggles to suppress her love for Rochester, 'in all women to let a secret love kindle within them'; for if it is unreturned, it must 'devour the life that feeds it', and if it is discovered and responded to, it will 'lead *ignis-fatuus*-like, into miry wilds whence there is no extrication'. Thus she seeks unsuccessfully to reason herself out of her apparently hopeless desire (169).

Yet in *Jane Eyre* 'the desire of being beloved' seems compelling, and paramount, displacing, rather than countered by, the soberer satisfactions which moralists and feminists recommend. Six years after the publication of *Jane Eyre*, one of Charlotte Brontë's few close friends, Harriet Martineau, lamented her 'incessant . . . tendency to describe the need of being loved'. 'It is not thus in real life', she maintained. 'There are substantial, heartfelt interests for women of all ages, and under ordinary circumstances, quite apart from love' (quoted in Allott, *The Brontës*, 172). Martineau was a dedicated campaigner for women's rights: her suspicion of what she called 'the need of being loved' was based on an acute sense of the social disadvantage which could make it an undermining obsession for women. Yet the rational common sense of her invocation of other 'interests' seems a curiously blunt response to the urgency of *Jane Eyre*. 'I know what *love* is as I understand it', wrote Brontë to Martineau, in passionate reply, 'and if man or woman should be ashamed of feeling such love, then there is nothing right, noble, faithful, truthful, unselfish in this earth' (quoted in Allott, *The Brontës*, 171). In *Jane Eyre*, that 'desire of being beloved' which her contemporaries deplored is presented neither as obsession nor as sin, nor even simply as romantic desire, but as an absolute primary need.

Jane Eyre is not simply a young woman lured by the *ignis fatuus* of romance. For the whole first third of the novel she appears not thus, but as a subjugated, unloved child. It is this which sets this novel apart from every other of its period – except that which its author perhaps knew best, her sister's *Wuthering Heights*. It is this which might lead us to think of *Jane Eyre* not merely as telling the singular story of Jane's self-reliance and fulfilment but as posing rather larger, more searching questions than might at first appear. In her portrayal of her heroine's childhood, Charlotte Brontë points toward a context very different from that which Jane invokes in her plea on behalf of womankind. It is a context which is signalled not, like those 'pronouncements' on women against which Jane argues so eloquently, by direct polemical engagement, but in quite a different way.

In the opening pages of the novel the child Jane's 'dependent' status is continually, accusingly stressed. 'You have no business to take our books', John Reed declares, when Jane is discovered reading in the breakfast-room window-seat. 'You are a dependant, mamma says; you have no money; your father left you none; you ought to beg, and not to live here with gentlemen's children like us' (11). 'You are less than a servant', says the lady's-maid, 'for you do nothing for your keep.' 'You are under obligations to Mrs Reed: she keeps you', warns Bessie. 'If she were to turn you off, you would have to go to the poorhouse.' 'I had nothing to say to these words', Jane recalls. 'They were not new to me: my very first recollections of existence included hints of the same kind. This reproach of my dependence had become a vague singsong in my ear; very painful and crushing, but only half intelligible' (13). If the adult Jane takes issue with what her society prescribes for woman, the child Jane is altogether more baffled by that which others tell her of her place within her world. 'Benefactress! benefactress!' she thinks. 'They all call Mrs Reed my benefactress; if so, a benefactress is a disagreeable thing' (34). 'I read these words over and over again', she says, of the tablet commemorating the foundation of Lowood Institution. 'I felt that an explanation belonged to them, and was unable fully to penetrate their import' (51). By presenting these authoritative 'words' from the perspective of the bewildered child, Charlotte Brontë makes them seem strange. And in doing so she prompts her reader to consider the nature of the social arrangements which such pronouncements justify.

As that reference to the 'poorhouse' suggests, the England of which these strange 'words' speak is that which had been ushered in by the controversial New Poor Law of 1834. This Act (of which Charlotte Brontë's father had been an impassioned opponent) defined the unfortunate as having not claims upon but 'obligations' to others, and institutionalised 'charity' in a way which meant that the 'poorhouse' was more a place of deterrence than a refuge for those in need. As soon as one is aware of this, a pattern of emphases in the novel which might otherwise seem incidental springs into sharp relief. 'Why do they call it an Institution?' Jane asks on her first day at Lowood, as she tries to forget 'the cold which nipped me without, and the unsatisfied hunger which gnawed me within'. 'It is partly a charity-school', Helen Burns replies. 'You and I, and all the rest of us are charity-children'(52). 'Charity', here, is something chilling and mystifying, its recipients a race apart; it is less to be welcomed than feared. 'Cold charity must be entreated before I could get a lodging', Jane agonises on her flight from Thornfield (341). This is a world in which those without resources are seen as hardly human at all. A 'rat', John Reed calls his cousin; 'like a mad cat', says Bessie (11, 12); ten years later her aunt recalls the fear the child's outburst inspired in her – 'as if an animal that I had struck or pushed had looked up at me with human eyes and cursed me in a man's voice' (251) . Such habits of thought are writ large in the wider society. The world into which Jane wanders, alone and destitute, after her flight from Rochester is a place in which there can be no reliance on others; in which want is met with suspicion and need means degradation. 'I blamed none of those who repulsed me', she says. 'I felt it was what was to be expected' (346). 'I drew near houses; I left them, and came back again, and again I wandered away: always repelled by the consciousness of having no claim to ask – no right to expect interest in my isolated lot' (345). 'Brought face to face with Necessity', she sums up her society's measure of human value in a telling series of appositions: 'I stood in the position of one without a resource, without a friend, without a coin' (344).

'But I was a human being', says Jane, 'and had a human being's wants' (342). *Jane Eyre*'s portrayal of this social world has always provoked anxiety. To some of its earliest reviewers Jane's was the voice of 'moral Jacobinism', 'the tone of mind and thought which has overthrown authority and violated every code human and divine abroad, and fostered Chartism and rebellion at home' (quoted in Allott, *The Brontës*, 90, 109). But more recent critics have found quite different causes for disquiet. If Jane is presented in the novel as a victim of a dehumanising society, her narrative seems shaped by that society's assumptions, even at points where her own experience might seem sharply to question them. That sense of 'dependence' as shame instilled in her as a child informs her later account of her homeless wanderings. She describes her efforts to obtain work and food as a 'moral degradation'; when she must 'ask relief for want of which I was sinking' she is, she says, 'brought low' (346, 345). 'I felt it would be degrading', she says, 'to faint with hunger on the causeway of a hamlet': privation, it seems, must be hidden from others' gaze (343). The dominant feeling is not of outrage, but of humiliation. And as her problems are resolved, the rebellious, excluded Jane becomes a pillar of this society. The woman who as a child of ten gave her 'furious feelings uncontrolled play' becomes a disciplinarian – instructing the pupils in her school 'in learning their tasks regularly' and 'acquiring quiet and orderly manners' (385); supervising the education which corrects Adèle's 'French defects' (474). She who refused to accept that 'it is your place to be humble, and to try to make yourself agreeable' is pleased to report that her erstwhile pupil has become 'a pleasing and obliging companion: docile, good-tempered and well-principled. By her grateful attention to me and mine, she has long since well repaid any little kindness I ever had it in my power to offer her' (13, 474). In the end, now a married gentlewoman of independent means, she retreats to domestic seclusion, far from that world whose rigours her story has exposed.

It is unsurprising, in view of all this, that where once *Jane Eyre* was condemned as radical, now it is seen as not nearly radical enough. For some present-day critics, intent on political correctness, Jane has begun to seem less a heroic Everywoman than one who becomes the mouthpiece of some of the most repressive features of the ideology of her time. Such readings as this might well give pause to the unreflective identification which many have felt with Jane Eyre. But they also, I think, leave much unaccounted for. For the ordinary reader's enduring sense that there is something subversive in this novel should not, I think, be seen as simply naïve. In the remainder of this essay, I wish to look a little more closely at that in the text which seems most to have prompted this feeling – that compelling, embarrassing insistence on love – in order to suggest that there might be another way of reading *Jane Eyre*.

Faced starkly with the fact of her economic 'dependence', the child Jane gives voice to another, and much more urgent need. 'You think I have no feelings', she says to Mrs Reed, 'and that I can do without one bit of love or kindness; but *I cannot live so . . .*' (38). It is the child's baffled recognition of this, as much as her rebellious anger, that dominates these opening pages. Throughout the narrative which follows her longing for 'love or kindness' is as urgent, as unquestionable as the instinct for life itself. 'If others don't like me', she declares to Helen Burns, 'I would rather die than live.' 'Hush, Jane! you think too much of the love of human beings', the latter replies (72). But Helen is dying: the imaginative weight of the novel is with Jane. It is only as her own sense of the world is acknowledged, as she is recognised with 'kindness' rather than labelled as a Liar, that the child for whom 'the present was vague and strange' and who could 'form no conjecture' of the future (51) finds her 'memory . . . improved', her 'wits . . . sharpened' and learns 'the first two tenses' of the French verb *to be* (78).

Love as the necessary condition for existence: this emphasis recurs throughout *Jane Eyre*. Even the dying Helen Burns is kindled into life in 'the presence and kindness of her beloved instructress' (76). The death-bound St. John Rivers comes to life when he sees his beloved: 'his cheek would glow, and his marble-seeming features . . . changed indescribably' (387). Gazing at her face in the glass, Jane finds 'hope in its aspect and life in its colour' as she thinks of Rochester's love (269). 'When once I had pressed the frail shoulder', says he of his first meeting with her, 'something new – a fresh sap and sense – stole into my frame' (329). Rescued from destitution, Jane is brought back to life not merely by being provided with food and drink and shelter, but by the 'reviving pleasure' she finds in her kinsfolks' society (368). She speaks at last of her reunion with Rochester as a triumphant culmination of this coming to life through love: 'I knew I suited him; all I said or did seemed either to console or revive him. Delightful consciousness! It brought to life and light my whole nature: in his presence I thoroughly lived; and he lived in mine' (460). Conversely, the withdrawal or absence of love is portrayed in *Jane Eyre* as an assault on life itself. 'Helen Burns was not here; nothing sustained me . . . I had meant to be so good, and to do so much at Lowood; to make so many friends, to earn respect, and win affection', says Jane, as she tells of her public shaming. 'Now, here I lay again crushed and trodden on; and could I never rise more? "Never", I thought; and ardently I wished to die' (71). 'To me, he was in reality become no longer flesh, but marble', she says of St. John Rivers' disapproval. 'I felt how, if I were his wife, this good man, pure as the deep sunless source, could soon kill me, without drawing from my veins a single drop of blood, or receiving on his own crystal conscience the faintest stain of crime' (433).

This kind of imagery, with its life and death urgency, runs right through *Jane Eyre*. It is to this that one must attribute much of the novel's distinctive power. Even when focused on the Byronic figure of a Mr Rochester, the longing which pervades the novel is less a desire for self-surrender than a longing for life itself. 'I love Thornfield: I love it, because I have lived in it a full and delightful life', says Jane. 'I have not been petrified . . . I see the necessity of departure; and it is like looking on the necessity of death' (265). These words are underwritten by one of the most powerful episodes in *Jane Eyre*: that central, disquieting scenario, in which Jane does leave Thornfield, falls away from all human recognition – 'Alas, this isolation – this banishment from my kind!' she thinks, at her worst extremity (353) – and faces a lonely, agonising death. For that image of Jane's destitution, at the centre of the novel, echoing all its earlier images of hunger, cold and isolation, is most centrally an image of the impossibility of surviving alone. She is 'a human being', and has 'a human being's wants' – wants which must be answered not by nature, but by the human world.

'"I should kill you – I am killing you": your words are such as ought not to be used: violent, unfeminine, and untrue', says St. John Rivers, when Jane refuses his proposal of marriage, on the grounds that he does not love her. His words prefigure the negative criticism *Jane Eyre* received when it appeared. Such critics condemned the novel, centrally, for its offences against 'propriety': its heroine's 'undisciplined' demand for self-fulfilment, its author's 'incessant . . . tendency to describe the need of being loved' (quoted in Allott, *The Brontës*, 108–9, 173). In part, of course, they were responding, in their very different ways, to such obvious challenges to 'conventionality' as Jane's unwomanly expressiveness, her outspoken declaration of an initially unrequited love. But we might see a deeper meaning in their accusations than this. For 'propriety' does not signify merely compliance to social conventions. In its root sense of 'individuality' (and perhaps also in its now obsolete meaning of 'property'), it points also toward that sense of the proper self as an autonomous entity, independent of others, which underpinned early nineteenth-century English society – that society whose arrangements so baffled the child Jane Eyre. To 'propriety' in this sense *Jane Eyre* offers a striking challenge. To consider some of the contexts which the novel itself invokes is to see the real significance of that insistence on 'the need of being loved' which so many of its readers have thrilled to, so many of its critics deplored. This, rather than its 'improper' depiction of a woman's 'independence' is its real offence against the 'proprieties' of early nineteenth-century English society; and even, arguably, against our own.

Further Reading

Penny Boumelha, *Charlotte Brontë* (Hemel Hempstead, Harvester Wheatsheaf, 1990). A critically incisive study of Brontë as a woman writer.
Terry Eagleton, *Myths of Power: a Marxist Study of the Brontës* (London, Macmillan – now Palgrave, 1975; 2nd edn, 1987). A ground-breaking Marxist analysis of the novels of the Brontë sisters. Eagleton's volume appeared before the real burgeoning of feminist criticism, and paid little attention to questions of gender. In a Preface to the second edition, he offers a critical account of the methodological assumptions which shaped *Myths of Power*, paying particular attention to the work's 'gender blindness' and to what he now sees as its other 'faults or exclusions'.
Elizabeth Gaskell, *The Life of Charlotte Brontë* (Oxford, Oxford University Press, 1974). One of the greatest biographies in the language, written shortly after Brontë's death by one of her closest friends.
Sandra M. Gilbert and Susan Gubar, *The Madwoman in the Attic: The Woman Writer and the Nineteenth-Century Literary Imagination* (New Haven, CT, Yale University Press, 1979). An influential work of American feminist criticism.
Heather Glen (ed.), *Jane Eyre: Contemporary Critical Essays* (Basingstoke, Macmillan – now Palgrave – *New Casebooks*, 1997). A selection of critical essays written in the past 20 years.

David Lodge, 'Fire and Eyre: Charlotte Brontë's War of Earthly Elements', in *The Language of Fiction: Essays in Criticism and Verbal Analysis of the English Novel* (London, Routledge & Kegan Paul, 1966), 114–43. A pioneering attempt to pay close attention to the language and imagery of *Jane Eyre*.

Raymond Williams, 'Charlotte and Emily Brontë', in *The English Novel from Dickens to Lawrence* (London, Chatto & Windus, 1970). A brief, suggestive essay on the Brontës in their time.

References

Miriam Allott, *The Brontës: the Critical Heritage* (London, Routledge & Kegan Paul, 1974).

Anon., *Woman: as she is, and as she should be* (2 vols, London, 1835).

Juliet Barker, *The Brontës* (London, Weidenfeld & Nicolson, 1994).

Charlotte Brontë, *Jane Eyre*, ed. Margaret Smith (Oxford, The World's Classics, 1993).

Angela Carter, 'Charlotte Brontë: *Jane Eyre*', in *Expletives Deleted* (London, 1992).

Sarah Ellis, *The Women of England* (London, 1839).

Anne Richelieu Lamb, *Can Woman Regenerate Society?* (London, 1844).

Adrienne Rich, 'Jane Eyre: The Temptations of a Motherless Woman', in *Of Lies, Secrets and Silences: Selected Prose 1966–1978* (London, Virago, 1980).

Mrs John Sandford, *Woman, in her Social and Domestic Character* (London, 1831).

Virginia Woolf, '*Jane Eyre* and *Wuthering Heights*' (1916), in *The Common Reader: First Series* (London, The Hogarth Press, 1968).

George Eliot: *Middlemarch*

Elisabeth Jay

George Eliot as a young woman, after a portrait by F. d'A. Durade.

Demonstrating a knowledge of the context of *Middlemarch* raises a series of apparently daunting problems. Which 'context' are we addressing: the early 1830s of the novel's setting, 1872, when it was published, or even the context in which readers of different age, sex and cultural backgrounds now read it? Are we supposed to know everything that happened between 1830 and 1872? Given George Eliot's apparently encyclopaedic knowledge, how can we hope to know as much? Should we bone up on nineteenth-century medical theories, or concentrate upon learning significant dates in the history of women's education?

One way of considering 'context' is to try to imagine what knowledge and experience the novel's first readers would have brought with them. Even those, like George Eliot herself, in their early fifties, were unlikely to have remembered the political events and scientific advances of 40 years before very clearly. As author she supplied such facts as she judged necessary to make her picture of that society seem plausible and com-prehensible. Whether £80 a year was really the going rate for the post that Caleb Garth offered Fred Vincy in 1830 is comparatively unimportant, but specifying the salary allowed readers to understand how serious Lydgate's debt of £1000 to Bulstrode was. Nor would George Eliot have expected all her women readers to have acquired the learning she had during an adult life spent working in a male environment as editor and reviewer on high-brow magazines. Indeed, 'short-sighted' Dorothea Brooke's mistaken belief that knowing Latin, Greek or Hebrew would transform her view of the world warns readers against confusing knowl-edge with understanding.

However, Eliot did write to interest those who, like Dorothea, possessed minds of a 'theoretic' cast. Of course we can no more enter the past entirely on its own terms, than we can claim to know what each of *Middlemarch's* first readers thought. We do, nevertheless, know that *Middlemarch* was directed primarily at those with money and time enough to be interested in subjects such as how women could best be prepared to contribute to society's well-being, or why choosing the right career had become more important in a society where family connections no longer dominated a man's lot in life. History, or the story of other people's doings, is, as the novel often reminds us, a mirror to which we bring our own reflection.

An eminent philosopher . . . who can dignify even your ugly furniture by lifting it into the serene light of science, has shown me this pregnant little fact. Your pier-glass or extensive surface of polished steel made to be rubbed by a housemaid, will be minutely and multitudinously scratched in all directions; but place now against it a lighted candle as a centre of illumination, and lo! the scratches will seem to arrange themselves in a fine series of concentric circles round that little sun. It is demonstrable that the scratches are going everywhere impartially, and it is only your candle which produces the flattering illusion of a concentric arrangement, its light falling with an exclusive optical selection. These things are a parable. The scratches are events, and the candle is the egoism of any person now absent . . .

(*Middlemarch*, 264 [ch. 27])

Middlemarch is always seeking to persuade us to test the individual point of view, or any theory that claims to rule out all others, against a broader, more inclusive, vision. By quoting a philosopher and offering a homely proof, the narrator, gender unspecified, ranges across intellectual issues, traditionally seen as men's concern, and the domestic practicalities, customarily associated with women's lives, to encourage readers to abandon these limiting categorisations and to transcend their self-centred preoccupations. However, if we distance ourselves from this guide for a moment, and turn the light shed by this 'parable' on the text itself we can perhaps begin to see ways in which the author can also be viewed as a 'person now absent', a historical 'ego', fixed within a particular place and time that limited her impartiality. She is, to late twentieth-century eyes, placed by that reference to 'a pier-glass . . . made to be rubbed by a housemaid', as a middle-class author writing for her peers in an era when domestic labour was cheap, plentiful and therefore always replaceable. Within the novel (ch. 36) Lydgate is criticised for thought processes that treat women and servants as lesser 'creatures', capable of being selected and adapted to his higher scientific purpose, but the passage quoted could be used to suggest that the narrator similarly disregards the individuality of servants, not through falsely applying scientific principles, but by virtue of the age's class assumptions. Mary Garth's servitude at Stone Court (ch. 14) is much deplored, but in what ways is her life harder than that of the other unnamed servants living in Featherstone's household? The tradespeople who gather in the Tankard in Slaughter Lane are named, but with a crude humour that undermines our ability to take seriously the opinions of a shoemaker called 'Limp' or a butcher called 'Byles', or the landlady, Mrs Dollop's, references to the high rate of child mortality among the poorest classes in Middlemarch (ch. 71). Their comically misinformed gossip acts as a barrier to our seeing the real economic insecurities of those 'odious tradesmen' who, Rosamond Lydgate feels, should be made to wait for payment so that she may continue a fashionable middle-class lifestyle (*Middlemarch*, 596 [ch. 58]).

It may seem inappropriate and unfair to fault a Victorian writer for failing to extend her imaginative empathy to all classes of society, but identifying different value systems at work helps us to recognise the way that our reading also has its own 'context', such as the events of our private lives, or topical issues, that lead us to take an interest in one character or theme rather than others. Today's readers, for instance, might feel that there is more to the environmental argument about changing the face of the land-scape to accommodate the coming of the railway, than is implied by allow-ing pro-conservation views to be expressed by 'Women both old and young' who 'regarded travelling by steam as presumptuous and dangerous', self-seeking landowners and drunken farm-labourers (*Middlemarch*, 553 [ch. 56]). A generation of readers in the 1980s, brought up on feminist theories and 'yuppie' assumptions, often found it difficult to find any point of contact with a text that wanted them to sympathise with a heroine 'who had given up a position and fortune to marry Will Ladislaw'. Wholly out of sympathy with the ideology that believed silent self-sacrifice to be a woman's highest duty, and marriage and motherhood her ultimate goal, these readers found themselves numbered with those who 'thought it a pity that so substantive and rare a creature should have been absorbed into the life of another, and be only known in a certain circle as a wife and mother'. They were inclined to neglect the force of the next sentence, written by a female author who had herself chosen to reject both silence and motherhood: 'But no one stated exactly what else that was in her power she ought rather to have done – not even Sir James Chettam, who went no further than the negative prescription that she ought not to have married Will Ladislaw' (*Middlemarch*, 836 [Finale]). Yet, by the early 1990s the BBC clearly thought that the times were ripe again for major financial investment in a televised version of *Mid-dlemarch*. The BBC Education pack, *Screening Middlemarch* (1994) includes a fascinating section on the commercial interests that coincided to enable the costly production of the same year.

> An earlier televised version (1968) was not successful, so it remained a challenging possibility as a high-profile, big budget production. WGBH [an American public broadcasting company] expressed an early interest, but a key factor for the BBC was the concern at senior level that because the BBC was due to have its Royal Charter renewed in 1996 and was therefore particularly vulnerable to Government scrutiny, it needed to commit itself to some large-scale productions with impeccable cultural credentials.
>
> (*Screening*, 63)

What these cultural credentials were this analysis does not pause to examine, observing only that 'The novel is in any case one of the most famous of nineteenth-century English fiction'. Perhaps the writer of this section was too close to the venture to see that this was not merely a period costume drama 'with impeccable cultural credentials', tapping into the beginnings of the English Heritage industry, but that the cultural concerns this particular novel portrayed, such as an interest in the complex ways in which society is more than the sum of its individuals, was also responding to a shift in the evaluation of how societies operate that would shortly lead Britain's voters to bring in a Labour government. (The Conservative Prime Minister Mrs Thatcher had nailed her colours to the mast by declaring that society was no more than the sum of its parts.) *Screening Middlemarch*, in any case, did not consider it worth investigating why the same novel, televised in 1968, had proved unsuccessful: the commercial fact seemed to have precluded further discussion.

Each generation of readers, then, brings its own 'lighted candle as a centre of illumination' for exploring the mirror of history; selecting, discarding and arranging the 'minute and multitudinous' events of the past, to form the pattern that best seems to explain the present. The Victorians were supremely interested in investigating and documenting their own lives and that of their society: it was an age of biography, of fact-gathering for parliamentary 'blue books', of exhibitions celebrating its own achievements. Sociology came to the fore as a separate discipline, and history became a useful instrument for measuring to what extent the much talked of nineteenth-century 'march of progress' had either improved upon the past, or cut their society adrift from its finest traditions. *Middlemarch's* subtitle, 'A Study of Provincial Life', offered the first signal that this novel was offering itself as an alternative genre through which to conduct sociological analysis. The novel's opening words, 'Who that cares much to know the history of man, and how the mysterious mixture behaves under the varying experiments of Time . . .' further advertised its intention of engaging in the contemporary debate. Those of her Victorian readers who were familiar with such much discussed books as Thomas Carlyle's *Past and Present* (1843), Charles Darwin's *The Descent of Man and Selection in Relation to Sex* (1871), or the work of her sociologist friend, Herbert Spencer, the 'eminent philosopher' from whose work she had taken the parable of the pier-glass, would not have missed these strong hints. For any more frivolous readers still uncertain as to the novel's intellectual agenda, the dinner-party in chapter 2 is used to draw attention to the foolish extremes that had been thrown up in the course of the debate about the uses of history: those who like

Casaubon retreat to the past 'like the ghost of an ancient, wandering about the world and trying mentally to construct it as it used to be, in spite of ruin and confusing changes', and those who, like Brooke, become so overwhelmed by the historical documentation they accumulate, that they never form any coherent view.

George Eliot certainly makes a great effort in that dinner party scene to get the period detail right. The book titles, famous names and political events are all, perhaps a shade ostentatiously, selected to fit her 1829 setting, but the issues touched upon, such as land reform, political economy, appropriate activities for young women, the debate over the Church of England's Protestant or Catholic heritage, and the relationship between Church and State, are all carefully chosen as concerns still relevant in 1872. In the midst of this fictional, pre-Victorian, provincial society George Eliot placed Dorothea, a girl some ten years older than she herself had been in 1829, and equally interested in improving the world. Dorothea, however, leads a life more sheltered and hampered by class and prospective inheritance than the young George Eliot who, when she entered Warwickshire's provincial society, encountered a group of friends whose thinking and lifestyle were far more unconventional than anything Middlemarch has to offer. Indeed, by choosing *Middlemarch* as the title, Eliot suggested that the novel would concern itself with a society which may include idealists, reactionaries and progressives, but does not look kindly upon exceptionality. Dorothea, for instance, does not become a famous writer, like her creator, or a famous campaigner, like Florence Nightingale, who complained that George Eliot had deliberately ignored the openings that existed in 1872 for female idealists such as Dorothea. Dorothea could, for instance, have found charity work in London's East End when she moved to the metropolis with Ladislaw (Nightingale, *Fraser's*, 567).

Instead, George Eliot created her fictional society to prove a particular hypothesis: that social change occurs gradually, by almost imperceptible stages. Even the way in which the novel was first published was designed to make readers realise this. In the eighteen-thirties Charles Dickens and his publishers had found a way of reaching a wider public by selling a novel more cheaply as a monthly, or, later, weekly serial than in the previously standard, expensive, three-volume, hardback format. To persuade readers to keep buying a novel in sections of four or five chapters at a time, authors often resorted to ending each part with a cliffhanger. When George Eliot's publishers agreed to break with this convention and publish *Middlemarch* in eight parts, at two-monthly intervals, she found a way of forcing readers to take stock of the slow, and comparatively undramatic, way in which small, apparently unrelated, decisions trigger a chain reaction. Through the novel's subtitle and by giving all but the first instalment titles that prompted the drawing of links and comparisons between different sets of characters, Eliot used her medium to persuade her audience to take a particular view of how society worked. (It is, of course, equally possible to read these instalment titles as either pandering to or teasing readers devoted to the sentimental or sensational fiction signalled by such topics as 'Three Love Problems', or 'Waiting for Death'.)

Victorian theories about society divided between those which envisaged society as a machine, with identifiable parts that could be rationally manipulated into working more efficiently, and those that saw it as a complex living organism. In the following passage, Eliot uses a metaphor derived from a development in instrument technology, but the real emphasis lies not on the mechanical advance, but upon how it enables us to recognise the intricate mobility of social life and the, at first sight invisible, forces at play which determine an individual's fate.

> Even with a microscope directed on a water-drop we find ourselves making interpretations which turn out to be rather coarse; for whereas under a weak lens you may seem to see a creature exhibiting an active voracity into which other smaller creatures actively play . . . a stronger lens reveals to you certain tiniest hairlets which make vortices for these victims while the swallower waits passively . . .
>
> (*Middlemarch*, 59–60 [ch. 6])

By 1872 many of George Eliot's contemporaries felt they could point to abundant evidence that they had lived through a period of extraordinarily rapid change: there had been two major benchmarks in electoral matters, the Reform Acts of 1832 and 1867; the railway had visibly transformed the landscape and the speed with which the centre could be connected with the provinces; and Britain's livelihood had definitively shifted from an agrarian to an industrial economy. Yet, despite the 1831 Reform riots, the Chartist campaign of the 1840s, or the 1866 agitation in Hyde Park, each, in turn, interpreted by doom-mongers as threatening incipient anarchy, rule by revolutionary mobs had been avoided and the nation had grown in economic prosperity. You might want to trace George Eliot's view of the differing significance of political reform as it affects class interest and as it is viewed by 'county' people like Mr Brooke, or Mrs Cadwallader (ch. 6) and town tradespeople like Mr Mawmsey, the grocer (ch. 51). It is also worth considering what benefit, if any, is directly attributable within the novel to the much heralded coming of the railway.

As landed wealth and aristocratic patronage slowly ceded influence to commercial interests, so the middling classes sought to review the efficiency of the national institutions and professional structures they had inherited. George Eliot's sense of the way that gradual changes often leave individuals stranded between one phase and the next is signalled when she shows Lydgate as caught uneasily between strong distaste for approaching an aristocratic relative for patronage and the 'desirability', he nevertheless feels, 'of its being known (without his telling) that he was better born' than the local physicians and apothecaries, whose trade practices seemed to threaten his conception of medicine as an honourable new 'profession' (ch. 15). Despite Lydgate's final capitulation to the social aspirations of a manufacturer's daughter, readers of *Middlemarch* in 1872 knew that many of the reforms Lydgate had so desired had occurred in the intervening years, even if his particular theories had been discredited. Looking at the recurrent pictures of the way in which local health affairs, concerning sanitation, the old Infirmary and the new Hospital, are managed (chs 18 and 71) will offer you a helpful guide to the range of vested interests that Eliot believed made themselves apparent in any reforming gesture. It is also noteworthy that the money necessary to save the new Hospital is finally offered not by local merchants and tradesmen, but from a traditional source of patronage: a widow who is a member of the landed gentry by both birth and marriage (ch. 76). The slow improvement of the world, the novel's last paragraph claims, is due just as much to awakening individuals to the need for self-discipline and self-regeneration, as to acts of parliament: an argument Eliot tries to clinch by showing us the specific effect Dorothea's unselfish impulses have had, while suggesting that the instant reforms that Will yearned for in his Parliamentary career had not materialised.

In stressing the importance of individual moral accountability George Eliot was also engaging with Victorian theories for interpreting society's workings: the leading social theorists of the day were agreed in believing that the social sciences could and should be developed upon models derived from contemporary scientific theories of development. The inferences that they drew from Darwin's biological work, which had established the uniform 'natural laws' governing the development of the species as a whole, as well as that of the individual organism, were often harnessed to a social model that assumed the slow and orderly evolution of the human race and favouring 'the survival of the fittest': this despite Darwin's own emphasis upon the functioning of chance that potentially challenged orderly models of development. Transferring observations originally applied to animal life to the study of humans, also raised ethical issues not implicit in in the fields of biology or zoology, such as what was meant by 'fittest': was this a physical, moral or intellectual capacity enabling survival? The move from a land-based to an urban economy, for instance, appeared to have encouraged the notion of the 'self-made' man, someone capable of seizing the opportunities on offer in a changing society faster than his fellow creatures. Bulstrode is Middlemarch's representative of this much discussed Victorian phenomenon. Eliot found a way of employing scientific developmental models to relate the individual to the larger processes of human society. Casaubon's clinging to the past and his pitiful failure to achieve a mature relationship, is presented to us in terms of the scientific discoveries that had recently been made about the way in which all embryos develop, not, as previously thought, swelling from a perfectly pre-formed dot to a larger version, but evolving in complexity: Casaubon is pictured as an undeveloped embryo, who has failed to evolve to fit the demands of the society in which he finds himself (ch. 10). In the Finale Eliot uses the format of a scientific law to present her social model: 'there is no creature whose inward being is so strong that it is not greatly determined by what lies outside it'. The 'fittest' in her society are those who recognise this universal law. Those who neglect it fall by the wayside whether their motives are initially good, as are Bulstrode's and Lydgate's, or whether their desire to shape the world to their own dictates springs from egotism as it does in the case of Featherstone and Casaubon. Learning to take others into account, and its moral application, 'sympathy', are thus built into George Eliot's world as an evolutionary law. Developing readers' sensitivity 'to what is apart from themselves, which may be called the raw material of moral sentiment' was, she believed, the supreme gift a novelist had to offer (Eliot, *Essays*, 270). *Middlemarch* repeatedly invites us to learn the distinction between a passive recognition of the extent to which we affect each others' lives and the moral energy, or 'sympathy' we require to apply that knowledge for the common good. Dorothea's marriage to Casaubon invites us to study these two stages as a developmental process, and the lesson is driven home by the comparison between Lydgate's lack of moral energy to 'be the more because she was less' in dealing with his wife and Rosamond's feeling that in Dorothea's offer of help she has been 'taken hold of by an emotion stronger than her own' (*Middlemarch*, 758 [ch. 75], and 797 [ch. 81]). Again this process is seen as occurring at the level of the individual, leaving room for debate over the kind of society that might hinder or best promote it.

England's rapid industrialisation was felt to have undermined the sense of interdependence that had been far more visible in rural communities. *Middlemarch*, it is true, does not depict grim urban conditions, but it is sig-

these developments were there in the novel for any of her readers who were already aware of these debates. Ladislaw's attitude to Mr Casaubon's outdated research project (ch. 21), and the Rev. Camden Farebrother's compromise between clerical duties and his scientific investigations (ch. 17) are two of the more obvious hints she drops. Although she remained intellectually sceptical, and critical of versions of Christianity that claimed sole rights of interpretation, George Eliot saw no reason to disturb others' religious beliefs whenever they did not lead to bigotry and divisiveness. Her position was close to Dorothea's:

I have always been thinking of the different ways in which Christianity is taught, and whenever I find one way that makes it a wider blessing than any other, I cling to that as the truest – I mean that which takes in the most good of all kinds, and brings in the most people as sharers in it.

(*Middlemarch*, 495 [ch. 50])

Making a list of clergymen and other Christian laymen and women in this novel will help you see how George Eliot felt that those who concentrated upon drawing up and enforcing codes for the way in which other people should live their lives, were almost inevitably distracted from showing practical sympathy for their day-to-day needs. One of the ways she achieves this is by focusing most of the religious activity in the novel within the Church of England: we hear about Methodists and Roman Catholics, and the social disadvantages of being a Nonconformist or Dissenter, but the point George Eliot wanted to stress is best made by showing how small differences of interpretation existing within the same wing of the Christian church could arouse bitterness and suspicion among those who should be living in brotherly love. She never claims, however, in the world of *Middlemarch* that religious believers have a monopoly on intolerance and insensitivity, or upon wanting to control the lives of others. By offering a vision of a spiritual life concerned to find the best in fellow human beings, rather than in pursuing ever-narrower definitions of God, George Eliot appealed to the growing number of her contemporaries who felt that Christ's life and teachings offered a moving picture of the human ideal rather than a historical record of God coming to earth. By setting the novel back in time, before the theories supplied by German criticism and scientific advances had been popularised, she avoided these debates and appealed to the increasing numbers of Christians who, as the century wore on, preferred to worship a unifying God of Love rather than a God of hellfire. You might ponder what message George Eliot intended to offer contemporary believers and unbelievers in the way that she makes Mrs

Bulstrode exhibit the face of Christian forgiveness to her husband in chapter 74.

Many of the clergymen in this novel have been ordained primarily as a matter of family expectation: traditionally, becoming a clergyman provided the younger sons of landowning families, who could not hope to inherit, with a home, an income, and social respect. Mr Cadwallader and Mr Farebrother both exemplify this route into the profession. However the wave of religious seriousness that had started with the Evangelical Movement's emphasis upon experiencing a highly personal conversion and relationship with God, gradually led people to expect that clergymen would have a vocational calling. Fred Vincy's plight illustrates something of the chaos that Victorians felt had been brought about as money started to flow out of stable commodities like land and into industry and speculative ventures. Fred's family see educating a son for the ministry as a new route to the social advancement that their money can purchase, while Fred himself is more inclined to hope for an old-fashioned inheritance from Featherstone. The novel suggests that trusting money to flow in the old ways through inheritance is becoming a thing of the past: Casaubon's views about Ladislaw's career are worth investigating (chs 37 and 46). Young men brought up to think of themselves as gentlemen, as Ladislaw, Fred Vincy and Lydgate have been, must look for careers that provide both a living and self-respect. Finding appropriate work for men of their status was still a concern in the 1870s. In Fred's case you may feel that George Eliot ducks the problem by returning him to a job, concerned with the land, that he obtains through family connections. Fred's final decision, however, fits into her larger design of declaring that when religious conviction no longer dictates a clear path of duty, being able to take pride in one's work must be the overriding factor in choosing a career. Caleb Garth's philosophy of work, uttered 'with the air of a man who felt himself to be saying something deeply religious' (ch. 56) would have struck a recognisable chord with a generation brought up on the writings of Thomas Carlyle. He had declared, that in a society where religious belief was waning and the universe seemed devoid of purpose, the old moral instruction, 'Know thyself' was impossible and had better 'be translated into this partially possible one, Know what thou canst work at' (Carlyle, Sartor Resartus, 124 [Book II, ch. 7.]) The moral lessons Middlemarch offers us suggest that his further advice, ' "Do the Duty which lies nearest thee", which thou knowest to be a Duty! Thy second Duty will already have become clearer', weighed equally strongly with George Eliot (Carlyle, Sartor Resartus, 148 [Book II, ch. 9.])

And what of the duty of the young women of Middlemarch? In raising this topic George Eliot was again sure of her readers' attention: in 1869

John Stuart Mill had argued the case for equal rights for both sexes in *The Subjection of Women*. Ben and Letty Garth, the coming generation of the Finale, are in open dispute over the assumption, colouring the thinking of men as different as Brooke, Lydgate, Sir James and Casaubon, that women are 'the weaker sex'. In mid-century a fear arose that gender distribution had become unbalanced, thereby risking a surplus of young women who could never hope to find husbands and become wives and mothers. What was to become of a generation of women, without adequate financial support from their families, who would endanger their status as 'ladies' if they looked for paid work outside the home? Governessing, running a school from home, as Mrs Garth does, and authorship, which Mary Garth takes to, proved standard solutions; but each of these occupations, if undertaken for money, left the women and their families on the very edge of social acceptability. Education was the cure the nineteenth century most frequently offered for a range of social ills, but whether a girl should receive the same education as a boy, and whether the better to share her husband's interests or for learning's own sake, remained vexed questions. It would be useful to trace the variety of opinions expressed in the novel by both men and women. Although Dorothea's sketchy education leaves her dissatisfied, it is not clear that her mistakes in life would have been averted had she had access to the university lectures being opened to girls in the 1870s. Neither can Rosamond's limited horizons and total self-satisfaction with the way she fulfils her wifely duties all be laid at the door of Mrs Lemon's Academy, 'the chief school in the county', where she has acquired her shallow 'accomplishments' (*Middlemarch*, 96 [ch. 11]). Mary Garth attended the same school, earning her way by helping with various duties, and she eventually writes a book based upon the classical education that had been reserved for men.

The fact that most people assume that Fred has written his wife's book, *Stories of Great Men, taken from Plutarch*, is George Eliot's joke at her audience's expense. Marian Evans had adopted and kept her male pseudonym, well after her real identity was quite widely known, partly to protect her privacy and partly because she was well aware that male authors commanded greater authority and were taken more seriously than women writers. Henry James, her nearest rival as an intellectually heavyweight novelist, remarked of *Middlemarch*, 'It raises the standard of what is to be expected by women . . . We know all about the female heart; but apparently there is a female brain too . . .' (James, *Letters*, i, 351). George Eliot was thin-skinned on this issue. In 1856, just before she had started writing fiction, she had published an essay entitled, 'Silly Novels by Lady Novelists' (Eliot, *Essays*, 301–24) in which, although she admitted that there had been some very fine women novelists, she found it a matter for regret that, because novel-writing, unlike poetry, had no rules and required no classical education, ill-educated women with time on their hands too often took to producing fiction. Some feminist critics today feel that she had absorbed her society's general contempt for women's abilities so thoroughly that she actually shared it.

You may feel that she was altogether too anxious to prevent her narrator, who displays a comprehensive knowledge of science, literature in several languages, philosophy and classical mythology, from ever being mistaken for a 'Lady Novelist'. A feeling that she is overanxious to display her learning, should, however, be kept separate from a dislike for the frequently used nineteenth-century convention that the story should be told by an all-seeing, all-knowing narrator. Modern British novelists, like Jeanette Winterson and Julian Barnes, have sometimes reverted to using a narrator who comments upon the characters and actions, but in the early twentieth century this convention went out of fashion and George Eliot's reputation consequently suffered.

George Eliot was right to assert that there were no rules for writing fiction. There were for Victorians no limits upon what could be discussed in a novel, other than those imposed by that society's concept of 'good taste'. (You might discuss what subjects of interest to modern-novel readers are missing from *Middlemarch*.) Moreover, it was common practice to use fiction as a way of interesting the middle- and upper-class reading public in topical issues: Disraeli, later to be Prime Minister, wrote three novels in the eighteen-forties because he thought they would get a better hearing for his ideas than political pamphlets could. The attention to realistic detail with which George Eliot composed *Middlemarch* owed much to the view that literature and its educational capacity could help to change the world. 'Contextual knowledge' is therefore vital for us to understand the work of a novelist who declared: 'It is the habit of my imagination to strive after as full a vision of the medium in which a character moves as of the character itself' (Eliot, *Letters*, iv, 97).

Further Reading

There are many brief 'life and times' books offering surveys of George Eliot's work, but all too few of them engage with why and how such knowledge might help a contextual *understanding* of her writing. Among those works specifically devoted to *Middlemarch*, Kerry McSweeney, *Middlemarch* (London, Unwin Critical Library, 1984) offers the clearest guide to the historical, social, religious and artistic ideas that informed her writing, while a briefer study, Karen Chase, *George Eliot. Middlemarch* (Cambridge, Cambridge University Press, 1991) includes a fairly full guide to the further reading then available.

A recent and extremely cheap CD-ROM, entitled *George Eliot's Middlemarch: A Guide for Students and Readers of the Novel* (obtainable from the Department of English Literature, Chester College of Higher Education, Parkgate Road, Chester, CH1 4BJ) understandably does not make use of much in the way of exciting graphics, but helps viewers understand something more of the complex web of *Middlemarch* as they access its multiple pathways.

The study guide that the BBC produced to accompany its 1994 televised version of the novel, *Screening Middlemarch: C19th Novel to 90s Television* (London: BBC Educational Developments, 1994) is an excellent teaching aid, providing thought-provoking exercises. It encourages the consideration of production values and, by helping us to understand some of the technical decisions that had to be made in transferring the novel from one medium to another, heightens an appreciation of the way in which Eliot's own narrative worked.

The following books and articles, as their titles imply, take up particular aspects of *Middlemarch*, in an interesting and accessible manner. The world of nineteenth-century ideas that informed the novel is opened up in Gillian Beer, *Darwin's Plots: Evolutionary Narrative in Darwin, George Eliot and Nineteenth-Century Fiction* (London, Routledge & Kegan Paul, 1983); Gillian Beer, 'Middlemarch and the Woman Question', *George Eliot* (Sussex, Harvester Press, 1986), 147–99; Sally Shuttleworth, 'Middlemarch: an experiment in time', *George Eliot and Nineteenth-Century Science: the Make-Believe of a Beginning* (Cambridge, Cambridge University Press, 1984), 142–74; and Nancy L. Paxton, 'Theories of Origin and Knowledge: *Middlemarch* and *The Study of Sociology*', *George Eliot and Herbert Spencer: Feminism, Evolutionism, and the Reconstruction of Gender* (Princeton, NJ, Princeton University Press, 1991), 171–97.

An account of the form in which the novel was originally published can be found in Carol A. Martin, 'A "Greater Trial of Readers' Faith and Patience": *Middlemarch*, a Bimonthly Serial', *George Eliot's Serial Fiction* (Columbus, OH, Ohio University Press, 1994), 182–210.

References

Thomas Carlyle, *Sartor Resartus*, first published in *Fraser's Magazine*, 1833–4. (London, J. M. Dent, 1959).

George Eliot, *The George Eliot Letters*, ed. G. S. Haight, 9 vols (New Haven, CT, Yale University Press, 1954–6, 1978).

——, *George Eliot 1819–1880: Essays*, ed. Thomas Pinney (New York and London, Columbia University Press and Routledge & Kegan Paul, 1963).

——, *Middlemarch: A Study of Provincial Life*, ed. Rosemary Ashton (Harmondsworth, Penguin, 1994).

Henry James, *Letters of Henry James: Vol. 1: 1843–1875*, ed. Leon Edel (London, Macmillan – now Palgrave, 1974).

Florence Nightingale, 'A "Note" of Interrogation', *Fraser's Magazine*, 87 (1873), 567–77.

10 The Novels of Thomas Hardy: *Tess of the d'Urbervilles*

Roger Webster

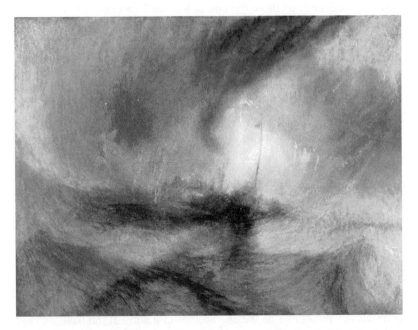

Snow Storm – Steam Boat off a Harbour's Mouth by J. M. W. Turner (1775–1851), exhibited 1842.

In this essay I intend to explore 'context' in several interrelated ways with reference to Thomas Hardy's fiction, especially *Tess of the d'Urbervilles*. The context of changing literary and artistic styles towards the end of the nineteenth century (what can be termed 'modernism'), and the impact of visual art (particularly Impressionism), were very significant in the development of Hardy's fictional style. Successive critical interpretations have shaped attitudes towards his fiction, and these also need to be considered in order to understand context at the point of reading or reception as opposed to that of writing or production. I will also look briefly at some additional forms of context linked to these areas, such as biographical and autobiographical material, the social, scientific and intellectual developments which influenced Hardy's writing, and more recently the adaptations of his novels into film, television and radio.

Hardy was not only interested in the process of writing, but also in the act of reading. Indeed, his views on reading in an essay called 'The Profitable Reading of Fiction' (1888) anticipate some of the more recent theories about the role of the reader which have had a profound impact on the ways in which we now think about literature and its study. Hardy suggests in this essay that the meanings which we discover in, or attribute to, a text may not necessarily be those the author intended: indeed there may be no finite or stable point of understanding at all. On reading, he says:

> The aim should be the exercise of a generous imaginativeness, which shall find in a tale not only all that was put there by the author, put he it never so awkwardly, but which shall find there what was never inserted by him, never foreseen, never contemplated. Sometimes these additions which are woven around a work of fiction by the intensive power of the reader's own imagination are the finest parts of the scenery.
>
> (*Selected*, 243)

Significantly, although Hardy was involved in the production of literature as a writer, he acknowledges that it is at its point of reception where much of its meaning may be generated: where, when, how and by whom a novel or a poem is read will be major determinants in arriving at an interpretation or understanding. For Hardy, then, the context of reading as well as that of writing is crucial to his novels.

In arriving at understanding, whether of a novel, an experience or a philosophical idea, Hardy stresses its provisional and tentative nature: 'We don't always remember as we should that in getting at the truth, we get only at the true nature of the impression that an object, etc., produces on us . . .' (*Life*, 247–8). Hardy frequently refers to his novels and poems as 'seemings' or 'impressions'; writing is for him provisional, always subject to revision and modification. The term 'palimpsest' which Hardy also employs on occasion, is suggestive of this. (A palimpsest is a manuscript on which subsequent writing is superimposed on the original text. Thus for Hardy, character or the novel form itself are best viewed as successive layers of experience or writing.) Gabriel Oak for example, in *Far from the Madding Crowd* (1874), is described thus: 'But man, even to himself, is a palimpsest, having an ostensible writing, and another beneath the lines' (273). The novel as a form is viewed in a similar way: 'What has been written cannot be blotted. Each new style of novel must be the old with added ideas, not an ignoring and avoidance of the old' (*Life*, 218). This theme of repetition and superimposition is central to Hardy's writing, especially his final novel, *The Well-Beloved* (1897), in which the central character Jocelyn Pierston marries successive generations of mother and daughter. This experimental repetitive structure departs from the conventions of nineteenth-century realism and anticipates a number of modernist innovations. Hardy's increasing preoccupation with the process of constructing fiction, and the introduction of a self-reflexive dimension in his writing, parallel developments in painting of the period and anticipate the techniques of later, more experimental novelists such as Marcel Proust or James Joyce.[1] One context, then, in which we can begin to appreciate Hardy's fiction is in relation to his own essays on fiction, his notebooks and autobiographical writing. His references to the visual arts, in particular the Impressionist movement in which he became very interested and on which he commented frequently, are particularly helpful in this respect.

If we turn to the qualities of language or discourse which we discover in Hardy's fiction, one of the first things that strikes the reader is the way in which the narrative frequently implies or draws on a context itself. One of the dominant features of Hardy's narrative voice is the number of references or allusions which the narrator makes to events, people, objects and other works of art both literary and non-literary. At one level there is a sustained narrative with characters, plot and landscape description, but beyond this the text is peppered with often quite explicit mention of a range of phenomena which belong historically and narratively on different planes. Many of these references and allusions are anachronistic, belonging to a period outside that in which the chronology of the story is set. For example in *Far from the Madding Crowd* the narrator compares the song of a farm worker to that of another shepherd in one of the Latin poet Virgil's *Eclogues* (c. 40–60 BC). On the one hand, this is an historical dislocation, but on the other it parodically reinforces the context of the pastoral tradition which is a major theme of the novel. This feature has become known as 'intertextuality' in critical theory, that is one text drawing on and synthesising other texts in weaving together its narrative. The following passage is from chapter 19 of *Tess of the d'Urbervilles* (1891) in which Tess and Angel Clare begin to assess each other whilst working together at Talbothays Farm.

> Tess, on her part, could not understand why a man of clerical family and good education, and above physical want, should look upon it as a mishap to be alive. For the unhappy pilgrim herself there was very good reason. But how could this admirable and poetic man ever have descended into the Valley of Humiliation, have felt with the man of Uz – as she herself had felt two or three years ago – 'My soul chooseth strangling and death rather than my life. I loathe it; I would not live alway.'
>
> It was true that he was at present out of his class. But she knew that was only because, like Peter the Great in a shipwright's yard, he was studying what he wanted to know. He did not milk cows because he was obliged to milk cows, but because he was learning to be a rich and prosperous dairyman, landowner, agriculturalist, and breeder of cattle. He would become an American or Australian Abraham, commanding like a monarch his flocks and his herds, his spotted and his ring-straked, his men-servants and his maids. . . . At first Tess seemed to regard Angel Clare as an intelligence rather than as a man. As such she compared him with herself; and at every discovery of the abundance of his illuminations, of the distance between her own modest mental standpoint and the unmeasurable, Andean altitude of his, she became quite dejected, disheartened from all further effort on her own part whatever.
>
> (*Tess*, 163–4)

Although this passage is presented from Tess's point of view, the narrator's language is not, in fact, always appropriate to her own use of language both spoken and thought. When she normally speaks it is in less formal or colloquial as opposed to 'literary' language, sometimes using dialect. (For example just before this extract she talks to Angel of 'This hobble of being alive . . .' [*Tess*, 162], 'hobble' being Dorset dialect for a perplexing problem.) Not only is the narrator's vocabulary external to Tess, so are the various culturally remote references to literary, biblical, historical and geographical figures and locations which probably would be beyond her knowledge. 'The Valley of Humiliation' is a reference to Bunyan's *Pilgrim's Progress* (1678), and 'the man of Uz' to the Old Testament Book of Job. There are further biblical references to Abraham and his great flocks in the Book of Genesis, and 'his spotted and ring-straked' is an allusion to Jacob's bargain with Laban that his hire should be the ringstraked or brindled and spotted sheep or goats among Laban's flocks (Genesis XXX). It is possible that Tess may have encountered these figures and narratives through her teacher or at her Sunday School, but it is unlikely that she would formulate her own, instinctive perceptions in such terms. It seems even less likely that she would know about Peter the Great working incognito in British and Dutch shipyards, or of the Andes mountain range. The latter reference is also ironic because Angel eventually emigrates to the remoteness of South America for a period following his marriage to Tess and the discovery of her illegitimate child.

Although these references might be considered inconsistent with the depiction of Tess's character, and therefore disruptive of the novel's surface realism, they can also be seen to function in ways which transcend this dimension and extend the possibilities of meaning in the narrative. With respect to Tess's character, the gap between language, culture and character is profoundly revealing in relation to the social gulf between Tess and Angel which is central to this passage and throughout the novel. Not only does Angel's educated social position place him above Tess, the omniscient perspective articulated through the narrator's discourse also serves to exclude her from the cultural framework shared by the narrator and Angel. In effect the novel uses cultural and educational values and allusions in order to frame and explore issues of class and power. It is only when we begin to understand the controlling contexts of class, education, religion, gender and, inevitably, language, that we can understand Tess's predicament as a rural working-class woman and mother of an illegitimate child in the nineteenth century.

It is important in this extract, and in Hardy's novels generally, not to confuse the narrator with the historical figure of the author – an error which has beset some Hardy criticism. It is worth making the obvious point that there is a very important distinction to be made between the figure that we read about in biographies of Thomas Hardy and the narrating voices in his novels or poems. (This is not to suggest that the figure which biographers construct is 'real' in any definitive sense; biography is arguably itself a form of narrative which utilises fictional techniques in the construction of character.) A review of *Tess of the d'Urbervilles* in 1891 by Richard de Gallienne of the *Star* makes no such distinction, as was normal at the time. It attacks 'Mr. Hardy' for 'continually delighting in those long Latin and Greek words . . .' and for using colour terms such as 'photosphere', 'heliolatries' and 'arborescence' (Cox, *Thomas Hardy*, 178–9). What is notable in this kind of approach is that the stylistic traits are read as authorial characteristics verging on personality flaws rather than as discursive features in a fiction. Biography and autobiography are important to the study of literature; they both provide valuable sources of information and knowledge which may shape our reading in highly productive ways. What we must guard against is allowing biographical approaches to dominate or determine our reading, to think of them as the most obvious or natural context at the expense of other kinds of narrative and knowledge which may provide more relevant and illuminating contexts.

For example, some biographical accounts of Hardy have tended to emphasise or exaggerate his pessimistic and fatalistic tendency in ways that have obscured more historically detailed approaches. Others have been condescending, viewing Hardy as a rural self-taught writer outside the classical and metropolitan cultural traditions of literature. The cosmopolitan novelist Henry James, for example, talked patronisingly of 'The good little Thomas Hardy'. The major source of much biographical information on Hardy is extremely informative, but it was very carefully shaped and edited and is crucially evasive in certain areas. Published under the name of his second wife, Florence Emily Hardy, *The Life of Thomas Hardy 1840–1928* (1962; first published in two volumes in 1928 and 1930 shortly after Hardy's death), was in fact written or ghosted by Hardy himself. He employed a number of other techniques to distance himself, including creating a third-person narrator who purports to be the voice of Florence, but this is clearly a device for controlling the biographical narrative. Florence's function is to provide the seal of apparently 'objective' authorship and so authenticate the supposed biography. Hardy thus contrives to leave behind an official and public account of his life, carefully editing out much information. We find little mention of his early childhood and family background, for instance, so that the class position which is emphasised is that of a middle-class writer mixing very much in literary and fashionable social circles. The deterioration of his marital relationship to his first wife Emma Gifford is also ignored: Hardy destroyed her notebook along with many other documents which would undoubtedly have provided a very different biographical perspective on many of his poems about her. I am not suggesting that we should dismiss *The Life of Thomas Hardy*: in fact in one way its construction reveals more than it conceals about Hardy's concerns and preoccupations with, for example, his own class position, close relationships, and sense of his standing in the relatively new profession of novelist. It also contains much detailed information on his literary, artistic and philosophical interests, which provide an invaluable context for reading his novels and poetry.

To illustrate this, I want to examine *Tess of the d'Urbervilles* in the light of a comment that is attributed to Hardy in *The Life of Thomas Hardy* and which provides both a biographical perspective on the novel and a wider artistic context through which to approach his fiction. Following a visit to the Society of British Artists in 1886, he is reported as stating that:

> The impressionist school is strong. It is even more suggestive in the direction of literature than in that of art. As usual it is pushed to absurdity by some. But their principle is, as I understand it, that what you carry away with you from a scene is the true feature to grasp; or in other words, *what appeals to your own individual eye and heart in particular* amid much that does not so appeal, and which you therefore omit to record.
>
> (*Life*, 184)

Hardy himself trained as an architect and always displayed a strong interest in the visual arts, keeping a notebook on painters in which he was particularly interested. All of his novels make explicit reference to a wide range of artists and painting techniques, and his second published novel, *Under the Greenwood Tree* (1872), was subtitled 'A Rural Painting of the Dutch School'. In novels up to *The Woodlanders* (1887) references are made mostly to classical painters from the Renaissance to the eighteenth century in order to heighten character or landscape descriptions. For example, in *The Return of the Native* (1878), Clym Yeobright's face is described as appearing 'in Rembrandt's intensest manner'(*Return*, 162), and figures in a night landscape silhouetted by fire 'caused their lineaments and general contours to be drawn with Düreresque vigour and dash' (*Return*, 45). Between writing *The Woodlanders* and *Tess of the d'Urbervilles*, Hardy developed a particular interest in more contemporary and experimental painting, especially French Impressionism and the work of the British painter J. M. W. Turner. (It might be helpful here to look at one or two reproductions of paintings by Turner and the Impressionists to get a feel for their work, for example 'Snowstorm and a Steamboat' [1842] or 'Rain, Steam and Speed' [1844] by Turner, and Claude Monet's 'Impression, Sunrise' [1874] or works by Paul Cézanne and Camille Pissaro.)

Hardy dismissed traditional styles of painting as the conventions of an outmoded realism:

> I don't want to see landscapes, *i.e.* scenic paintings of them, because I don't want to see the original realities – as optical effects, that is. I want to see the deeper reality underlying the scenic, the expression of what are sometimes called abstract imaginings.

The 'simply natural' is interesting no longer. The much decried, mad, late-Turner rendering is now necessary to create my interest. The exact truth as to material fact ceases to be of importance in art. . . .

(*Life*, 185)

Turner's innovative, modern technique is again stressed in a note dated 1889:

Turner's water-colours: each is a landscape *plus* a man's soul. . . . What he paints chiefly is *light as modified by objects*. He first recognises the impossibility of really reproducing on canvas all that is in a landscape; then gives for that which cannot be reproduced a something else which shall have upon the spectator an approximate effect to that of the real.

(*Life*, 216)

Locating *Tess of the d'Urbervilles* in the context of these developments in nineteenth-century visual art offers illuminating ways of reading and, at the level of the development of the novel form, can assist in placing Hardy's fiction in relation to literary tradition. This also sheds interesting light on some of the more negative critical judgements which have been passed on Hardy's prose fiction style.

The narrative in *Tess of the d'Urbervilles* contains a number of unusual terms referring to light and colour which are linguistically foregrounded throughout the novel. Each phase of the novel accentuates different colours and uses light and shade to reflect Tess's state. Indeed, it could be argued that Tess's character is rendered in a discourse which attempts to present her, paradoxically, as beyond language: beyond, that is, the established and conventional discourses of social control and class. During her idyllic period at Talbothays farm, when she falls in love with Angel Clare, she dissolves into nature, light and colour:

Her affection for him was now the breath and life of Tess's being; it enveloped her as a photosphere, irradiated her into forgetfulness of her past sorrows, keeping back the gloomy spectres that would persist in their attempts to touch her – doubt, fear, moodiness, care, shame. She knew that they were waiting like wolves just outside the circumscribing light, but she had long spells of power to keep them in hungry subjection there.

A spiritual forgetfulness co-existed with an intellectual remembrance. She walked in brightness, but she knew that in the background those shapes of darkness were always spread. They might be receding, or they might be approaching, one or the other, a little every day.

(*Tess*, 236–7)

The use of colour, light and shade suggests Tess's emotional state, but Hardy employs an unusual scientific term 'photosphere' which is taken from astronomy. Its mid-nineteenth-century meaning, according to the Oxford English Dictionary, was 'the luminous envelope of the sun (or a star), from which its light and heat radiate', and significantly, both Impressionism and Turner's use of colour were grounded in similar scientific theories of light.[2] By using terms such as 'polychrome' (*Tess*, 161), 'phosphoresence' (170), 'aqueous light' (169), and 'a pollen of radiance' (235), Tess becomes indistinct and nebulous, in a state of suspension 'conscious of neither time nor space'(162). It is as if she has become (as Hardy said of Turner's paintings) 'light as modified by objects' (*Life*, 216). Form is present in the background, with its dark connotations of memory for Tess, but at this stage 'she was in a dream wherein familiar objects appeared as having light and shade and position, but no particular outline' (*Tess*, 211), and 'she moved about in a mental cloud of many-coloured idealities, which eclipsed all sinister contingencies by its brightness' (254).

Later in the novel, when Tess has been abandoned by Angel Clare, and has moved to the harsh landscape at Flintcomb-Ash farm, we find Tess now surrounded by 'an achromatic chaos of things', 'a disordered medley of grays' (335). Here it is the sharp materiality of the landscape which is stressed, combining with Alec's reappearance – 'flints in bulbous, cusped and phallic shapes' (331) and the 'black angularities' (352) of Alec's face. Tess's social exclusion and oppression by established religion are reinforced by Angel's parents' attitudes. His father is a vicar, and the biblical epigraphs emblazoned in the landscape which heighten her sense of guilt, are ironically painted by Alec during his temporary religious conversion. A scene from this phase of the novel in chapter 47 which has received considerable attention (especially after its striking portrayal in Roman Polanski's film *Tess* [1979]) is that when Tess and Izz Huet work on the steam threshing machine. It is worth quoting this at length to illustrate how Hardy builds his affects.

It is the threshing of the last wheat-rick at Flintcomb-Ash Farm. The dawn of the March morning is singularly inexpressive, and there is nothing to show where the eastern horizon lies. Against the twilight rises the trapezoidal top of the stack, which has stood forlornly here through the washing and bleaching of the wintry weather.

When Izz Huett and Tess arrived at the scene of operations only a rustling denoted that others had preceded them; to which, as the light increased, there were presently added silhouettes of the two men on the summit. They were busily 'unhaling' the rick, that is, stripping off the thatch before beginning to throw down the sheaves; and while this was in progress Izz and Tess, with the other women-workers, in their whitey-brown pinners, stood waiting and shivering, Farmer Groby having insisted upon their being on the spot thus early to get the job over if possible by the end of the day. Close under the eaves of the stack, and as yet barely visible, was the red tyrant that the women had come to serve – a timber-framed construction, with straps and wheels appertaining – the threshing-machine which, whilst it was going, kept up a despotic demand upon the endurance of their muscles and nerves.

A little way off there was another indistinct figure; this one black, with a sustained hiss that spoke of strength very much in reserve. The long chimney running up beside an ash-tree, and the warmth which radiated from the spot, explained without the necessity of much daylight that here was the engine which was to act as the *primum mobile* of this little world. By the engine stood a dark motionless being, a sooty and grimy embodiment of tallness, in a sort of trance, with a heap of coals by his side: it was the engineman. The isolation of his manner and colour lent him the appearance of a creature from Tophet, who had strayed into the pellucid smokelessness of this region of yellow grain and pale soil, with which he had nothing in common, to amaze and to discompose its aborigines.

What he looked he felt. He was in the agricultural world, but not of it. He served fire and smoke; these denizens of the fields served vegetable, weather, frost, and sun. He travelled with his engine from farm to farm, from county to county, for as yet the steam threshing-machine was itinerant in this part of Wessex. He spoke in a strange northern accent; his thoughts being turned inwards upon himself, his eye on his iron charge, hardly perceiving the scenes around him, and caring for them not at all: holding only strictly necessary intercourse with the natives, as if some ancient doom compelled him to wander here against his will in the service of his Plutonic master. The long strap which ran from the driving-wheel of his engine to the red thresher under the rick was the sole tie-line between agriculture and him.

While they uncovered the sheaves he stood apathetic beside his portable repository of force, round whose hot blackness the morning air quivered. He had nothing to do with the preparatory labour. His fire was waiting incandescent, his steam was at high pressure, in a few seconds he could make the long strap move at an invisible velocity. Beyond its extent the environment might be corn, straw, or chaos; it was all the same to him. If any autochthonous idlers asked him what he called himself, he replied shortly, 'an engineer'.

(*Tess*, 372–3)

The visual qualities of this passage are very evocative. The colour spectrum is reduced to dark ominous forms, and the only primary colour emphasised is that of the red threshing machine itself. Red always poses a threat to Tess in the novel's colour symbolism (for example Alec is described much earlier as 'one who stood fair to be the blood-red ray in the spectrum of her young life' [71]). With the notable exception of the engineer, who seems not of this world, the human figures are reduced and marginalised by the awesome mechanical power. The dynamic tensions between nature and machine, between colour, light and form, between tradition and technological progress, are very reminiscent of some of Turner's paintings which Hardy specifically mentions in his notebooks: paintings like 'Snowstorm and a Steamboat' (1842), 'The Burial of Wilkie' (1842), and 'Rain, Steam and Speed' (1844).

The visual emphasis in this passage combines with other discourses to describe a world in which Tess and Izz have no control whatsoever, where the all-powerful machine becomes a symbol of a rapidly changing social order concentrated in this image. Although the threshing machine represents at one level modernity and changes in time and space, just as the train which took the milk from Talbothays farm to London does earlier in the novel, much of the language which is used to express its impact is drawn from mythological and biblical sources. Again, most of the narrator's references – such as *'primum mobile'* referring to Ptolemy's cosmological system, or 'Tophet', a biblical allusion to a place near Jerusalem where fires were kept constantly burning suggesting Hell – are likely to be beyond Tess's and Izz's knowledge and cultural horizons, as would terms derived from Latin and Greek such as 'aborigines' and 'autochthonous', both meaning original inhabitants or natives. To refer to the agricultural labourers in such a way implies linguistic alienation, forms of language and knowledge to which they are denied access yet which exercise power over them and convert them from individuals into social types. A similar kind of alienation and division of labour is expressed graphically in the image of the 'long strap which ran from the driving-wheel of his engine to the red thresher . . . the sole tie-line between agriculture and him'. This pictorial depiction of the growing division or mediation between labour and product, between worker and machine, between rural community and mass production, graphically reinforces the theme of social division and exclusion which runs throughout the novel. It is reflected in the divorce between character and language.

It might be helpful at this stage to turn to the context in which Hardy's novels have been read and interpreted, and in particular to consider briefly some of the ways that literary critics have responded to his fiction. The critical reception of a novel can exert a very significant influence on the ways in which we respond to it: almost as if it has been read for us before-hand and we need to be aware of these shaping forces. The range and variety of approaches we find indicate not only that his fiction is very diverse, but also that attitudes to his work have changed significantly over more than a hundred years in line with the cultural and critical contexts in which it has been read. Peter Widdowson's *Hardy in History: A Study in Literary Sociology* (1989) suggests that we need a 'critiography' (6) in order to understand how literature is studied in different critical contexts, and how these affect our understanding and evaluation of, in this instance, Hardy's novels. Indeed, the novels offer an illuminating case study of how literary texts are affected by the passage of time, how they impact on their readers, and how their reception by readers and critics may in turn shape and modify further responses. For example, Hardy's novels have been frequently read with reference to what has often been called the 'back-ground' of nineteenth-century rural life particularly in Dorset. Merryn Williams's *Thomas Hardy and Rural England* (1972), for instance, approaches *Tess* in relation to changing agricultural conditions in the period.

In understanding descriptions of nineteenth-century rural life and in considering how technology and industry began to impact on traditional activities, a socio-historical approach can be illuminating. Other critics, however, have chosen to identify and emphasise more universal and time-less qualities and have located Hardy's fiction in the grand European tra-ditions of the novel or made comparisons with Greek classical tragedy. This often coincides with a concentration on Hardy's characters, in par-ticular a focus on major figures such as Michael Henchard in *The Mayor of Casterbridge* (1886) or Clym Yeobright in *The Return of the Native* (1878) as tragic heroes. In the 1960s and 1970s, when critical responses to fiction began to stress narrative form in particular, we find a number of approaches which examine the fictional structures in Hardy's novels, such as Barbara Hardy's *The Appropriate Form: An Essay on the Novel* (1962) or Ian Gregor's *The Great Web: The Form of Hardy's Major Fiction* (1974). Some of these critics found Hardy's fiction wanting in terms of form, 'fixing the complexities of life into a predetermined and dogmatic pattern' according to Barbara Hardy (*Appropriate Form*, 4–5), or 'Like lumps of uncooked por-ridge, his concepts hang suspended in the novel or poem, indigestible and tasteless' in Richard Carpenter's assessment in *Thomas Hardy* (1964: 22–3). Others stressed unity of form and vision in his fiction, as Penelope Vigar does in *The Novels of Thomas Hardy: Illusion and Reality* (1974); while Gregor emphasised the integration and organic wholeness of Hardy's world-view, able to contain complexities and contradictions, as suggested by the metaphor of 'the great web of human doings' found in *The Wood-landers* (1887: 52). With the impact of feminist theory and criticism in the 1980s, critics have also addressed the representation of women; for example Penny Boumelha in *Thomas Hardy and Women: Sexual Ideology and Narrative Form* (1982), argues that Hardy's innovative narrative form permits a radical portrayal of women characters. Sue Bridehead and Arabella Donn, for example, in *Jude the Obscure* (1896), represent in quite different ways fundamental departures from conventional nineteenth-century depictions of womanhood. The impact of more recent critical approaches such as poststructuralism, new historicism and cultural materialism has also been significant. Rather than viewing Hardy's fiction as a straightforward reflection of history, John Goode's *Thomas Hardy: The Offensive Truth* (1988) explores the tensions between the novel form, specific historical contexts of gender, class and culture, and considers the expectations of Hardy's contemporaneous readership alongside those of subsequent critical responses. Roger Ebbatson's *Hardy: The Margin of the Unexpressed* (1993) addresses what have been frequently considered Hardy's minor novels, stories and essays as a way of challenging the traditional view of 'Hardy as a kind of cultural monument' (Ebbatson, *Hardy*, 7). Ebbatson employs a range of theoretical approaches which reveal the ways in which Hardy's fictional writing is inextricably enmeshed with the contradictions and power structures of nineteenth-century society. Critical writing, then, is a major context and shaping force in our reading of Hardy's novels, and criticism itself explicitly or implicitly employs a range of contexts and assumptions in order to establish or validate an interpretation.

Alongside critical and academic responses we should not forget that a number, but by no means all, of Hardy's novels have always been extremely popular. (How widely read are *The Hand of Ethelberta* (1876) or *A Laodicean* (1881) for example?) Few other writers whom we might designate 'serious' or 'classical' in terms of the ways in which they have been positioned historically, culturally and commercially, have at the same time sold so widely. Whilst occupying a central position in the English academic curriculum, his novels have also had a much wider circulation through book clubs, radio and television serials and film adaptations. Hardy's novels have a wider appeal and history of readership alongside the narrower context of the academy, and their transmission into other media has become an increasingly important feature of his position as a novelist, arguably bridging the gap between popular and high culture. This also raises interesting questions about the kind of audience which Hardy was writing for, and how it may have changed over the last hundred years given this wide and varied circulation. We might consider, as examples of recent contexts, how viewing film versions such as John Schlesinger's *Far from the Madding Crowd* (1967), Roman Polanski's *Tess* (1979), or Michael Winterbottom's *Jude* (1996) affects our reading of the novels. We should recognise that versions of the novels in different media now have a significant impact on the way in which we respond to the written text; indeed many people may now view film or television adaptations before reading the novels. You may wish to consider whether the cinematic text should – or can – be a faithful reproduction of the literary text. What elements of each medium make direct translation difficult? Certainly the visual emphasis in Hardy's writing lends itself very well to cinematic form, in ways that film directors have exploited. You might consider the imaginative uses of colour and optical effects in the cinematography of Polanski's *Tess*, or the grainy black and white combined with exaggerated perspective in the opening of Winterbottom's *Jude*.

Hardy frequently favoured geological and evolutionary images in his poetry and fiction to describe the shaping forces of time and nature on life as well as on the landscape.[3] We in turn can draw on such images to help us understand how the accretions of responses to his writing have shaped and possibly determined the ways in which we respond. In other words the *text* and *context* relationship is a dynamic one. Text and context are in dialogue with one another, and the contextual pressures on a work should not be seen as limiting or circumscribing meaning. We might also consider that the text/*context* relationship is potentially reversible, so that Hardy's novels may be used as contextual material for other texts. There are many possibilities here: we can read Hardy's novels in relation to each other, or other nineteenth- and twentieth-century novels in relation to Hardy's fiction. Moving beyond fiction, we might want to use the novels themselves as context or sources for historical writing on agricultural conditions in Dorset – as J. H. Bettey has in *Rural Life in Wessex 1500–1900* (1977) – or for situating more contemporaneous writing such as Richard Jeffries' essays on agricultural conditions. To use Hardy's own words, 'Experience *unteaches* – (what one at first thinks to be the rule in events)' (*Life*, 176). Context does not simply 'explain' or 'fix' the meaning of a novel; rather it opens up new possibilities of interpretation, and may well modify or even undermine our initial responses and assumptions. We need then to consider not only the contemporaneous contexts in which Hardy's fiction was *written*, but also the subsequent critical and cultural frames in which the novels are *read*.

The extended passage concerning the threshing machine quoted above from *Tess of the d'Urbervilles* raises questions about the ways in which we should read the novel. What kind of reader is implied? A major expectation in reading the nineteenth-century realist novel has been to look for forms of coherence and resolution, to seek or maybe to impose a unified structure and meaning on the narrative. *Tess of the d'Urbervilles* has been read by some critics within a tradition, or context, which emphasises this approach to reading, and the result has been, I would argue, either to distort the novel so that some areas of the text are emphasised at the expense of others, or to suggest that Hardy's writing doesn't offer a harmonious literary experience, and therefore should be relegated to a position below authors deemed as 'great' writers. An influential example of this is to be found, famously, in F. R. Leavis's *The Great Tradition* (1948) in which he quotes from Hardy's rival Henry James that '*Tess of the d'Urbervilles* is chock-full of faults and falsity', and goes on to speak of Hardy's 'clumsy' writing in *Jude the Obscure* (1895) (Leavis, *Great Tradition*, 34). More recently, David Lodge, in his essay on *Tess of the d'Urbervilles* in *Language of Fiction* (1966), quotes from another critic, Vernon Lee, who accuses Hardy of a 'slackening of attention', 'vagueness' and 'confusion of thought'. Lodge concludes:

> Sometimes his various 'voices' subtly make their points and modulate smoothly into one another; at other times they seem to be interrupting and quarrelling between themselves. Alternately dazzled by his sublimity and exasperated by his bathos, false notes, confusions, and contradictions, we are, while reading him, tantalised by a sense of greatness not quite achieved.
>
> (Lodge, *Language of Fiction*, 188)

In reading *Tess of the d'Urbervilles* mainly at a level of close textual analysis, Lodge loses the wider social contexts of the novel and the historical themes and issues which are addressed. The lack of resolution for the reader, the refusal by the text to coalesce into a harmonious whole, the denial of a comfortable ending or view of the world, are characteristics which we would not now necessarily consider artistic defects. The emphasis on coherent form ignores what we can term the ideological contexts of writing: the underlying shaping forces which lie behind language and form that operate on a writer, character or reader in areas such as nationhood or the family. The lack of any conventional resolution in terms of the plot and human relationships in *Tess of the d'Urbervilles*, or the novels which precede and follow it, *The Woodlanders* and *Jude the Obscure*, must be viewed in the socio-historical contexts of class and gender: these texts refuse to conceal these problems by illusory means in the form of a 'happy ending', and thereby do not condone marital and social relations involving inequality and exploitation. We should not forget that Hardy was on occasion viewed as a scandalous novelist: *Jude the Obscure* was burnt by a bishop on its publication for its radical representation of sexual relations and unconventional portrayal of the family. The effect of these tensions on the reader and critic should not lead to a purely literary and aesthetic judgement (ranking authors in relation to each other against some supposed, universal, self-evident standard of greatness is itself a highly questionable activity). The 'unresolved conflict' which Lodge points to in the narration should be read as indicative of wider unresolved conflicts in nineteenth-century society and beyond.

In his journals, Hardy frequently talks of art as a form of distortion, of 'disproportioning' (*Life*, 229). What he valued was what he termed 'the idiosyncratic mode of regard' (*Life*, 225). Significantly, these terms anticipate some twentieth-century theories on art and literature, such as Bertolt Brecht's concept of 'estrangement' or 'alienation effect' whereby the reader or audience is made to see beyond the work's artistry into its construction, so there can be no pretence or illusion.[4] This in turn serves to reveal and question the relations of power and social organisation with which the work of art engages. Hardy's later fiction can be read as a critique not only of the nineteenth-century social order, but also of literary and artistic conventions. Just as the 'long strap' which links the steam engine to the thresher reveals the power relations operating between technology, nature and society in the passage from *Tess*, so the fictional text reveals the relations between society and artistic production as readers are confronted with a narrative which challenges fictional decorum. Hardy makes the experience of reading, whether we recognise it or not, a process of both learning and *un*learning. In other words, art can make the familiar contexts in which we read, think, and live seem *un*familiar or strange so that we see them anew and maybe recognise the contradictions and inequalities which compose 'normal' or conventional art and life. Hardy's fiction was produced in, and has subsequently been subject to and processed by, various complex social, cultural and historical forces which we need to acknowledge in our reading. Further, the novels can be seen to question dominant orthodoxies in their content and in their form, challenging readers to question their relationship to fiction in ways that might extend beyond fiction and the act of reading.

Notes

1. Hardy's interest in form and repetition is recognised by Proust in a passage in his epoch-making novel, *A la recherche du temps perdu* (1920), where

the central character, Marcel, explains that a great writer or artist creates the same work over and over throughout his life. The idea of repetition in fiction has become a very significant feature of modernist and postmodernist writing, both imaginative and theoretical or critical, so that rather than fiction apparently reflecting in a faithful mirror-like way some external and pre-existing reality, it has become increasingly preoccupied with its own language and structure, inward looking and self-reflective. Patricia Waugh's *Metafiction* (1984) is a very good introduction to this feature of modernist writing which Hardy anticipates.

2. It is another interesting parallel between Turner and Hardy that they both, in their respective media, progress from a concentration on *chiaroscuro* – an emphasis predominantly on contrasting light and shade as in Turner's 'The Shipwreck' (1805) or Hardy's *The Return of the Native* (1878) – towards a much wider use of the colour spectrum as in Turner's 'The Fighting "Temeraire"' (1838) or *Tess of the d'Urbervilles* (1891). Turner developed his use of colour and perspective through scientific theories, but also significantly was strongly influenced in the 1830s and 1840s by the German writer Goethe's *Zur Farbenlehre* or *Treatise on Colour* (1810) in which light and colour are linked to character and the emotions.

3. Hardy was very interested in the theories of Charles Darwin, as references in *The Life of Thomas Hardy* reveal; it is stated that, 'As a young man he had been among the early acclaimers of *The Origin of Species*' (*Life*, 153), which was published in 1859. He was friendly with Darwin's followers such as Thomas Huxley, Leslie Stephen and Herbert Spencer, and was familiar with the latter's phrase 'the survival of the fittest' which has become so strongly identified with Darwinism. His novels display many reflections of evolutionary ideas.

4. Hardy is quoted as stating in 1890, 'Art consists in so depicting the common events of life as to bring out the features which illustrate the author's idiosyncratic mode of regard; making old incidents and things seem as new' (*Life*, 225), and 'Art is a disproportioning – (*i.e.* distorting, throwing out of proportion) – of realities, to show more clearly the features that matter in those realities, which, if merely copied or reported inventorially, might possibly be observed, but would more probably be overlooked. Hence "realism" is not Art' (*Life*, 229). These ideas anticipate some of the radical earlier twentieth-century theories which have been associated with modernism and experimental art, such as Brecht's 'estrangement effects', or Shklovsky's concept of 'defamiliarisation', which suggest that experimental art can perform much more active and disruptive functions than traditional passive realist works have done. (See Webster, *Studying Literary Theory* [69–70], for a discussion of these concepts.)

Further Reading

There is an abundance of critical writing on Hardy – indeed D. H. Lawrence said of his novels that, 'if one wrote everything they give rise to, it would fill the Judgement Book' ('Study of Thomas Hardy', in *Phoenix I*, Heinemann, London, 1936: 410). Most of the critical works mentioned in the essay above offer helpful approaches to Hardy's fiction. I would recommend especially Peter Widdowson, *Hardy in History: A Study in Literary Sociology* (1989) and John Goode, *Thomas Hardy: The Offensive Truth* (1988), the former being more accessible and covering a wider range of material. On historical context in nineteenth-centural rural England, Merryn Williams, *Thomas Hardy and Rural England* (London, Macmillan – now Palgrave, 1972) reads Hardy's novels revealingly in the light of social and agricultural conditions. J. B. Bullen, *The Expressive Eye: Fiction and Perception in the Work of Thomas Hardy* (Oxford, Oxford University Press, 1986) is an extended discussion on Hardy's visual imagination and relationship to the visual arts, and Joan Grundy, *Hardy and the Sister Arts* (London, Macmillan – now Palgrave, 1979) considers the importance of music and drama as well as painting. Robert Gittings, *Young Thomas Hardy* (London, Heinemann, 1975), *The Older Hardy* (London, Heinemann, 1978), and Michael Millgate, *Thomas Hardy: A Biography* (Oxford, Oxford University Press, 1982) are informative biographical studies. J. A. V. Chapple, *Science and Literature in the Nineteenth Century* (London, Macmillan – now Palgrave, 1986) provides useful contextual material on Darwin, Lyell and others.

References

Richard Carpenter, *Thomas Hardy* (Boston, Twayne, 1964).

R. G. Cox (ed.), *Thomas Hardy: The Critical Heritage* (London, Routledge, 1970).

Roger Ebbatson, *Hardy: The Margin of the Unexpressed* (Sheffield, Sheffield Academic Press, 1993).

Ian Gregor, *The Great Web: The Form of Hardy's Major Fiction* (London, Faber, 1974).

Barbara Hardy, *The Appropriate Form: An Essay on the Novel* (London, Athlone, 1962).

Florence Emily Hardy, *The Life of Thomas Hardy 1840–1928* (1962: London, Macmillan – now Palgrave, 1975). First published in two volumes as *The Early Life of Thomas Hardy 1840–1891* (1928), and *The Later Years of Thomas Hardy 1892–1928* (1930).

Thomas Hardy, *A Pair of Blue Eyes* (1873: London, Macmillan – now Palgrave, 1975).

——, *Far from the Madding Crowd* (1874: London, Macmillan – now Palgrave, 1974).

——, *The Return of the Native* (1878: London, Macmillan – now Palgrave, 1974).

——, *The Woodlanders* (1887: London, Macmillan – now Palgrave, 1974).

——, *Tess of the d'Urbervilles* (1891: London, Macmillan – now Palgrave, 1974).

——, *The Well-Beloved* (1897: London, Macmillan – now Palgrave, 1975).

——, *Selected Poetry and Non-Fictional Prose*, ed. Peter Widdowson (Basingstoke, Macmillan – now Palgrave, 1997).

F. R. Leavis, *The Great Tradition* (1948: Harmondsworth, Penguin, 1974).

David Lodge, 'Tess, Nature and the Voices of Hardy', in *Language of Fiction* (London, Routledge, 1966).

Marcel Proust, *A la recherche du temps perdu*, Vol. III (Paris, Pléiade, 1954).

Patricia Waugh, *Metafiction: the Theory and Practice of Self-Conscious Fiction* (London, Methuen, 1984).

Roger Webster, *Studying Literary Theory* (London, Arnold, 1996).

Peter Widdowson, *Hardy in History: A Study in Literary Sociology* (London, Routledge, 1989).

11 Virginia Woolf: *Mrs Dalloway* and *A Room of One's Own*

Marion Shaw

Portrait of Virginia Woolf (1882–1941).

Virginia Woolf (1882–1941) was born Virginia Stephen. As a writer she has always been known by her married name, Virginia Woolf, and it is by this name that she is referred to throughout this essay.

In this essay I am going to base most of my discussion on one novel by Virginia Woolf, *Mrs Dalloway*, and one of her non-fiction works, *A Room of One's Own*. I shall consider these works in several contexts: the circumstances of Virginia Woolf's early life, her position as a woman writer during the first 30 years of the twentieth century, the place she occupies in the literary movement known as Modernism, and how her style of writing registers this movement. I shall also cross-refer between the two works, using each as a context for the other. My main critical approach in this essay is a feminist one, but this inevitably shades into biographical, historical and aesthetic considerations.

It is particularly fitting to view Virginia Woolf in context because she was one of the first writers to consider seriously and at length the relationship between an author's historical and personal situation and his or her work. She was, in fact, interested in a work of art's context. This question particularly interested her in relation to women writers. She wanted to know why women had not written as much as men, why some of what they had written was flawed, and why certain kinds of writing – the drama and poetry – had hardly been written by women at all. Her conclusions were that this was because historically women had been deprived of education, money, status and a room of their own in which to write. The example she used was Charlotte Brontë, who 'had been starved of her proper due of experience [and] made to stagnate in a parsonage', and whose books were 'deformed and twisted' as a result. Woolf thought that Charlotte Brontë 'had more genius in her than Jane Austen' but because of her frustration at her situation she 'will write in a rage where she should write calmly. She will write foolishly where she should write wisely . . . She is at war with her lot. How could she help but die young, cramped and thwarted?' (Woolf, *Room*, 70).

These passionate sentiments are extracted from one of Woolf's most famous books, *A Room of One's Own*. It is interesting that the tenses of the verbs change in this passage, from a past tense – 'Brontë *had* more genius in her' – to an imperative future tense and a present tense – 'She *will* write foolishly . . . She *is* at war . . .' The sense of urgency and stress this transition creates tells us more about Woolf than it does about Brontë, as though the 'deformed' nature of Brontë's novels is a danger for Woolf, a model of writing which is a present and future threat. Woolf's anxieties about her life as a woman writer are shaping her response to the topic. These anxieties should be seen in the context of women's general position at this time and how this affected their writing.

A Room of One's Own was based on two lectures read to women undergraduates at Newnham and Girton Colleges, Cambridge, in 1928, on the subject of women and fiction. The timing was significant because in May of that year women finally attained the right to vote on equal terms with men. Politically the young women in Woolf's audience at Cambridge were now entitled to full citizenship; economically they would still have far to go but those who listened to her were at least being educated almost to the same level as men. Cambridge would not permit women to be awarded degrees until 1944 but in 1928 they were allowed to take the degree examinations. 1928 also saw the opening of the Shakespeare Memorial Theatre in Stratford-on-Avon and this visible reminder of the greatest English poet-dramatist raises the question of why there has not been a female Shakespeare. Woolf's fantasy in *A Room of One's Own* is that there was one, that Shakespeare had a sister, as talented as he but, unable to survive in the male world of the Elizabethan theatre, she killed herself: 'who shall measure the heat and violence of the poet's heart when caught and tangled in a woman's body?' (Woolf, *Room*, 50).

Now, however, in 1928, at this crucial time in women's history, with the vote captured and higher education within reach at least for some, Woolf's concern is with the future for women writers and the possibility that in 'another century or so . . . the dead poet who was Shakespeare's sister will put on the body which she has so often laid down' (Woolf, *Room*, 112). The necessary condition of her arrival is intellectual freedom and 'intellectual freedom depends upon material things'. But it is an intellectual and material freedom which must be part of the common life of women because that is the context in which great art flourishes. Woolf claims, perhaps slightly extravagantly, that if all women have £500 a year and rooms of their own; if they have the courage to 'escape a little from the common sitting-room', and to face the fact that 'there is no arm to cling to, but that we go alone', then the conditions will be right for Shakespeare's sister to be born again (Woolf, *Room*, 112).

The feminist movement in Britain at this time was relatively subdued, compared with the pre-war excitements of the suffrage campaigns. At such a time it would have been easy for Woolf to ignore these concerns. Why she chose instead to write polemical feminist essays can perhaps be considered in the context of her own development both as a woman and as a woman writer. The relation between life and art is complex and biographical criticism can be treacherously reductive. Nevertheless, Woolf's fiction frequently uses her own family experiences, and her memoirs, diaries, journals and letters habitually weave together the personal and the artistic in a way which invites a similar contextual approach. The Cambridge lectures which became *A Room of One's Own* were something of a stock-taking exercise, a middle-aged woman (she was 46 at the time, old enough to be the mother of those in her audience) drawing on her experiences as a writer to make a political statement to her successors, the 'starved but valiant young women' students at Cambridge who may become the next generation of writers.

Unlike the young women in her audience, as a daughter in a Victorian middle-class family she had been educated privately at home, sometimes with tutors, mostly alone and self-directed. She envied her brothers the intellectual companionship of university; 'There's nothing like talk as an educator I'm sure', she wrote in 1903. 'I have to delve from books, painfully and all alone, what you get every evening sitting over your fire and smoking your pipe with Strachey etc. No wonder my knowledge is scant' (Woolf, *Letters*, I, 77). To have scant knowledge, to be trapped in narrow circumstances instead of 'practical experience, intercourse with her kind and acquaintance with a variety of character', had been the limitations imposed on Charlotte Brontë, who had known, 'no-one better, how enormously her genius would have profited if it had not spent itself in solitary visions over distant fields'.

For Woolf to avoid this Victorian legacy she had to move away from the influence of her parents, particularly her mother, Julia Stephen, who had died when Woolf was 13, leaving a painful memory of a beautiful, intensely maternal and self-sacrificing figure who would feature in much of Woolf's fiction. Not to be trapped by this ideal, whom Woolf referred to as 'the angel in the house', was made more difficult by her father, Leslie Stephen, who expected his daughters to follow in their mother's footsteps. When Leslie Stephen died in 1904, although she was full of grief and remorse at his death, Woolf was also liberated. Many years later, in November 1928, not long after giving her Cambridge lectures, she remembered her father on the day of his birthday: 'He would have been . . . 96, yes, today; & could have been 96, like other people one has known; but mercifully was not. His life would have entirely ended mine. What would have happened? No writing, no books: – inconceivable' (Woolf, *Diary*, III, 208).

After her father's death, Virginia Woolf and her sister Vanessa set up home in Gordon Square, in the Bloomsbury district of London, to live an experimental, emancipated, bohemian existence very different from their earlier life. 'There was', Woolf later wrote, 'something in the atmosphere; something hostile to the old traditions of the family; something [which] my mother would have disapproved of for her daughters' (Lee, *Virginia Woolf*,

208). Visitors to the new home included artists and writers, intellectuals and wits; the talk was intense, competitive, abstract yet also gossipy, sometimes hilarious, sometimes infuriating: altogether the environment in which a budding journalist – Woolf was by now writing for the *Times Literary Supplement* and the *Cornhill* – and an aspiring novelist might flourish. These were the early days of what has come to be known as the 'Bloomsbury Group', whose members over the years included Clive Bell, Roger Fry, Lytton Strachey, Maynard Keynes, Duncan Grant, Dora Carrington, E. M. Forster and Leonard Woolf. Sometimes thought of as elitist and 'arty' (Woolf herself often criticised it as snobbish and socially irrelevant), the Bloomsbury Group, particularly during the war years and the 1920s, was a forum for progressive thought and art of all kinds and a bulwark against what its members saw as the erosion of civilised values. 'There was always', Woolf wrote later, 'some new idea afoot; always some new picture standing on a chair waiting to be looked at, some new poet fished out from obscurity and stood in the light of day' (Woolf, 'Old Bloomsbury', 214–15).

By the time Woolf gave her lectures at Newnham and Girton Colleges, she had published five novels, a fictional biography (*Orlando*), a number of short stories and essays, and numerous book reviews. She had become, in fact, an established writer, one who earned money – her income from writing in 1928 was £1434 – and who had all the space and privacy she could wish for. Why should she still be fretting about women and fiction? Perhaps there was a lingering resentment at her 'cramped and thwarted' background – 'I should have liked a closer & thicker knowledge of life . . . I get such a tingling & vitality from an evenings talk like that', she wrote enviously after meeting the students at Cambridge (*Diary*, III, 201) – but more powerful was her desire for a tradition of female writing. This is one respect in which *A Room of One's Own* is itself a highly contextual study: it describes the material and educational deprivation of women writers of the past, it explores the current struggle for women (like Woolf herself) to find a writing identity, and it imagines a future for women of 'freedom and fullness of expression'. All these concerns cluster round two figures in Woolf's fiction: the mother and the daughter. 'For we think back through our mothers if we are women', she wrote in *A Room of One's Own* – and she might have added that we also think forward through our daughters (*Room*, 76).

In the context of past writing, Woolf s interest in the mother–daughter relation is historically significant. Although nineteenth-century fiction had paid lip service to a maternal ideal, in actuality mothers had featured little; their ineffectuality or their absence through death had been a useful plot device for freeing the heroines of Victorian novels for adventure. With the growth of the women's movement towards the end of the Victorian age, and a move towards sexual equality, the 'problem' of Victorian mothers with modern daughters came to represent a profound change in the lives of women generally. The literary climate reflected this change, and the conflicts, reconciliations, betrayals and recuperations of the mother–daughter relationship become a major preoccupation of the domestic novel of the war and interwar years. Woolf's intense autobiographical interest in the mother–daughter relation must be seen in this context of contemporary writing on the subject by novelists like Elizabeth Bowen, Ivy Compton-Burnett, May Sinclair and Jean Rhys. These were matched in this preoccupation by a new generation of women psychologists. Karen Horney, Melanie Klein and others sought to revise the male-biased thinking of Sigmund Freud to acknowledge the maternal influence on women's development. Women's psychology, Horney wrote in 1924, 'is determined by innate identification with the mother, not by disappointed identification with the father' (quoted in Sayers, 92). Even more interesting was Melanie Klein's view of artistic creativity not as Freudian sublimation of instinctual drives but as a wish to repair relations with others, particularly with the mother.

Woolf's most obvious reparation and recuperation of the mother–daughter theme is in the most autobiographical of her novels, *To the Lighthouse* (1927). If Mrs Ramsay is the adored but repressive and eventually negated Victorian mother, the daughter figure is split among many characters: the little girls, Rose and Cam, benefit from their mother's comforting and protective presence; the grown-up Pru, whose life is modelled on her mother's, dies in childbirth, sacrificed, like her mother and by her mother, to the maternal role; and Lily Briscoe, the artist, the one who escapes but does not forget all that Mrs Ramsay signified. Mrs Ramsay (she is given no first name) is the full embodiment of maternal figures in Woolf's earlier fiction, perhaps particularly of one who exists as a ghost on the edge of the previous novel, *Mrs Dalloway* (1925). Mrs Dalloway – Clarissa – is the wife of an MP and the novel tells of a day in her life, 13 June 1923, when she gives a party. One of the guests at the party knew her as a girl: ' "Dear Clarissa!" exclaimed Mrs. Hilbery. She looked to-night, she said, so like her mother as she first saw her walking in a garden in a grey hat. And really Clarissa's eyes filled with tears. Her mother, walking in a garden!' (Woolf, *Dalloway*, 193). There are subtle evocations in this description of the Victorian mother; she belongs to an innocent first world of childhood (a garden of Eden) yet her grey hat suggests both the formality of this world and its erasure into ghostliness, washed away by time as well as by

Clarissa's tears: 'But alas, she must go', Clarissa thinks as she turns away from the memory, called to her hostess duties and dismissing her mother's presence from the party.

Clarissa Dalloway is a transitional figure, born in the Victorian period (she is 52 at the time of the novel) yet surviving the watershed of the war into a modern age of motor-cars, aeroplanes, shell-shocked war veterans, and new opportunities for women. Woolf's preoccupation with history is expressed in this novel through the context of generational change: the memory of Clarissa's mother in her late Victorian clothes, Clarissa herself, and her daughter, Elizabeth, a 17-year-old schoolgirl, 'queer-looking', Peter Walsh thinks (*Dalloway*, 61), not like her mother, very serious, 'like a hyacinth sheathed in a glossy green . . . a hyacinth that has had no sun' (*Dalloway*, 134). She is the true, post-war new woman, and she shares with Lily Briscoe, the artist in *To the Lighthouse*, 'Chinese eyes in a pale face', and a sense of future opportunities beyond the conventional roles for women, beyond what her mother, and certainly her grandmother, would ever have thought to do. Elizabeth is 'quite determined, whatever her mother might say, to become either a farmer or a doctor' (*Dalloway*, 150). When Elizabeth makes this resolution she is riding on the top of an omnibus up the Strand, having escaped the confines of her mother's house and also the grasp of an alternative mother-figure in the novel, the 'bitter and burning' spinster Miss Kilman, who coaches Elizabeth in history. Motor omnibuses first ran in London in 1905, so to ride on one is still quite a modern thing to do. This omnibus passes Somerset House:

> It looked so splendid, so serious, that great grey building. And she liked the feeling of people working. She liked those churches, like shapes of grey paper, breasting the stream of the Strand . . . It was so serious; it was so busy. In short, she would like to have a profession. She would become a doctor, a farmer, possibly go into Parliament if she found it necessary, all because of the Strand . . . She penetrated a little farther in the direction of St. Paul's. She liked the geniality, sisterhood, mother-hood, brotherhood of this uproar. It seemed to her good.
>
> (*Dalloway*, 149–51)

In *A Room of One's Own* Woolf quotes the passage from Charlotte Brontë's *Jane Eyre* where Jane climbs to the roof of Thornfield and looks over the fields at the distant view and longs for 'a power of vision which might over-pass that limit; which might reach the busy world, towns, regions full of life I had heard of but never seen' (*Room*, 69; *Jane Eyre*, ch. 12). Elizabeth Dalloway fulfils Jane Eyre's vision, moving through a world which Woolf carefully historicises in relation to women's twentieth-century opportunities. The Parliamentary Qualification of Women Act of 1918 allowed women to be elected as members of parliament and the Sex Disqualification (Removal) Act of 1919 had abolished all existing restrictions upon the admission of women into professions, occupations and civic positions, so Elizabeth's ambition to have a profession, to be an MP if necessary, is both realisable and a mark of her modernity.

The geography of central London becomes a map of Elizabeth's emancipation, and her movement through a world which though anchored in the past looks to a future both troubled and challenging. The eighteenth-century elegance of Somerset House on the Strand housed in 1923 some of the most important government offices, particularly the Public Record Office. Elizabeth will be part of that public record, not subsumed like her mother and her grandmother into domestic obscurity. Even more significant is that she travels down the Strand, that conduit between the West End of London, where the Dalloways live, to Fleet Street and St Paul's and out towards the beginnings of the East End, where in two months' time there will be a London Dock strike, heralding the industrial unrest and economic slump of the years to come. This oblique allusion to the 'other' London is one instance of the rich contextual fabric of *Mrs Dalloway*, just as the occasional mention of worrying 'news from India' by one of the characters signals the beginnings of the end of empire and, by implication, of the way of life of the Dalloways and their class. But Elizabeth is not to be trapped in the old systems, riding her omnibus towards this future like a frontiersman, 'like the figure-head of a ship', not needing a chaperone in these post-war days, going further than her mother, who goes only as far as Bond Street to buy flowers: 'no Dalloways came down the Strand daily: she was a pioneer, a stray, venturing, trusting' (*Dalloway*, 151). The 'busy world, towns, regions full of life' that had been Charlotte Brontë's dream become, literally, for Elizabeth her familiar place: 'She liked the geniality, sisterhood, motherhood, brotherhood of this uproar. It seemed to her good.'

Mrs Dalloway is generally regarded as Woolf's first experimental work, in fact her first Modernist novel; not only is the subject matter new, but the style in which the novel is written is also unconventional. To many critics, this style would be the hallmark of Modernism. Of course, to describe Woolf as a modernist is to place her in another and very complex context, that of an artistic phase in the Western world which began around 1910 and seems to have come to an end by 1930. An example from *Mrs Dalloway* of Woolf's own variety of a Modernist style is the moment of Elizabeth's decision to return home – 'But it was later than she thought

... She turned back down the Strand' – and how she achieves this – 'Calmly and competently, Elizabeth Dalloway mounted the Westminster omnibus.' The thought and action are separated in the text by a paragraph which is not spoken through her consciousness nor does it even seem to be about her. The narrative voice is speculative, uncertain, by no means an authorial or authoritative voice but detached, indeterminate:

> A puff of wind (in spite of the heat, there was quite a wind) blew a thin black veil over the sun and over the Strand. The faces faded; the omnibuses suddenly lost their glow. For although the clouds were of mountainous white so that one could fancy hacking hard chips off with a hatchet, with broad golden slopes, lawns of celestial pleasure gardens, on their flanks, and had all the appearance of gods above the world, there was a perpetual movement among them. Signs were interchanged, when, as if to fulfil some scheme arranged already, now a summit dwindled, now a whole block of pyramidal size which had kept its station inalterably advanced into the midst or gravely led the procession to fresh anchorage. Fixed though they seemed at their posts, at rest in perfect unanimity, nothing could be fresher, freer, more sensitive superficially than the snow-white or gold-kindled surface; to change, to go, to dismantle the solemn assemblage was immediately possible; and in spite of the grave fixity, the accumulated robustness and solidity, now they struck light to the earth, now darkness.
>
> (*Dalloway*, 152)

This strange description of clouds over London is not necessary to whatever 'plot' *Mrs Dalloway* has. Wedged between Elizabeth's decision to act and the act itself it becomes what Woolf herself called a 'moment of being' when the daily business of life, the routines of linear time, are interrupted by the mind's escape into reverie, symbolism, and introspection. To Woolf, this was an alternative reality with its own time, at odds with or complementing linear or clock time. These interlocking times are encapsulated in the image which accompanies the striking of Big Ben throughout *Mrs Dalloway*: 'The leaden circles dissolved in the air.' Nothing is more solid than lead yet the circles of its solidity become like the clouds of the 'moment of being' described in Elizabeth's journey down the Strand. Time during the early years of the twentieth century was indeed losing its fixity, Einstein's first theory of relativity in 1905 having shown that time and space are indivisible, that there is no absolute time, that both time and space are relative. A total eclipse of the sun in 1919, which Woolf saw, had demonstrated the truth of this theory. Ernest Rutherford's work on the atom came to an important conclusion in that year also. Writers, composers and artists of the period, particularly those who have become known as Modernists, expressed this sense of relativism, vividly demonstrated in a picture like Picasso's *Les Demoiselles d'Avignon* (1907), in which five women are painted in a series of planes, angles and ovals. Such a picture was deeply shocking and controversial because it challenged the familiar and accepted conventions of representational painting, the 'realism' which had dominated much nineteenth-century art. Painting of this kind was brought sharply into view for the British public in the Post-Impressionist Exhibition which Roger Fry, one of Woolf's Bloomsbury friends, organised in 1910. The description of clouds over London in *Mrs Dalloway* may seem arbitrary and controversial but it caught the tone of an important direction in intellectual and artistic life of the period. Its characteristics of achronicity, narrative indeterminacy, impressionistic reverie and absence of linear plot are those of Modernism, though it is, of course, a version of Modernism highly individual to Woolf.

In creating her own style as a Modernist writer, Woolf reacted strongly against Edwardian novelists like Arnold Bennett who, she thought, described only the exterior life of their characters, the houses they live in, the work they do and the clothes they wear but not those moments of their being when their memories and imaginations are in free fall, are in an impressionable, alternative time. As Woolf famously wrote in 1919:

> the mind receives a myriad impressions – trivial, fantastic, evanescent, or engraved with the sharpness of steel. From all sides they come, an incessant shower of innumerable atoms . . . Life is not a series of gig lamps, symmetrically arranged; life is a luminous halo, a semi-transparent envelope surrounding us from the beginning of consciousness to the end.
>
> (Woolf, 'Modern Fiction', 8)

To the new writers of Woolf's generation, the Edwardian conventions were worn out. It was the task of these new writers to convey the 'unknown and uncircumscibed spirit' of modern consciousness and to do so 'we are suggesting that the proper stuff of fiction is a little other than custom would have us believe'. In planning *The Waves* (1931), which critics believe to be her most experimental novel, Woolf wrote that what she wanted to do was 'give the moment whole; whatever it includes'. What had to be excluded in this approach was the 'appalling narrative business of the realist: getting on from lunch to dinner: it is false, unreal, merely conventional' (Woolf, *Diaries*, III, 209). A new relation between the inner and the outer lives of her characters had to be created – 'some combination of them ought to be possible'. In *The Waves*, an almost plotless novel in which the thoughts of six characters, from childhood to middle age, interweave to form a composite meditation, externality is refracted and fractured through the consciousness of the characters, as in this extract where Susan sees two servants kissing:

> I saw Florrie in the kitchen garden . . . as we came back from our walk, with the washing blown out round her, the pyjamas, the drawers, the nightgowns blown tight. And Ernest kissed her. He was in his green baize apron, cleaning silver . . . and he seized her with the pyjamas blown out hard between them. He was blind as a bull, and she swooned in anguish . . . Now though they pass plates of bread and butter and cups of milk at tea-time I see a crack in the earth and hot steam hisses up; and the urn roars as Ernest roared, and I am blown out hard like the pyjamas, even while my teeth meet in the soft bread and butter, and I lap the sweet milk.
> (Woolf, *Waves*, 20–1)

A 'real' Edwardian household is evoked here, with its work, routines, energies and prohibitions but the 'moment' of seeing Florrie being kissed is, to use Woolf's word, 'saturated' with Susan's sensations, impressions and emotions, and overspills the clock time of its happening into the alternative time of memory, re-enactment and fantasy.

The kind of writing in this passage and in the one about the clouds in London is often described as 'stream of consciousness'. It has become an umbrella label to cover a range of styles by Modernist writers, but it was first used in literary criticism in 1918 by the writer May Sinclair who applied it to Dorothy Richardson's autobiographical, sequential novel *Pilgrimage*. It has been subsequently used of the work of other of Woolf's contemporaries, particularly that of James Joyce whose *Ulysses* (1922), like *Mrs Dalloway*, has little plot, takes place on one day, and is full of the thought processes, sense impressions and imaginings of its characters. Woolf also reviewed *Pilgrimage* (a later part; there would eventually be 13) in 1923, praising its concern 'with states of being and not with states of doing. Miriam [the protagonist of *Pilgrimage*] is aware of "life itself"; of the atmosphere of the table rather than of the table; of the silence rather than the sound'. Particularly interesting is Woolf's claim that what Richardson has done has:

> invented, or, if she has not invented, developed and applied to her own uses, a sentence which we might call the psychological sentence of the feminine gender. It is of more elastic fibre than the old, capable of

stretching to the extreme, of suspending the frailest particles, of enveloping the vaguest shapes. Other writers of the opposite sex have used sentences of this description and stretched them to the extreme. But there is a difference. Miss Richardson has fashioned her sentence consciously, in order that it may descend to the depths and investigate the crannies of Miriam Henderson's consciousness. It is a woman's sentence, but only in the sense that it is used to describe a woman's mind by a writer who is neither proud nor afraid of anything that she may discover in the psychology of her sex.

(Woolf, *Women and Writing*, 191)

Modernism in England has often been thought of as a particularly male enterprise, dominated by four writers: Eliot, Yeats, Joyce and Lawrence. This view has been challenged recently, mainly due to the rise of feminist criticism since the early 1970s which has not only seen Woolf given her rightful place amongst the great writers of the twentieth century but has paid critical attention to other modernist women writers – Djuna Barnes, Katherine Mansfield, Dorothy Richardson and Gertrude Stein, for example. But it is not just a matter of mere numbers. What Woolf daringly suggests in her comments on the form of Richardson's novels, is that Modernism, far from being a male preserve, is a feminine art form. The 'women's sentence', with its elastic texture, its capacity for stretching to the extreme, or suspending the frailest particles, is the Modernist sentence. Though it might sometimes be written by men, it is 'the psychological sentence of the feminine gender'.

This brings together the contexts this essay has discussed: Woolf's own feminism and its roots in her Victorian childhood, the generational changes in the lives of women during the early years of the century, the tradition of women's writing and its future development, and the Modernist movement and its stylistic characteristics. It also brings us back to *A Room of One's Own* which seems to summarise these links in its discussion of the relation between gender and style. The problem for an aspiring woman novelist, Woolf maintains, has been that 'there was no common sentence ready for her use'. The forms of language have been shaped by men 'out of their own needs and for their own uses'. The young women who listened to Woolf give her Cambridge lectures are exhorted to consider what such a sentence might be, and what shape such sentences might build into the 'arcades and domes' of fiction. Woolf gives some suggestions on what the novels should be about: they might be about women and work, or women and friendship, neither of which have been explored before. But the form the writing will take is more difficult because it will have to express a woman's psychology as never before. Woolf imagines a young woman, Mary Carmichael, writing her first novel, called *Life's Adventure*, and considers what her modern sensibility, which is 'very wide, eager and free', might have achieved in its experimentation:

> It feasted like a plant newly stood in the air on every sight and sound that came its way. It ranged, too, very subtly and curiously, among almost unknown and unrecorded things; it lighted on small things and showed perhaps that they were not small at all. It brought buried things to light and made one wonder what need there had been to bury them at all. [Mary Carmichael] had – I begin to think – mastered the first great lesson; she wrote as a woman, but as a woman who has forgotten that she is woman, so that her pages were full of that curious sexual quality which comes only when sex is unconscious of itself.
>
> (Woolf, *Room*, 92)

It was because Charlotte Brontë was angry at her position as a woman who had no money, no privacy, no dignity, no tradition on which to draw, that her books, in Woolf's view, are deformed and twisted: 'She left her story, to which her entire devotion was due, to attend to some personal grievance' (Woolf, *Room*, 73). But as Woolf very well recognises, personal emotion, aroused by 'the relation of human being to human being', is what shapes a novel, and if that relation is based on a social system which deprives one half of the population of rights and responsibilities, then the 'integrity' of a novelist like Charlotte Brontë will be spoiled by 'an acidity which is the result of oppression'. Woolf's belief is that the emotion which gives rise to a novel must be distilled into 'a structure leaving a shape on the mind's eye, built now in squares, now pagoda shaped, now throwing out wings and arcades, now solidly compact and domed' (*Room*, 71). If the emotion is too raw, as in the sexual anger of Charlotte Brontë, then this 'shape' will be distorted, 'nothing appears whole and entire'. So it comes back to a question of context again: the context has to be appropriate for women to be able to write great work, for Shakespeare's sister to be born again. And the context has to be right not just for women writers but also for the Elizabeth Dalloways of the world who will be farmers, doctors or even politicians.

A Room of One's Own is regarded as one of the great feminist documents of the twentieth century and its influence on feminist criticism has been incalculable. Its elegant and playful style and its sinewy argument cannot, however, disguise how it itself is full of contradictions and anger. Its 'shape' is not perfect and perhaps it has the more endeared itself to us because of that. The greatest dislocation in the book is between its political and its aesthetic purposes, between its feminist message and its Modernist desire to 'give the moment whole, whatever it may include'. Woolf's terror at the Victorian inheritance of self-sacrifice and deprivation fuels the passion with which she lectured to the young women at Cambridge but her writer's sense of the need to keep that sexual anger within artistic proportions cuts across her feminism. Her description of Charlotte Brontë – 'She is at war with her lot' – is appropriate to Woolf herself. The context in which she wrote was highly complex and her novels struggle to accommodate the contradictions of her situation and to contain the problematic relation between Modernism and feminism. In *A Room of One's Own* she recommends that Mary Carmichael should 'learn to laugh, without bitterness, at the vanities – say rather peculiarities, for it is a less offensive word – of the other sex'. In *Mrs Dalloway*, Peter Walsh has a corresponding adventure to Elizabeth's in which he follows an unknown young woman up Piccadilly and down Oxford Street: 'he was an adventurer, reckless, he thought, swift, daring . . . a romantic buccaneer, careless of all those damned proprieties, yellow dressing-gowns, pipes, fishing-rods . . . and respectability . . . He was a buccaneer' (*Dalloway*, 58). Peter is, in fact, a stalker, and he is also, unlike Elizabeth, trapped in worn-out romantic conventions which are the glamorous face of sexual predatoriness. Yet his 'vanities' are obliquely presented, there is no explicit condemnation of his behaviour, but through the 'stream of [his] consciousness' we are given an affectionate delineation of his 'peculiarities'. In the pagoda shape of the novel nothing juts out disharmoniously or jarringly disturbs its aesthetic symmetries. Politics and art are if not reconciled then at least held precariously in balance so that criticism of Peter may be inferred by readers rather than thrust upon them, as perhaps it might have been if Charlotte Brontë, in Woolf's opinion, had been the author.

Further Reading

In many respects Virginia Woolf is her own best critic and I recommend the various collections of essays cited below. As she is also a great writer of informal prose, students may wish to consult her diaries and letters, details of which have also been given. In addition, you may wish to consult:

Lyndall Gordon, *Virginia Woolf: A Writer's Life* (Oxford, Oxford University Press, 1984).

Virginia Woolf, A *Woman's Essays*, ed. Rachel Bowlby (London, Penguin, 1992).

Alex Zwerdling, *Virginia Woolf and the Real World* (London, University of California Press, 1986).

References

Hermione Lee, *Virginia Woolf* (London, Chatto & Windus, 1996).

Janet Sayers, *Mothering Psychoanalysis* (London, Hamish Hamilton, 1991).

Virginia Woolf, *The Waves* [1931] (Harmondsworth, Penguin, 1964).

——, *A Room of One's Own* [1929] (Harmondsworth, Penguin, 1970).

——, *Mrs Dalloway* [1925] (London, Penguin, 1992).

——, 'Old Bloomsbury' in *Moments of Being*, ed. Jeanne Schulkind (London, Grafton, 1989).

——, 'Modern Fiction' in *The Crowded Dance of Modern Life*, ed. Rachel Bowlby (London, Penguin, 1993).

——, *Women and Writing*, introd. Michèle Barrett (London, The Women's Press, 1979).

——, *The Letters of Virginia Woolf*, ed. Nigel Nicolson and Joanne Trautmann, 6 vols (London, Hogarth Press, 1975–80).

——, *The Diary of Virginia Woolf*, ed. Anne Olivier Bell and Andrew McNeillie, 5 vols (London, Penguin, 1982).

12 The Poetry Of Sylvia Plath

Rick Rylance

Sylvia Plath reading her poems in *New Yorker*, August 1958. ©Mortimer Rare
Book Room, Smith College, Copyright Estate of Ted Hughes.

The poetry of Sylvia Plath (1932–63) is notoriously distressing, and for most readers this is the first and paramount fact in the experience of reading her work:

> The smile of iceboxes annihilates me.
> Such blue currents in the veins of my loved one!
> I hear her great heart purr.
>
> (Plath, *Collected*, 189)

The feelings of unease a verse like this creates (taken from a typical, but not widely cited poem called 'An Appearance') arise from a number of sources: there is an extremity of emotion which seems incongruous in relation to the object that apparently causes it (here annihilation by a refrigerator); and there is the disconcerting proximity of the homely and the grotesque in which everyday objects are twisted to the limits of recognisability. Things seem alarmingly out of customary proportion. Often, this goes hand in hand with an obscurity in the literal meaning. What are these blue currents – refrigerator fluid? electricity? cheese? Who is the loved one – a child? the machine itself? Anyway, why should a refrigerator annihilate the speaker? The poem continues:

> From her lips ampersands and percent signs
> Exit like kisses.
> It is Monday in her mind: morals
>
> Launder and present themselves.
> What am I to make of these contradictions?
> I wear white cuffs, I bow.

You have now read the first half of the poem and the mood has not relaxed nor its obscurity become plain (nor will it during the remainder). Indeed, the poem takes confusion as a key topic: 'What', the speaker asks, 'am I to make of these contradictions?' So, here is someone in an everyday place, apparently a kitchen, in state of considerable disturbance. The chain of images takes us through the apparatus of housekeeping and its (traditionally female) routines – the refrigerator (whose motor purrs like a loved one), the bill for the shopping that emerges from the cash register in a blur of figures and symbols which 'exit like kisses', the laundry (conventionally done on Monday), the serving of meals to the family like a waitress: 'I wear white cuffs, I bow.' Later, there are lines on the sewing machine, the television, and child-bearing which is itself reduced to instrumentality ('How her body opens and shuts – / A Swiss watch, jewelled in the hinges!') Here is someone observing her own predicament with an apparently helpless detachment.

There is also the startling juxtaposition of the human and the mechanical. The kitchen in this poem seems to be a proto-cyber world where machines kiss, have veins and become loved ones. Its images draw upon the shiny new world of 'white-goods', domestic technologies marketed in America in the 1950s and at British housewives slightly later. But they also have a relation to more fearful imaginings in the popular culture of the period, especially in science fiction and horror writing: a world of untrustworthy technology which comes (it is feared) to dominate its makers, of mysterious forces or creatures that snatch one's willpower or humanity. A major component of the 'structure of feeling' in Sylvia Plath's work (to use a term coined at the time by the critic Raymond Williams) is powerlessness, of dizzied helplessness and enraptured suspicion. But alongside this, and awkwardly and unclearly related to it, is a sense of outrage, of a vigorous, creative imagination resisting, but captivated by, the forces that threaten to desolate it.

What are the contextual pressures that create such a complex structure of feeling? In Plath's work there are many possible sources: there is her situation as a woman balancing creative, professional and domestic lives in a period notorious for its stereotyped visions of femininity; there is her situation as a parent which creates the aching paradox whereby love cements one to enthralment; and there is her individual situation as a woman whose personal history contained fearful episodes of despair. Much of the contextual commentary on Plath's work has focused on these areas, and there are strong, legitimate reasons for this (though this essay will point in somewhat different directions). Plath's life has always exerted a tragic fascination, ending as it did in suicide following the failure of her marriage to the poet Ted Hughes. Alone, with two young children, an American exile in England, separated from her family, and with a history of deep mental trouble, Plath killed herself on 11 February 1963 in her flat in London. Her reputation as a writer was then breaking (as we now say), but her subsequent fame, and the establishment of her reputation as one of the best of mid-twentieth-century poets writing in English, arrived laden with tragic, renewable legend. The biographical context has recently been given a fascinating, revisionary twist, and a whole set of new materials, by the publication of Ted Hughes's own poetic account of their life together in his best-selling *Birthday Letters* (1998). Hughes's volume, too, was tinged with mortality. Already ill when it was published, he died of cancer some months later. So there is already a legendary and somewhat oppressed quality ascribed to Plath's work which is derived from its biographical context. But biography has its limitations as a key to interpretation. Placing together rival accounts of shared experiences by Plath and Hughes is intriguing and can be significant. *Birthday Letters* contains direct replies to some of Plath's best-known poems like 'The Rabbit Catcher', for instance. It can generate perspectives in which differences of perception and interpretation in close, sexual relationships might be explored, not least from the divergent viewpoints of a man and a woman. But there is also much to be said about the limits of such an approach to context.

For one thing, discussion arising from biography can be merely trivial. For another, what happens in a poem is not simply a record of a life-experience. One of Plath's best-known poems, 'Daddy', has frequently been excavated for its biographical significance, but Plath herself was careful to distinguish between her own life and that of the poem's speaker. Reading it for BBC radio in October 1962, three months before her death, she commented thus:

> Here is a poem spoken by a girl with an Electra complex. Her father died while she thought he was God. Her case is partly complicated by the fact that her father was also a Nazi and her mother very possibly part Jewish. In the daughter the two strains marry and paralyse each other – she has to act out the awful little allegory once over before she is free of it.
>
> (*Collected*, 293)

It is striking that she speaks quite deliberately of a created character ('a girl with an Electra complex'), and not of herself. The speaker is immature – 'a girl' – and not, like Plath herself, a woman turned 30 with two children. The speaker of the poem seems to be a quite consciously created 'type' with apparently easily diagnosed symptoms. An 'Electra complex' is a psychoanalytic term, coined by Jung, to designate little girls' erotic fascination with their fathers which, he believed, they must overcome to establish mature, independent adulthood. To further distance the poem, we might also note that the family history Plath creates for her speaker was, in fact, not her own – her father was not a Nazi, though he was of Polish-German origin, and her mother was raised as a Catholic. Plath's own religious background lay in Protestant Unitarianism for which, her letters suggest, she retained a fondness.

Plath describes this girl's experience as an 'allegory'. An allegory is a literary term for a story which carries an explicit, symbolically coded message. For example, Bunyan's *Pilgrim's Progress* tells of a physical journey which represents the Christian path to salvation. So the question is what might this allegory be in Plath's poem? What might this case-history represent? In 'Daddy', Plath creates a recognisable figure in mid-twentieth-century history. This figure is the second-generation product of the gigantic – often forced – movements of European populations (and accompanying deaths) which uniquely typifies that period. The 'girl' in 'Daddy' is the child of migrant parents whose family history stretches confusingly back into the most disturbing historical episodes of the last century. The family carries within it the obscure psychological burden of association with an atrocious history, that of the Nazi Holocaust. This is a subject that preoccupied Plath. Twentieth-century history, her poems declare, is inescapable and devastating, and its effects are passed down the generations through and within the psychological and imaginative dynamics of families. This opens a crucial contextual perspective. As the created characters who populate the poems testify, in urgent personal voices, she is interested not just in individual tragedies (though she is intensely interested in them too), but in *representative* ones. Her poems are psychological but also historical 'allegories'. The 'girl with an Electra complex' is compelled to display and repeat her symptoms as the migrant families struggle to reconcile themselves with their origins. Though Plath was using the word casually, and her work lacks the exact, carefully coded system of meanings characteristic of classical allegory, one can see in her poems a series of structured levels of significance, in which the more general level enfolds the particular. Thus the personal psychological crisis is unfolded within family dynamics which in turn are shaped by the public and historical life of her period which we, in part, share. It is in the exploration of the interrelationship between these layers of experience that Plath's major achievement lies, and this widens and adjusts the frame of our contextual understanding. She is creating characters whose predicaments are closely and intelligently related to situations perceived as general and representative.

But before we leave the biographical context of Plath's work there is another issue to explore. It has often been remarked that 'Daddy', like much of her best-known work, is full of self-drama. This has alienated readers who find in it an uncontrolled indulgence at odds with what they take to be art's proper analytical distance. Plath's poetry, some feel, lacks propriety and self-control, and she has been accused of being a writer whose work is 'merely' personal in a self-indulgent, emotionally bombastic way. Sometimes this charge has very serious dimensions: the apparent appropriation of Jewish experience in Holocaust poems like 'Daddy' or 'Lady Lazarus' disturbs those who see a false rhetorical opportunism which makes use of appalling tragedy for reasons of perverse self-dramatisation. In 'Daddy' Plath writes:

> I thought every German was you.
> And the language obscene
>
> An engine, an engine
> Chuffing me off like a Jew.
> A Jew to Dachau, Aushwitz, Belsen.
> I began to talk like a Jew
> I think I may well be a Jew.
>
> (*Collected*, 223)

The point about extravagant, inauthentic self-dramatisation seems clear, but we should not rush to conclusions. Once again, statements like this should be understood as utterances in character (the character of 'a girl with an Electra complex'). The point is that they are so outrageously hyperbolic. The psychology here is one in which the speaker is immaturely reaching for extreme self-images to validate her feelings: she is dramatising her predicament in the borrowed clothes of genuine atrocity. In so doing, she abandons a degree of responsibility for her situation by making herself the passive victim of an irreversible, guiltless fate. We can see a similar element in the poem with which we began this essay.

The speaker in 'An Appearance' is also 'annihilated' by (somewhat less extreme) circumstances to the point where her behaviour can be understood, even by herself, to be a kind of acting. The title of the poem plays on the different meanings of the word 'appearance'. There is, first, the difference between appearance and reality: a materially affluent lifestyle with all the latest domestic gadgets is contrasted with the inner torment of their owner. But appearance is also a theatrical term used in phrases like 'Arnold Schwarzenegger is making an appearance at the local theatre'. The poem makes much of the idea that the self is a performance: the loved one exits with kisses as a celebrated actor leaves the stage, morals 'present themselves' as actors do, the speaker bows. In the contrast between deceptive appearance and distressed inner reality, and in the cognate idea of social behaviour as performance, there is a deep inauthenticity in the lives of these speakers. And in this situation, sometimes life can be acted out in the borrowed costumes of atrocious history as a desperate reaching towards a borrowed significance. As the cynical speaker of 'Lady Lazarus' puts it following her failed suicide attempt: 'It's the theatrical / comeback in broad day' (*Collected*, 245–6).

The idea of the essential hollowness and inauthenticity of modern life was much in the cultural air in the 1950s and 60s. One of Plath's early champions, her friend the critic A. Alvarez, included her work in his enormously influential anthology *The New Poetry* (1962, revised to include Plath in 1966). Alvarez's introduction to the volume was called 'Beyond the Gentility Principle' and in it he argued that British postwar life had become stagnant and complacent, unable to acknowledge, as he put it, 'the dominant public savagery' of the era: 'two world wars, the concentration camps, genocide, and the threat of nuclear war' (Alvarez, *New Poetry*, 26). Alvarez made an analogy between the individual personality that represses traumatic experience, or disturbing desires, and the state of a culture that 'pretends that life . . . is the same as ever, that gentility, decency and all the other social totems will eventually muddle through' (Alvarez, *New Poetry*, 27–8). It is easy to see the relevance of this connection between individual psychological situations and the wider cultural and social conditions to Plath's work.

Probably uniquely among the writers featured in this volume, Sylvia Plath wrote her own essay on 'Context'. It was commissioned, though not actually published, by the *London Magazine* in 1962. In that year a number of separate negotiations to abandon the nuclear arms race between 'West' and 'East' were abandoned, and the year culminated, in October, in the Cuban Missile Crisis bringing the world to the brink of nuclear war. Plath begins her essay on 'Context' in this way: 'The issues of our time which preoccupy me at the moment are the incalculable genetic effects of fallout and a documentary article on the terrifying, mad, omnipotent marriage of big business and the military in America – "Juggernaut, The Warfare State" by Fred J. Cook in a recent *Nation* [an American magazine]' (Plath, 'Context', 92). In Plath's own view, it is the Cold War and the growth of the 'military-industrial complex', as it had just been named (in 1961) by the retiring American President Dwight D. Eisenhower, that provides the key contextual element for her late work.

Fred Cook's essays on 'The Warfare State' affected Plath deeply. A letter to her mother in December 1961 apologises for not writing 'but I got so awfully depressed two weeks ago by reading two issues of *The Nation* – "Juggernaut, the Warfare State" . . . and then another article about the repulsive shelter craze for fallout, all very factual, documented, and true, that I couldn't sleep for nights with all the warlike talk in the papers' (Plath, *Letters Home*, 437–8). The direct connection of depression to political events is revealing. But the issues which this letter and the essay on 'Context' raise do not stop at personal despair. Her letter continues with an analysis of the grip of military power structures on everyday life, and, in a larger frame, the complicity of these structures with the legacy of Nazi Germany, some of whose scientists and military personnel were recruited to the Cold War effort: 'I am horrified at the US selling missiles (without warheads) to Germany, awarding former German officers medals. As the reporter for the liberal Frankfurt paper says, coming back to America from his native Germany, it is as if he hadn't been away' (*Letters Home*, 438). The creation of NATO in 1949, and its subsequent expansion (West Germany joined in 1954), took Germany back into the fold of military nations defending 'civilised' values from Communist peril. Plath is very clear about the connection she made between the military-industrial complex of the Cold War and the pathologically militarised society of wartime Germany. (This, of course, furnishes an important additional context for her so-called 'Nazi' poems.) Her analysis ends wishing that 'England had the sense to be neutral, for it is quite obvious she would be "obliterated" in any nuclear war, and for this reason I am very much behind the nuclear disarmers here' (*Letters Home*, 438). This dread of obliteration, featured in poems like 'An Appearance', surfaces regularly in her writing. In other letters, she records her attendance with Ted Hughes at Campaign for Nuclear Disarmament (CND) rallies in London. The theme of imminent nuclear catastrophe, and more importantly the state of high anxiety it generated, was well established between the two poets. Hughes's collection *Lupercal* a year earlier, which is dedicated to Plath, featured a poem called 'A Woman Unconscious' which begins:

> Russia and America circle each other;
> Threats nudge an act that were without doubt
> A melting of the mould in the mother,
> Stones melting about the root.
>
> (Hughes, *Lupercal*, 15)

In his first collection, *Hawk in the Rain* (1957), also dedicated to Plath, Hughes meditated, in 'The Ancient Heroes and the Bomber Pilot', on the difference between these heroes and the new 'V-Bomber' pilots who, 'at a turn of [a] wrist', can obliterate cities, shake the earth in its frame, and stop the centuries. 'My heart', Hughes concludes, 'is cold and small' – like the earth after nuclear war (Hughes, *Hawk in the Rain*, 57).

Plath's essay on 'Context' balances these fears against her personal, domestic and artistic concerns:

> Does this influence the kind of poetry I write? Yes, but in a sidelong fashion. I am not gifted with the tongue of Jeremiah, though I may be

sleepless enough before my vision of the apocalypse. My poems do not turn out to be about Hiroshima, but about a child forming itself finger by finger in the dark. They are not about the terrors of mass extinction, but about the bleakness of the moon over a yew tree in a neighbouring graveyard. . . . In a sense these poems are deflections. I do not think they are an escape. For me the real issues of our time are the issues of every time – the hurt and wonder of loving; making in all its forms – children, loaves of bread, paintings, buildings; and the conservation of life of all people in all places, the jeopardising of which no abstract doubletalk of 'peace' or 'implacable foes' can excuse.

(Plath, 'Context', 92)

Here again we have that stunned paradox discoverable everywhere in Plath's work: the contrast between an appalled, fascinated sense of threatening obliteration, and an emphasis on creativity. These two sides of her work are in a relation of 'macro' to 'micro' but, as she says, this does not mean that the latter is of negligible value.

Plath puts clearly and intelligently a major general issue connected with the analysis of the contexts of literary works. All literary works are written in contexts which shape them to a degree, but these do not entirely determine the nature of a poem nor exhaust its achievement, just as enveloping circumstances do not often entirely exhaust the individual. The distinctiveness of a literary work, in a sense, is that which *resists* the contextual pressures of which it is aware. A poem reduced to 'religious or political propaganda' (in Plath's words from 'Context') becomes an empty poem, unresponsive to the distinctive humanity of its creation. In 'Context', Plath makes clear that part of the triumph of poetry (its 'great use' as she puts it) lies in the pleasure and freedom it stimulates as a response to distressing and oppressive environments. Poems 'deflect', but do not 'escape', the circumstances which surround, condition and shape them. This was a position increasingly adopted during the 1950s. Its clearest and most influential exposition is that of the French Existentialist philosopher and novelist Jean-Paul Sartre in *What is Literature?* (1948: translated into English 1950), a book that directly influenced numbers of younger British writers. The Existentialists argued that works of literature, in their commitment to exploring predicaments and resisting conventional explanations, profoundly enacted the distinctively human values of creativity and freedom.

It may seem strange to discuss a poet like Plath, whose work is so notoriously given over to rage and despair, in terms of freedom and creativity. But this is the paradox entailed in art of all kinds that takes human suffering as its theme: it can simultaneously portray, and free itself from, devastation. There is a famous poem called 'Futility' by the First World War poet Wilfred Owen which encapsulates the seeming paradox. Written following the death of a comrade in the trenches, it closes with an unanswered question: 'O what made fatuous sunbeams toil / To break earth's sleep at all?' (Owen, *Poems*, 135). Part of the answer arises from the fact that the poem itself represents a *creative* response to carnage, although the feelings it describes are those of meaninglessness and futility. Sylvia Plath's poetry – and the implication that her work is a form of war poetry is not too far from the mark – creates similar responses.

Critics – and readers for examinations of various kinds – like to look for tidy meanings, what Sartre called, dismissively, the 'message' of the work found by critics 'for their own convenience' (Sartre, *What is Literature?*, 154). He emphasises that the distinctiveness of literature is its ability to explore the multiple, and overlapping, directions in which human situations and responses can point. There is therefore a danger, in the study of literary context, that too close a correlation between text and context will result in the oversimple conversion of the former into the latter because there are few exact, direct correlations between a literary work and its historical and social circumstances. We deal throughout with a world of interpretation: poems interpret events, readers interpret poems. Contextual knowledge enriches rather than explains both processes. As a person, Plath could be hyper-conscious of the slow infiltration of socio-political conditions into ordinary life, and the anxieties of living in the nuclear age. In October 1961 she worries about the levels of Strontium 90 – the radioactive isotope of the metal strontium and an important element in nuclear fallout – rumoured to be found in milk (*Letters Home*, 434). From time to time, such details find their way obliquely into the poems. In 'Nick and the Candlestick', for instance, written a year later during the Cuban Missile Crisis, she writes of her love for her baby son, Nicholas:

Let the stars
Plummet to their dark address,

Let the mercuric
Atoms that cripple drip
Into the terrible well,

You are the one
Solid spaces lean on . . .
         (*Collected*, 241–2)

The important point is not so much that Plath's poetry is consistently alert to, and makes use of, the nuclear particulars. It is that the 'structure of feeling' she inhabits is part of an overarching context: in this case a climate of military and political tension which hollows out meaning and betrays certainties in a world on the edge of a new kind of holocaust. Plath captures this finely in 'solid spaces', the poem's closing oxymoron: in nuclear blast space becomes solid, solids become space. In the psychological climate of nuclear anxiety, reliable solids too become empty. In poems like 'An Appearance' (written six months earlier in April 1962) she creates an atmosphere of frenzied tension which is easy to connect to the feeling of the moment. The connection is facilitated because Plath's perception was not singular. Fellow writers, like the novelist Doris Lessing, made the same graphic connection between personal, domestic tension and an awareness of imminent catastrophe. After all, this was a culture which could name the latest sexy swimsuit after the atom-bomb tests at Bikini Atoll. In *The Golden Notebook* (1961), Lessing's major novel on this theme, she describes the 'H-Bomb Style' in ladies' hairdressing: 'the "H" is for peroxide of hydrogen, used for colouring. The hair is dressed to rise as from a bomb-burst, at the nape of the neck' (Lessing, *Golden Notebook*, 241). Lessing did not invent this: she is quoting from a description in the *Daily Telegraph*.

I have been arguing that literary works of distinction, like the poems of Sylvia Plath, take the pressures of their contextual moment, absorb its influences, and resist and respond to them. Literary works are not passive creations just as their authors are not passive creatures. Plath's poetry is shaped by the pressures of its time in its depiction of a particular crisis in postwar life and its record of a 'structure of feeling' that results from it. But her work also provides an incisive analytical commentary on these conditions which is best observed in the way individual poems unfold. This essay, therefore, will close with an analysis of one such poem, 'The Munich Mannequins'. (It might be worthwhile re-reading the poem now so its details are fresh.)

'The Munich Mannequins' was completed on 28 January 1963. We know this because Plath kept punctilious records of the dates on which her work was written. At this stage of her life she composed in fast bursts of controlled inspiration – sometimes writing two or three poems a day – which responded to events around her. She was attentive to newspapers, magazines and other media, and her work sometimes reacts directly to particular events. 'Thalidomide' (8 November 1962), for instance, continues her concern with biological mutation also addressed in the 'nuclear' poems, but was written in response to revelations of the catastrophic effects of the drug thalidomide given to women during pregnancy which caused gross foetal deformities. Other poems are similarly responsive. 'The Courage of Shutting Up' (2 October 1962) reacts in part to the political crisis in Burma at this time (see Rylance, 'Fellow Travelling'). 'Brasilia' (1 December 1962) has, for its context, the controversial construction, widely derided in the West, of the city of Brasilia in the Amazon jungle to serve as an alternative administrative capital for Brazil relatively free of colonial corruptions and associations. In these cases, Plath shows herself attentive to another major issue in the postwar world: that of de-colonisation and the struggles for economic and cultural independence in postcolonial nations.

Plath herself never visited Munich so, with respect to 'The Munich Mannequins', we might begin by asking why the location was important to her. Most critics set it aside and read the poem as a general attack on the reduction of women to inhuman dolls or dummies. This is understandable, for there is ample evidence that this was an abiding concern in her work. One of her best-known poems, 'The Applicant', for example, features a parody marriage bureau in which the woman is introduced as a 'living doll' (Collected, 221–2). The poem was written in the same year – 1962 – that the Barbie doll was introduced to British children. But if this continues to be a concern in 'The Munich Mannequins' it is so, it seems to me, additionally rather than centrally. One might ask, if the mannequins are the focus, why is the poem set in Germany?

One cynical answer might be that it allows Plath to capitalise gratuitously on lurid associations with Nazism. But in January 1963 there were other, more intelligent reasons for writing a poem about Germany. The Berlin wall had been erected 18 months earlier and Germany was, in many Western minds, a plausible site for the third world war. On 16 January, 12 days before the poem was written, the Russian Premier Nikita Khrushchev, in a widely reported speech delivered in Berlin, announced Russia's new 100 megaton bomb and issued a warning that a nuclear war would kill 800 million people. On 22 January, France and West Germany signed a military co-operation treaty, and just before Christmas NATO had announced the establishment of a consolidated, multilateral nuclear strike force that would include, for the first time, the use of American Polaris missiles in British submarines. So the military constellations were, once again, gathering around Germany, and their imaginative consequences can perhaps be detected in the poem's depiction of a dead cityscape and of Munich as a 'morgue between Paris and Rome'. 'The Munich Mannequins' unites the ghastly heritage of the second war with the even more ghastly prospect of the third.

But there are other contextual factors in play in this poem, for Munich was at the centre not just of one of the imaginary battlefields of the Cold War, but also of Germany's widely admired, and widely resented postwar recovery, the 'economic miracle' led by Chancellor Konrad Adenhauer. 'The Munich Mannequins', it will be noted, is in its most literal aspect a poem about window shopping, and window shopping, what is more, for luxury goods:

> These mannequins lean tonight
> In Munich, morgue between Paris and Rome,
>
> Naked and bald in their furs,
> Orange lollies on silver sticks.
>
> *(Collected*, 263)

The swish shop windows of Munich are connected to the couturier capitals of Paris and Rome on an axis that coincides with a battlefront and frontier definitions of the affluent consumer culture of 'the West'. The poem works by the typical Plath technique of superimposition. Scenes of consumer affluence (shopping for furs in the 'economic miracle') mingle with the buried – and conveniently forgotten – memory of historical atrocity (the Nazi past imaged in unanswered telephones), and the prospect of nuclear annihilation. These are laid one on top of another, just as the swirl of domestic apparatus and situations are laid one on another in 'An Appearance'. But – and this is an indication not only of Plath's ingenuity, but also of her ability to encapsulate the ramifying forces of complex situations – the contextual facets of this poem are not yet exhausted.

In December 1962 Britain applied to join what was then called the European Economic Community (now the EU) after rather snootily standing aloof from the Treaty of Rome signed by Germany, France and four others in 1957 (the Paris, Rome, Munich ellipse emerges once more). The reasons for this abstention are familiar, and still disfigure British political debate: 'little-England' nationalism, late-imperial faith in the Commonwealth and Britain's 'world role', and the 'special relationship' with the United States were among them. The latter was a factor which particularly irked France's President Charles de Gaulle, and for this and other reasons he vetoed Britain's application to join the Common Market on 14 January 1963, two weeks before 'The Munich Mannequins' was written. The poem offers a vision of Europe as Britain was poised on the cusp of European integration.

Of course, 'The Munich Mannequins' is not, in any particular sense, a 'Common Market poem'. It is not engaged, in detail, with that issue any more than it is engaged in detail with Germany's 'economic miracle' or the other contextual factors in play in its composition. Sometimes, writers attend to specific public issues, or treat a controversial topical subject, but

Plath's work is not really of this kind. She is not especially interested in the details of a particular argument or event, but in the imaginative apprehension of a structure of response and feeling which includes a great diversity of elements. 'The Munich Mannequins', and related poems with European themes like 'Getting There' or other 'Nazi' poems like 'Daddy' and 'Lady Lazarus', offer an imaginative apprehension of the fragmented European situation in its historical, cultural, economic, political and ethical mutations. This vision is offered at a particular, defined moment as it appeared to an American born of a migrant family whose European antecedents loomed exceptionally large in her imagination. 'The Swarm' (3 October 1962) is an example. It juxtaposes a ordinary occurrence (a stray swarm of bees at loose in 'our town') against an imagistic panorama of post-Napoleonic European history from Paris to Moscow ('O Europe', the poem sarcastically ends, 'O ton of honey!' [*Collected*, 217]). These poems represent intelligent efforts to come to terms with an historical situation understood as both a traumatic legacy and a perilous present. They translate these perceptions into a singularly revealing and resonating discernment of a general situation, and an imagistic anatomy of recent and prospective history, which is locked into, and revealed through, the vivid realisation of intense personal predicaments.

All distress has a context; most instances have many; Plath had legion. One may choose to understand her work as a response to the particular circumstances that affected women in the 1950s; or – in its intense depiction of acute states from the point of view of those suffering from them – as a contribution to the evolving debate on the politics of mental health; or – as in this essay – as a major imaginative apprehension of the circumstances of the Cold War. But the important point is that these are not exclusive choices. They were not so for Plath, and should not be so for her readers. Context is multifaceted, and these facets interlock. The 'structure of feeling' of her work includes all of them, but most importantly it also includes the too often overlooked fact that, in the face of devastation, human beings also create, with life, skill and intelligence.

Further Reading

The 1990s produced several historical studies which make one feel that Plath's blood-soaked understanding of Europe's last century was neither exaggerated nor irrational. The reader might look on the last two chapters of Norman Davies's *Europe: A History* (London, Pimlico, 1997), and Mark Mazower's *Dark Continent: Europe's Twentieth Century* (London, Penguin,

1998), and despair. Because Plath dated her poems so carefully, her work can be illuminated by consulting year-by-year reference works such as *Chronicle of the Twentieth Century* (London, Longman/Chronicle, 1988), which is regularly updated in supplementary volumes.

Raymond Williams's telling concept of the 'structure of feeling' was introduced in *The Long Revolution* (1961: Harmondsworth, Penguin, 1965), see esp. 64ff. It is elaborated in his *Marxism and Literature* (Oxford, Oxford University Press, 1977), 128–35, and discussed in his *Politics and Letters: Interviews with New Left Review* (London, Verso, 1979), 156ff.

There is a good deal of contextually related criticism on Plath. Claire Brennan (ed.), *The Poetry of Sylvia Plath* (Cambridge, Icon Books, 1999) is a useful guide. Chapter 10 of Alan Sinfield's *Literature, Politics and Culture in Postwar Britain* (Oxford, Blackwell, 1989) makes a good case for her representative centrality. For a particular angle see chapter 8 of Elaine Showalter's *The Female Malady: Women, Madness and English Culture, 1830–1980* (London, Virago, 1987). The study of the Cold War and its influence on British culture in the 1950s and 60s is an evolving field. Sinfield (*Literature, Politics and Culture*) and Robert Hewison, *In Anger: Culture in the Cold War* (London, Weidenfeld & Nicolson, 1981) are helpful.

Overall, the most stimulating and ambitious book on Plath remains Jacqueline Rose's *The Haunting of Sylvia Plath* (London, Virago, 1991).

References

A. Alvarez, 'Introduction: The New Poetry, or Beyond the Gentility Principle', in Alvarez (ed.) *The New Poetry*, revd edn (Harmondsworth, Penguin, 1966).

Ted Hughes, *The Hawk in the Rain* (London, Faber, 1957).

——, *Lupercal* (London, Faber, 1960).

——, *Birthday Letters* (London, Faber, 1988).

Doris Lessing, *The Golden Notebook* (1961: London, Panther, 1972).

Wilfred Owen, *The Poems of Wilfred Owen*, ed. Jon Stallworthy (London, Chatto & Windus, 1985).

Sylvia Plath, *Letters Home: Correspondence 1950–1963*, ed. Aurelia Schober Plath (London, Faber, 1976).

——, 'Context', in *Johnny Panic and the Bible of Dreams and other Prose Writings* (London, Faber, 1977), 92–3.

——, *Collected Poems* (London, Faber, 1981).

Rick Rylance, 'Fellow Travelling With Feminist Criticism', in Kate Campbell (ed.), *Critical Feminism* (Buckingham, Open University Press, 1992), 157–81.

Jean-Paul Sartre, *What is Literature?* trans. Bernard Frechtman (London, Methuen, 1967).

13 Harold Pinter

Vincent Gillespie

Harold Pinter, photograph by Barry Ryan.

No one forgets a good teacher. Certainly not Harold Pinter: 'Joe Brearley fired my imagination. I can never forget him.' In 1945, at the age of 15, Pinter was cast by Brearley in the title role of a school production of *Macbeth*. To mark the occasion, his parents gave him a copy of the *Collected Plays of Shakespeare*. Pinter added to this a copy of *Ulysses*, which he placed on the bookshelf in the living room: 'My father told me to take it off the shelf. He said he wouldn't have a book like that in the room where my mother served dinner' ('Speech of Thanks', 59–60).

This anecdote economically sketches out the parameters of the young Pinter's social, cultural and literary contexts. At one extreme, we find the still-radical Joyce, soon augmented by Hemingway, Lawrence, Dostoevski, and Kafka and later enriched by Beckett, Arthur Miller (who all left their mark on the prose and theatre works), and the poetry of Rimbaud, Dylan Thomas, Yeats and Eliot (all of whose influences are apparent in Pinter's early poetry). At the other end of the historical spectrum, we find the work of England's greatest dramatic technician and poet ('Shakespeare dominated our lives'), reinforced under Brearley's guidance by the intoxicating verse of his Jacobean contemporary John Webster ('That language made me dizzy' ['Speech of Thanks', 59–60]).

Shakespeare and Webster: Joyce and Hemingway. Pinter's distinctive voice, remarkably consistent from his earliest prose pieces in the late 1940s, is a striking blend of the poetic and the bathetic, a dazzling mix of genres and styles. In its often subliminal literary allusiveness, his work is an echo-chamber of his wide reading, his enthusiastic theatre-going and his assimilation of the styles and techniques of American and European film:

> I'm well aware that my work is packed with literary references. Of course I am. I know what they are too. [Laughs.] I'm writing away and in the act of that writing, these references occur. It happens very quickly; a kind of intuition is involved.
>
> (Gussow, *Conversations*, 124)

But above all else, Pinter's work is powerfully attentive to the mechanics and magic of theatrical technique. 'The first time I went to a theatre', reports Pinter, 'as far as I remember, was to see Donald Wolfit in Shakespeare. I saw his Lear six times and later acted with him in it, as one of the king's knights' ('Writing for Myself', 9). After an unhappy experience in drama school, Pinter learned the theatre the hard way, slogging round provincial Ireland in the repertory company of one of the last of the great actor-managers, Anew McMaster. Pinter's time in Ireland was an education in many ways, but in his portrait of Mac's Othello he gives an insight into an important dimension of theatrical practice: the ability to capture and hold an audience:

> [H]e stood, well over six foot, naked to the waist, his gestures complete, final, nothing jagged, his movement of the utmost fluidity and yet of the utmost precision: stood there, dead in the centre of the role, and the great sweeping symphonic playing would begin, the rare tension and release within him, the arrest, the swoop, the savagery, the majesty, the repose.
>
> ('Mac', 29)

Pinter notes the repose at the heart of Mac's movement and display, a feature he also observed in his Lear:

> At the centre of the performance was a terrible loss, desolation, silence. He didn't think about doing it, he just got there. He did it and got there.
>
> ('Mac', 32)

Later on, Pinter spent a season in Donald Wolfit's company in England. Here too he learned by observation the theatrical alchemy of gesture and silence:

> Wolfit was standing high up on a rostrum with all the light on him ... he stood with his back to the audience with a cloak around him and there came the moment when the man downstage finished his speech and we all knew, the play demanded it, that Wolfit or Oedipus was going to turn or speak. He held the moment until one's stomach was truly trembling and the cloak came round; a tremendous swish that no one else has ever been able to achieve, I think. And the savagery and power that emerged from such a moment was extraordinary.
>
> (quoted Billington, *Life and Work of Pinter*, 47)

Again, attentiveness to the stillness and silence at the heart of Wolfit's performance characterises this comment. This can be compared to the stillness and silence of Aston at the end of *The Caretaker*, deaf to the increasingly desperate and incoherent pleas of Davies, solid in his position of visual power at the upstage window (the stage direction reads: *Aston remains still, his back to him, at the window*). Or to Mick's silent possession of the stage at the beginning of that play:

Mick is alone in the room, sitting on the bed. He wears a leather jacket.
  Silence
He slowly looks about the room looking at each object in turn. He looks up at the ceiling, and stares at the bucket. Ceasing, he sits quite still, expressionless, looking out front.
  Silence for thirty seconds.

Here Pinter's theatrical common-sense is allied to a profound understanding of the menace of silence. As the curtain goes up, the audience is greeted with a cluttered stage full of strange and incongruous objects, including a Buddha, a gas stove, several electrical appliances (later significant reflections of Aston's obsession with electro-convulsive therapy), everything, in fact, including the proverbial kitchen sink. Mick's perusal of the room allows the audience to take in the contents without missing crucial dialogue. More importantly the scene establishes Mick in 'possession' of the room: Aston and Davies who enter next are *de facto* interlopers into someone else's space. This is Mick's context not theirs, and the following action takes place on his territory. Finally, Mick's expressionless gaze at the audience allows them to experience at first hand a frisson of Mick's menace, here reinforced by the unpredictable silence held for a theatrically daring thirty seconds (try it and see). When that menace is later turned against Davies, therefore, there is a ready-made swell of sympathy for the character that can be tapped directly and economically.

Similarly in *The Homecoming* (1965), theatrical tableaux of great force mark the end of both acts. Act 1 closes with Max forcing his returning (prodigal) son Teddy to hug him, asserting parental power over the escaped child, and briefly recreating a normal family hierarchy in this hugely dysfunctional social context. And at the end of Act 2, Ruth sits enthroned centre stage *'relaxed in her chair'* with all the men of the family defining their relationship to her by various postures of pleading, sexual desire and childlike trust. 'So often, below the word spoken is the thing known and unspoken'('Writing for the Theatre', 13). The visual language of theatre can be eloquent in this regard.

Pinter's play with silence and position on stage is already taking shape in his early prose. In particular his *Kullus* (1949) and *The Examination* (1955) map out the physical and linguistic context of many later theatrical encounters. The latter describes a Kafkaesque interrogation where no word is spoken, interspersed by breaks which are equally silent. Pinter annotates the different qualities of silence in these episodes, noting how the interrogator has established in the room 'selected properties' (note the theatrical term) of a blackboard, a window and a stool. He also observes, again in a very theatrical way, that, once closed, the door of the room loses significance. The writing here dramatically choreographs a silent tussle for power and superiority:

> When the door opened. When Kullus, unattended, entered, and the interim ended. I turned from all light in the window, to pay him due regard and welcome. Whereupon without reserve or hesitation, he moved from the door as from a shelter, and stood in the light from the window. So I watched the entrance become vacant, which had been his shelter. And observed the man I had welcomed, he having crossed my border. Equally I observed the selected properties, each in its place . . . Whereupon I offered Kullus the stool, the which I placed for him. He showed, at this early juncture, no disregard for my directions; if he did not so much obey, he extended his voluntary co-operation.
>
> ('The Examination', 104)

Kullus enters like a Shakespearean character ('unattended'), abandoning the 'shelter' of the doorway and crossing the 'border' into the interrogator's space, where the 'properties' are ready prepared and the character seems willing to take the interrogator's 'directions'. Meanwhile, the interrogator turns from the visually 'strong' position of the lighted window, and commands the room with his back to the source of light (a theatrical trick replicated in several later Pinter plays). This is drama without words: the raw material for Pinter's comedies of menace is already gathered here, and Kullus, in his powerful and commanding silences, provides the prototype for the quietly dangerous stillness and watchfulness of many later characters in the plays: 'For he journeyed from silence to silence, and I had no course but to follow' ('The Examination', 103). This is the immediate context of many of Pinter's plays:

> I have usually begun a play in quite a simple manner; found a couple of characters in a particular context, thrown them together and listened to what they said, keeping my nose to the ground. The context has always been, for me, concrete and particular, and the characters concrete also. I've never started a play from any kind of abstract idea or theory.
>
> ('Writing for the Theatre', 10)

The germ of my plays? I'll be as accurate as I can about that. I went into a room and saw one person standing up and one person sitting down, and a few weeks later I wrote *The Room*. I went into another room and saw two people sitting down, and a few weeks later I wrote *The*

Birthday Party. I looked through a door into a third room, and saw two people standing up and I wrote *The Caretaker.*

('Writing for Myself', 10)

Pinter is an intensely visual and practical dramatist, as these teasing comments reveal. The physical disposition of the characters on stage, and the mechanics of getting them there and getting them off again are all fundamental to what he has called the 'necessary shape' of his plays, a shape to be discovered not just in the writing but also in their production: 'A rehearsal period which consists of philosophical discourse or political treatise does not get the curtain up at eight o'clock.' For Pinter, that rehearsal period allows exploration of the play's inner spaces ('Sometimes I learn quite a lot from rehearsals') and the discovery of the key images that make the play cohere:

[T]he image must be pursued with the greatest vigilance, calmly, and once found, must be sharpened, graded, accurately focussed and maintained ... [T]he key word is economy, economy of movement and gesture, of emotion and its expression, both the internal and the external in specific and exact relation to each other, so that there is no wastage and no mess.

('Shakespeare Prize', 41)

This pragmatic search for the right image is a function of Pinter's own theatrical training, his experience on stage of the traditional 'well-made' play, and the disciplined tension involved both in listening to his characters and in shaping their utterance:

I don't regard my own characters as uncontrolled, or anarchic. They're not. The function of selection and arrangement is mine. I do all the donkey work, in fact, and I think I can say I pay meticulous attention to the shape of things, from the shape of a sentence to the overall structure of the play. This shaping, to put it mildly, is of the first importance. But I think a double thing happens. You arrange *and* you listen ... And sometimes a balance is found, where image can freely engender image and where at the same time you are able to keep your sights on the place where the characters are silent and in hiding. It is in the silence that they are most evident to me.

('Writing for the Theatre', 14)

The silent inner spaces of a Pinter character are where its dramatic integrity can be found. On one level they reveal themselves in the much-parodied stage directions *Pause* and *Silence* (the difference between them being that in the former one must feel that the thought processes of the character are still in full spate, even if no words are spoken, whereas the latter suggests the chilly bleakness of the completed thought). On other levels they reveal themselves through the resistance to explicit propagandising and heavy-handedly politicised plots. Pinter reacted against the programmatic neatness of some contemporary theatrical resolutions, and the heart-on-the-sleeve political engagement of some of his fellow dramatists in the 1950s and early 1960s:

> To supply an explicit moral tag to an evolving and compulsive dramatic image seems to be facile, impertinent and dishonest. Where this takes place it is not theatre but a crossword puzzle. The audience holds the paper. The play fills in the blanks. Everyone's happy.
>
> ('Writing for the Theatre', 12)

Pinter's dramatic world, though no less political than those of his contemporaries, as recent writings and interviews have shown, prefers a more oblique approach:

> A character on the stage who can present no convincing argument or information as to his past experience, his present behaviour or his aspirations, nor give a comprehensive analysis of his motives is as legitimate and as worthy of attention as one who, alarmingly, can do all these things. The more acute the experience the less articulate its expression.
>
> ('Writing for the Theatre', 11)

Complete self-knowledge and coherent self-expression are more 'alarming' than acute inarticulacy in the theatrical world of Harold Pinter. Indeed his own attitude to his characters is close to that attributed by Pinter to Shakespeare in *The Dwarfs* (1952–6, revised 1989):

> He never uses a communication cord or a lifebelt, and what's more, he never suggests he's got one handy for your use or his . . .
> – The point about Shakespeare, Pete said, thumping the table, is that he didn't measure the man up against the idea and give you hot tips on the outcome.
>
> (*The Dwarfs*, 133)

These comments themselves replay remarks made in his earlier 'A Note on Shakespeare' (1950):

He amputates, deadens, aggravates at will, within the limits of a particular piece, but he will not pronounce judgement or cure. Such comment as there is is so variously split up between characters and so contradictory in itself that no central point of opinion or inclining can be determined.

('Note on Shakespeare', 5–6)

What matters to Pinter is the consistency and integrity of his characters, the still silences at the centre of his turning worlds.

Not that the characters in the plays are necessarily outwardly silent. As Pinter commented in 1962:

There are two silences. One when no word is spoken. The other when perhaps a torrent of language is being employed. This speech is speaking of a language locked beneath it. That is its continual reference. The speech we hear is an indication of that which we don't hear . . . One way of looking at speech is to say that it is a stratagem to cover nakedness.

('Writing for the Theatre', 14–15)

Many of Pinter's characters have a tactical talkativeness that masks a deeper strategic silence: 'So often, below the word spoken, is the thing known and unspoken' ('Writing for the Theatre', 13). In *The Caretaker*, Aston's obsessive searching out and attempted mending of electrical equipment, and his longing for the deferred utopia of his garden shed, are revealed in his long quasi-soliloquy at the end of Act 2 to be a function of his psychiatric problems and their brutalising treatment. Davies reveals in his serenades to Sidcup a Beckettian longing for identity and context invested in his 'papers', as precious to him as the Holy Grail and probably every bit as mythical:

DAVIES: A man I know has got them. I left them with him. You see? They prove who I am! I can't move without them papers. They tell you who I am. You see! I'm stuck without them.

Davies needs constantly to construct temporary contexts for himself, but of all the characters he is the least comfortable with speech and the least skilful in its deployment. His dismissal from the café that has led to his encounter with Aston, for example, has been brought about by his refusal to take out a bucket of rubbish. He objects because this violates a silent hierarchy he has invoked ('They got a boy there for taking out the bucket. I wasn't engaged to take out buckets': note the social aspiration implicit in 'engaged'). Mick, an astute and taciturn observer of Davies's power plays against his brother, later turns that need against him when in Act 3 he redefines the role Davies has created for himself in the household from caretaker (complete with brass bells by the front door) to 'first class painter and decorator' and 'interior designer', wrong footing the increasingly self-confident and querulous Davies ('You get a bit out of your depth sometimes, don't you?'). Indeed the tussles between Mick and Davies range from the silent (the subliminal message of the Electrolux in Act 2 is that Davies is a piece of filth that needs cleaning up) through the slapstick (the frantic game of pass the parcel with Davies's bag) to the torrentially verbal.

The opening of Act 2, for example, is a virtuoso performance of comic cross-examination with Mick's dazzling shifts of linguistic register from the polite to the menacing ('I'm awfully glad. It's awfully nice to meet you. *Pause.* What did you say your name was?'). Even more striking is Mick's exploitation of Davies's vulnerability as an 'outsider' both geographically and socially. At the end of Act 1, Aston has broached Davies's origins with him to little effect:

ASTON: You Welsh?
Pause
DAVIES: Well, I been around, you know ... what I mean ... I been about ...
ASTON: Where were you born then?
DAVIES: (*darkly*) What do you mean?
ASTON: Where were you born?
DAVIES: I was ... uh ... oh, it's a bit hard, like, to set your mind back ... see what I mean ... going back ... a good way ... lose a bit of track, like ... you know ...

In Act 2, Mick dazzles Davies with pyrotechnic displays of his local knowledge. Whereas Davies talks about places outside of Greater London (Sidcup, Watford), Mick's knowledge of East London bus routes and pubs, and his implied network of cousins, uncles and friends bludgeon the solitary Davies into cowed silence.

It turned out he was born in the Caledonian Road, just before you get to the Nag's Head. His old mum was still living at the Angel. All the buses passed right by the door. She could get a 38, 581, 30 or 38A, take her down the Essex Road to Dalston Junction in next to no time.

To be honest, I've never made out how he came to be my uncle's brother. I've often thought that maybe it was the other way round. I mean that my uncle was his brother and he was my uncle. But I never called him uncle. As a matter of fact I called him Sid. My mother called him Sid too. It was a funny business. Your spitting image he was. Married a Chinaman and went to Jamaica.

Mick also browbeats Davies with technical and legal jargon, threatening to draw him deep into a world of official contracts, solicitors, personal medical advisors, insurance firms and other institutions with which he knows the paperless Davies is incapable of dealing. This is language as blunt instrument, words as weapons of power and intimidation (see Knowles, 'The Caretaker').

Language, and in particular the language of the establishment in its various manifestations, is for Pinter a political issue. The skilful exploration into social cliché and political doublespeak, his expositions of euphemism and circumlocution have always been at the heart of Pinter's own social and political context and agenda, an agenda that has been expressed with increasing clarity and vigour in recent years. An important strand in many of his plays is a refracted version of the kind of interrogation first explored in *The Examination* and refined by Mick in *The Caretaker*. At its most obvious, it structures the post-Suez Cold War paranoia of a play like *The Hothouse*, written in the 1958 but only published in 1980; at its most elegant it is mutely gestured towards in the disempowerment of speech in *Mountain Language* (1988). In a recent interview, Pinter has said:

> Political theatre now is even more important than it ever was, if by political theatre you mean plays that deal with the real world, not with a manufactured or fantasy world.
>
> ('Writing, Politics', 74)

This links back revealingly to a comment made by Pinter in the 1960s:

> I'm convinced that what happens in my plays could happen anywhere, at any time, in any place, although the events may seem unfamiliar at first glance. If you press me for a definition, I'd say that what goes on in my plays is realistic, but what I'm doing is not realism.
>
> ('Writing for Myself', 11)

The psychological and artistic freedom gained by Pinter's decision to avoid an explicitly 'engaged' or 'realistic' theatre of overt political comment should not, therefore, be assumed to indicate a lack of concern or engagement in those plays with 'real' issues. Rather than address 'issues' or incidents in history, Pinter draws our attention to the ways in which we use and abuse language in our attempts to coerce life into a bearable pattern, and in our politics:

> What all this adds up to is a disease at the very centre of language, so that language becomes a permanent masquerade, a tapestry of lies. The ruthless and cynical mutilation and degradation of human beings, both in spirit and body, the death of countless thousands – these actions are justified by rhetorical gambits, sterile terminology and concepts of power which stink. Are we ever going to look at the language we use, I wonder? Is it within our capabilities to do so? Do the structures of language and the structures of reality (by which I mean what actually *happens*) move along parallel lines?
>
> ('Oh, Superman', 213)

While political corruption and state power are more explicitly explored in recent pieces like *Party Time* and *The New World Order* (1991), where the interrogators are 'keeping the world clean for democracy', even in *The Caretaker* Mick's verbal bludgeoning of Davies, Aston's silent rejection of him at the end of the play, and Davies's often incoherent attempts at manipulation and assertion are as eloquent an exploration of the corrupt use of power and the subversion of order as anything in the Shakespeare Pinter so admires:

> MICK: . . . Say the word and I'll have my solicitors draft you out a contract. Otherwise I've got the van outside, I can run you to the police in five minutes, have you in for trespassing, loitering with intent, daylight robbery, filching, thieving and stinking the place out. What do you say?

Goldberg and McCann in *The Birthday Party* (1958) have sometimes been seen as more explicitly politicised than many of Pinter's characters. Representing the unnamed organisation from which Stanley is a renegade, they exude suave menace (Goldberg) and barely suppressed neurosis (McCann) in a manner that parallels the *film noir*ish hitmen of *The Dumb Waiter* (written in 1957 but first performed in 1960). McCann's lachrymose nostalgia for Ireland might suggest one kind of organisation (in his poem *A View of the Party*, Pinter describes him as a man 'with a green stain on his chest' [*Various Voices*, 161]), but Goldberg's unsettling cultural lurches between the persona of a family-loving Jewish boy and a British patriot with an eye on the cricket scores (though Pinter himself is both of these) makes an easy identification of the organisation impossible. Which, of course, is the point. In a letter to Peter Wood, the director of the first production, Pinter, while typically disclaiming any special insight into the 'meaning' of the play, has this to say about Goldberg and McCann:

> We've agreed: the hierarchy, the Establishment, the arbiters, the socio-religious monsters arrive to effect alteration and censure upon a member of the club who has discarded responsibility . . . towards himself and others.
>
> ('On *The Birthday Party* I', 11–12)

This perhaps goes some way to explaining the kaleidoscopic array of registers and styles of speech that the characters bring to bear. They are all these things and they are none. Is McCann's repeated use of the word 'sir' in his speeches to Stanley a reflection of Stanley's rank in the organisation, or just a reflection of McCann's Irish idiom? Is Goldberg called Simey or Nat (or even Benny)? Are his various recreations of idyllic homecomings to mother and wife ('The sun falling behind the dog stadium.') memory or imagination? Did Stanley ever play his concert? Was the 'very big doctor' who provided Meg's pink childhood bedroom, and the 'little sisters and brothers in other rooms, all different colours' perhaps called Barnardo?

These questions jostle alongside the more formal interrogation scenes conducted by Goldberg and McCann in a style that blends the menace of Hemingway and Hollywood with the knockabout farce of music hall sketches and the patter of stand-up comedians. (By his own admission Pinter is a cultural child of his era, equally at home with film as he is with books.) The style and subject matter of the questioning in Act 2 lurch from the trivial and impossible ('Why did the chicken cross the road?') to the profound and impossible ('Do you recognise an external force, responsible for you, suffering for you?'; 'Is the number 846 possible or necessary?'). But they are all rhetorical questions, building up a head of linguistic steam for the repeated assertion that Stanley is 'dead'. In Act 3 the now speechless Stanley, whom Pinter describes as 'on the edge of utterance' and who here in his speechlessness 'approximates nearer to the true nature of himself than ever before and certainly ever after' ('On *The Birthday Party* I', 11), is bombarded not by questions but by assertions and promises, as if the former interrogators are now reprogramming him with the promise of a utopian but highly eclectic new life, using the stock clichés of social aspiration:

McCANN: A day and night service.
GOLDBERG: All on the house.

McCANN: That's it.

GOLDBERG: We'll make a man of you.

McCANN: And a woman.

GOLDBERG: You'll be re-orientated.

McCANN: You'll be rich.

GOLDBERG: You'll be adjusted.

McCANN: You'll be our pride and joy.

GOLDBERG: You'll be a mensch.

McCANN: You'll be a success.

GOLDBERG: You'll be integrated.

Paradoxically, it is when the interrogators are within sight of the successful completion of their mission that we see them at their most vulnerable.
McCann, it is true, has been on edge throughout, like a nervous actor
fearful of being left stranded on stage ('What about this, Nat? Isn't it time
someone came in?'), but Goldberg, who has oozed self-assurance, unexpectedly drifts to the brink of a philosophical abyss in the last of his
meditations on his family history:

All my life I've said the same. Play up, play up and play the game. Honour
thy father and thy mother. All along the line. Follow the line, the line,
McCann, and you can't go wrong. What do you think. I'm a self-made
man? No! I sat where I was told to sit. I kept my eye on the ball. School?
Don't talk to me about school. Top in all subjects. And for why? Because
I'm telling you, I'm telling you, follow my line? Follow my mental? Learn
by heart. Never write down a thing. And don't go too near the water.
And you'll find – that what I say is true.
Because I believe that the world . . . (*Vacant*) . . .
Because I believe that the world . . . (*Desperate*) . . .
BECAUSE I BELIEVE THAT THE WORLD . . . (*Lost*) . . .

Goldberg's entire presence in the play has been an act of smoke and
mirrors, a series of de-contextualised verbal conjuring tricks to charm
Meg, Petey and Lulu (especially Lulu). But these arabesques of self-
characterisation have concealed a void within. The language spoken has
been little more than 'a constant stratagem to cover nakedness'. The
clichés and aphorisms trotted out so confidently at the start of the speech
begin to falter and stumble in the face of the kinds of rhetorical questions
that Goldberg and McCann had earlier used to bring Stanley to the point
of silence. However extensive the repertoire of artificial cultural contexts
Goldberg can construct for himself ('LULU: I bet you were a good husband.

GOLDBERG: You should have seen her funeral.'), ultimately he has no world view, no philosophy, no moral framework, no context for the formulaic cultural gestures that he has acted out. Pinter has spoken of the nausea he feels when confronted by this kind of language:

> Such a weight of words confronts us day in, day out . . . the bulk of it a stale dead terminology; ideas endlessly repeated and permutated become platitudinous, trite, meaningless.
>
> ('Writing for the Theatre', 13)

Goldberg has shown us a glimpse of his own heart of darkness, of the ideological void that characterises 'the hierarchy, the Establishment, the arbiters, the socio-religious monsters':

> Most political systems talk in such vague language, and it's our responsibility and our duty as citizens of our various countries to exercise acts of critical scrutiny upon that language.
>
> ('Writing, Politics', 74)

Of course in Pinter the typical arena for such acts of critical scrutiny is the single room rather than the world stage. In one respect this is a reflection of the theatrical context in which he worked as an actor and for which he started writing. A travelling repertory company is likely to find single box sets easier to transport and erect than more complicated designs, and the small casts allow an intimate, chamber music feel to the playing. But, as the early prose pieces show, Pinter can create infinite riches in a seedy room:

> – The rooms we live in open and shut . . .
> – They change shape at their own will, he said. I would have no quarrel, I wouldn't grumble, you see, if these rooms would remain the same, would keep to some consistency. But they don't. And I can't see the boundaries, the limits which I've been led to believe are natural. I'm all for the natural behaviour of rooms, doors, staircases, the lot. But I can't rely on them.
>
> (*The Dwarfs*, 11–12)

In one way this is a sinister version of Shakespeare's hymn in *Henry V* to the imagination's power to convert the theatre's wooden O into the fields of Agincourt, but it also signals the battle for stability and quiet possession of space and language. The lives that are acted out in these rooms aspire to and invoke the condition of the mundanely routine, but are rarely allowed to achieve it for long. Meg's morning rituals in *The Birthday Party* are both a liturgical invocation of the pleasures of tedium and a kind of magic spell warding off change:

MEG: Here's your cornflakes . . . Are they nice?
PETEY: Very nice.
MEG: I thought they'd be nice . . . You got the paper?
PETEY: Yes.
MEG: Is it good?
PETEY: Not bad . . .

MEG: Is Stanley up yet?
PETEY: I don't know. Is he?
MEG: I don't know. I haven't seen him down yet.
PETEY: Well then, he can't be up.
MEG: Haven't you seen him down?
PETEY: I've only just come in.

The rhythms and repetitions of speeches like these, with the lyrical balancing of 'up' and 'down' (the opening of *The Room* has a similar riff), owe something to the patter of the music hall, and maybe to the film comedies of Laurel and Hardy, the Marx Brothers or Abbott and Costello. But they often establish the bylaws of living in Pinter's rooms. Sometimes (in fact nearly always), of course, those rhythms will be disrupted by an external force that challenges the rest and quietness of the room's inhabitants. In *The Dumb Waiter* (written in 1957 and first produced in 1960), for example, the hitmen Ben and Gus are waiting in a basement room for instructions concerning their next job. Realising that they have no way to light the gas stove, they are surprised by the arrival under the door of an envelope containing matches:

GUS: Well, they'll come in handy.
BEN: Yes.
GUS: Won't they?
BEN: Yes, you're always running out, aren't you?
GUS: All the time.
BEN: Well, they'll come in handy.
GUS: Yes.
BEN: Won't they?
GUS: Yes, I could do with them. I could do with them too.

This beautifully balanced writing shows us the characters tossing the same phrases back and forward, each unwilling to change the shape of the phrase or to move the conversation forward, and each refusing to grapple with the real issue underlying this passage: where have the matches come from, and who has sent them? The tension between them erupts in a indirect way, and comically dramatises a struggle for control as desperate as anything in Pinter:

BEN: Go on, go and light it.
GUS: Eh?
BEN: Go and light it.
GUS: Light what?
BEN: The kettle.
GUS: You mean the gas.
BEN: Who does?
GUS: You do.
BEN: (*his eyes narrowing*) What do you mean, I mean the gas?
GUS: Well, that's what you mean, don't you? The gas.
BEN: (*powerfully*) If I say go and light the kettle I mean go and light the kettle.
GUS: How can you light a kettle?
. . .
BEN: Light the kettle! It's common usage!
GUS: I think you've got it wrong.
BEN: (*menacing*) What do you mean?
GUS: They say put on the kettle.
BEN: (*taut*) Who says?
　　They stare at each other, breathing hard.
(*Deliberately*) I have never in all my life heard anyone say put on the kettle.
GUS: I bet my mother used to say it.
BEN: Your mother? When did you last see your mother?
GUS: I don't know, about –
BEN: Well, what are you talking about your mother for.
　　They stare.
. . .
BEN: (*vehemently*) Nobody says light the gas! What does the gas light?
GUS: What does the gas – ?
BEN: (*grabbing him with two hands by the throat, at arm's length*) THE KETTLE, YOU FOOL!

At stake here is Ben's position as 'senior partner' of the team, and the dynamic between them is similar to that between Goldberg and McCann.

The squabble comically spirals out of control over which is the appropriate figure of speech, swooping through a typical Pinter allusion ('When did you last see your mother/father?', taking us firmly back into the world of interrogation, and of one-sided interrogation at that) and landing with a slapstick resolution when Ben shakes Gus warmly by the throat, with his arms extended to signal the comic stereotype of the tableau that is thus created.

A final example comes from Pinter's first play, *The Room* (1957), where Mr and Mrs Sands have arrived in Rose's room, shattering her illusion of security with the news that the room is up for rent. Usurping Rose's space, they settle themselves in so completely that, centre stage, they launch into a full blown argument that speaks volumes beneath its trivial exterior:

> *He perches on the table.*
> MRS SANDS: You're sitting down!
> MR SANDS: (*jumping up*) Who is?
> MRS SANDS: You were.
> MR SANDS: Don't be silly. I perched.
> MRS SANDS: I saw you sit down.
> MR SANDS: You did not see me sit down because I did not sit bloody well down. I perched!
> MRS SANDS: Do you think I can't perceive when someone's sitting down?
> MR SANDS: Perceive! That's all you do. Perceive.
> MRS SANDS: You could do with a bit more of that instead of all that tripe you get up to.
> MR SANDS: You don't mind some of that tripe!
> MRS SANDS: You take after your uncle, that's who you take after!
> MR SANDS: And who do you take after?
> MRS SANDS: (*rising*) I didn't bring you into the world.
> MR SANDS: You didn't what?
> MRS SANDS: I said, I didn't bring you into the world.
> MR SANDS: Well, who did then? That's what I want to know. Who did? Who did bring me into the world?
> *She sits, muttering. He stands, muttering.*

Again we see here Pinter's skill in picking up oddities in register and lexis ('I perched.'; 'Perceive!') to highlight tension between the couple, alongside the hint of other problems and disagreements between them (perhaps of a sexual nature: 'some of that tripe'). The typical chasm of existence and identity suddenly and unexpectedly yawns under the couple ('Who did bring me into the world?') which leaves each of them muttering alone, communication broken, answers denied. This is as profound in its way as anything in Sartre, but it is delivered through slick action and deadpan humour rather than portentous debate and debilitating angst. Pinter's comic timing, honed in his short review sketches, comes partly from his experience in milking an audience on stage as an actor, and partly from the comedy of Joyce and Beckett:

> [T]he key word is economy, economy of movement and gesture, of emotion and its expression, both the internal and the external in specific and exact relation to each other, so that there is no wastage and no mess.
>
> ('Shakespeare Prize', 41)

What remains fundamental is shape: the shape of a line, of a scene, of a whole play, and the shapely integrity and consistency he allows his characters in resistance to the norms of theatrical resolution:

> A play is not an essay, nor should a playwright under any exhortation damage the consistency of his characters by injecting a remedy or apology for their actions into the last act, simply because we have been brought up to expect, rain or shine, the last act 'resolution'.
>
> ('Writing for the Theatre', 12)

Once again, it is Pinter's assessment of the theatrical achievement of Shakespeare that offers one of the best insights into his own art:

> – How can moral judgements be applied when you consider how many directions he travels at once? Hasn't he got enough troubles? Look at what he gets up to. He meets himself coming back, he sinks in at the knees, he forgets the drift, he runs away with himself, he falls back on geometry, he turns down blind alleys, he stews in his own juice, and he nearly always ends up losing all hands. But the fabric, mate, never breaks. The tightrope is never at less than an even stretch. He keeps in business, that's what, and if he started making moral judgments he'd go bankrupt like the others . . . He laid bare, that's all.
>
> (*The Dwarfs*, 133)

In July 1949, Pinter sought to be excused National Service on grounds of conscience. His Headmaster, T. O. Balk, wrote a reference to the court that spoke of Pinter's need for 'self-control and self-discipline', adding:

He has always been prone to select the pleasant, the attractive and the easy in his life and to discard the drab, the unattractive and the difficult.

(Guardian, 30.12.99, 3)

But then, teachers don't always get it right, do we?

Further Reading

Biography
The best starting place is the excellent recent study: Michael Billington, *The Life and Work of Harold Pinter* (London, Faber, 1996).

Works
Plays One, Two, Three, Four, now published by Faber and Faber in the series *Faber Contemporary Classics*. These volumes collect all the plays up to the 1980s in good texts. They were previously published by Methuen, and may be in libraries in this guise. Several volumes include important interviews with or speeches by Pinter, and some key early prose works. More recent plays (like *Moonlight*, *Ashes to Ashes* and *Celebration*) appear as single volumes published by Faber. There are filmed versions of early productions of several plays (especially *The Caretaker* and *The Homecoming*) and archive footage of early TV broadcasts of some shorter plays.

The Dwarfs (London, Faber, 1990).
Pinter's only novel, written in the early fifties. An important exploration of many key themes and obsessions.

Poems and Prose 1949–1977 (London, Methuen, 1978).
Collected Poems and Prose (London, Faber, 1991).
Various Voices: Prose, Poetry, Politics 1948–1998 (London, Faber, 1998).
Some of the (pretty awful) poems offer readings of the plays. The prose, mostly written before the plays, is fascinating in its exploration of theatrical motifs and themes that later recur in the drama.

Pinter's screenplays are also important and fascinating, and are mainly collected together by Faber. Key scripts include *The Servant*, *Accident*, *The Quiller Memorandum*, *The French Lieutenant's Woman* and *The Proust Screenplay*. *The Heat of the Day* and *The Trial* are available separately.

Interviews and Speeches

Malcolm Page, *File on Pinter* (London, Methuen, 1993).

Mel Gussow, *Conversations with Pinter* (London, Nick Hern, 1994).

The collected plays also contain some speeches and interviews. Michael Billington's study has a lot of first-hand material and gives a listing of interviews with Pinter (391–2). Pinter is a very acute, subtle and open-minded reader of his own material.

Criticism

There are cartloads of articles on Pinter, many of them of limited interest. There is even a journal (*Pinter Review*) dedicated to him. One starting point is Steven H. Gale, *Harold Pinter: An Annotated Bibliography* (Hall, 1978). Some of the best books follow:

William Baker and Stephen Tabachnik, *Harold Pinter* (London, Oliver & Boyd, 1973).

Katherine Burkmann and John Kundert (ed.), *Pinter at Sixty* (Bloomington, Indiana University Press, 1993).

Bernard Dukore, *Harold Pinter* (London, Macmillan – now Palgrave, 1982).

Martin Esslin, *Pinter the Playwright* (London, Methuen, 1982: previously published as *The Peopled Wound*, 1970).

Steven Gale, *Critical Essays on Harold Pinter* (London, Hall, 1990).

Lois Gordon (ed.), *Harold Pinter: A Casebook* (London, Garland, 1990).

Ronald Knowles, *Understanding Harold Pinter* (Columbia, SC, University of South Carolina Press, 1995) [despite being published in the USA, Knowles is one of the most acute British readers of Pinter].

References

Harold Pinter, 'A Note on Shakespeare' (1950), in *Various Voices*, 5–7.

——, 'The Examination' (1955), in *Various Voices*, 102–7.

——, 'On *The Birthday Party* I' (1958), in *Various Voices*, 8–14.

——, 'A View of the Party' (1958), in *Various Voices*, 160–2.

——, 'Writing for Myself' (1961), in *Plays: Two* (London, Methuen, 1977: now published London, Faber), 9–12.

——, 'Writing for the Theatre' (1962), in *Plays: One* (London, Methuen, 1976: now published London, Faber), 9–16.

——, 'Mac' (1966), in *Various Voices*, 26–33.

——, 'On being awarded the 1970 German Shakespeare Prize in Hamburg', in *Various Voices*, 38–42.

——, 'A Speech of Thanks for the David Cohen British Literature Prize for 1995', in *Various Voices*, 57–61.

——, 'Oh, Superman' (1990), in *Various Voices*, 204–13.

——, *The Dwarfs* (London, Faber, 1990).

——, 'Writing, Politics and *Ashes to Ashes*' (1996), in *Various Voices*, 72–88.

——, *Various Voices: Prose, Poetry, Politics 1948–1998* (London, Faber, 1998).

Michael Billington, *The Life and Work of Harold Pinter* (London, Faber, 1996).

Mel Gussow, *Conversations with Harold Pinter* (London, Nick Hern, 1994).

Ronald Knowles, '"The Caretaker" and the "point" of laughter', *Journal of Beckett Studies*, 5 (1979), 83–97.

14 The Novels of Graham Swift

Peter Widdowson

Portrait of Graham Swift by Mark Dovat.

All of Graham Swift's fiction to date was published, if not written, between 1980 and 1996: in other words, it all 'belongs', in some sense, to the late-twentieth-century Britain of Tory Governments – principally those of Mrs Thatcher, and then latterly of John Major. And that, we might well claim, is the context in which Swift's novels and short stories have been produced and read. But before reflecting on the relationship of contemporary texts to their context, I want to consider those key terms 'text' and 'context' in a little more detail.

The word 'text' is derived from the Latin verb *texere, textum* – 'to weave or construct, anything woven', while the noun *textus* means 'a weaving; web; texture' and – significantly – '*context*'. 'Context' itself derives from the Latin verb *contexere, contextum* – 'to weave together/woven in with', and from the noun *contextus* – 'connection; coherency'. It is readily apparent, therefore, that etymologically our English words are very closely related: indeed, if *textus* can also mean 'context', we might say that the terms are inseparable: text is 'woven in with' its context, just as context is 'weaved together' with text. The contexts, in this respect, are an implicit dimension of the text, while the text is inescapably inscribed by its contexts.

Now this sense of the symbiotic interpenetration of a literary text and its context (the real world encompassing the text and to which it alludes) will be true of all texts in all periods of history. Ancient, medieval, Renaissance and eighteenth-century texts, for example, are all *produced* within specific historical and cultural contexts, and are indelibly marked by them. Hence, a great deal of modern criticism rightly concerns itself with trying to establish what those contexts were, and with reading literary texts of the period in the light of them. But with historical literary texts, there is a further context which has to be taken into account, and which sets up potential confusions for understanding them: this is the variable historical contexts in which they are read and made meaningful. They are *reproduced* throughout succeeding history in terms of the social and cultural conditions of the periods in which they are read. Some contemporary critical approaches attempt to study this transhistorical process in which the reception of a text will vary quite significantly from historical period to historical period. With contemporary literature, however, text and context are coterminous in a much more immediate sense. There is no earlier moment of *production* for the cultural historian to research which will help to explain the nature of the text; and the moment of *reproduction* will more or less coincide with that of the contemporary text's production. Of course, this is not absolute, since reading Swift's fiction now during New Labour's government of Britain may subtly change the way we react to it. Nevertheless, to read contemporary writing 'in context' is a different exercise to reading older texts in their – reconstituted – historical context (including their modern reproduction), for it means attaining a rather different kind of historical sense – that is, a sense of the historical moment as it is being spontaneously lived and experienced. Text and context thus seem to be 'woven together' in a more simultaneous and inextricable way than is the case with past texts and contexts. In other words, to read Swift's fiction as it comes out requires an attempt to situate it in its present cultural ambience and to try and decipher what it tells us about – and what positions it takes up towards – the world which determines it and which it addresses. This implies a more engaged mode of reading: what we may call a 'politics of reading'.

In this respect, we are left to judge whether the context the text alludes to is one we can square with the world we experience in our daily lives – whether we think: 'yes, that is how it seems; I can recognise or identify with that'; or whether we think: 'no, this is merely the jaundiced view of an over-fastidious intellectual novelist alienated from the dynamics of contemporary culture'. In either case, however, the mindset which thus delineates the world is part of the context in which the texts get written and read, its disillusion being as much a product of the world it views as is its possible accuracy of depiction. It is worth bearing in mind, too, that with a sophisticated, self-conscious novelist like Swift, all his representations of the contextualising world are those of his first-person narrators, and can never be taken unproblematically to be the unmediated views of the author. Swift, in other words, can always escape the accusation that *he* may feel like this by reminding us that it is Tom Crick (in *Waterland*, 1983) or Harry Beech (*Out of this World*, 1988) or Bill Unwin (*Ever After*, 1992) who is 'speaking' and offering such a partial view. Nevertheless, there seems to be little indication in the novels' fabric that the narrators are indeed 'unreliable narrators' as usually understood (that is, those strategically angled to reveal themselves as untrustworthy). It does not seem, in other words, that they are being subjected to that kind of structural irony as part of the novels' overall project – but the reader must, of course, decide this for her or himself. This responsibility represents the 'politics of reading'; and while it is true of our experiencing of all writing to some degree, it is particularly insistent with contemporary texts, which have no established credentials as 'great works', have not been interpreted by generations of critics, and are not located in an already historically constructed context. They are products of the world we inhabit, and it is our spontaneous engagement with them which will define their meaning and value.

There are, of course, many contexts in which it would be possible to situate Swift's novels in their present cultural ambience: for example, in that of the modern market-driven world of book publishing and selling; of literary prizes like the Booker Prize (which Swift's most recent novel, *Last Orders*, won in 1996), with all the media hype such events engender; of Swift's own past and present biographical context; of the state of the novel genre as it mutated and evolved in the late twentieth century; of the literary tradition (*Ever After*, for example, uses *Hamlet* extensively as a contextualising motif or 'intertext', whilst *Last Orders* seems to allude structurally and thematically to the Prologue of *The Canterbury Tales*, to T. S. Eliot's poem *The Waste Land*, and to William Faulkner's novel *As I Lay Dying*). But in the limited space available, what the present essay will offer is a preliminary reading of Swift's novels which identifies those elements in them that are symptomatic of the late-millennial world in Britain. It will propose that his fiction depicts a world still bearing the presence of its pasts, but in which most certainties have evaporated and which is characterised by an empty and meretricious simulacrum of what human life is capable of – a world, in shorthand, recognisable as 'postmodern', where, as the narrator says in *Waterland*, we seem to have reached 'the End of History' (Swift, *Waterland*, 17). But what the novels also seem to propose is the possibility of salvaging some vestiges of humanity from the postmodern wasteland by way of 'love', a conspicuous theme in contemporary British fiction (sympomatised, perhaps, by the title of Doris Lessing's novel, *Love, Again* [1996]). This 'new humanism', if such I may call it, is embattled, tentative and replete with uncertainty, as Swift is only too well aware. But his fiction also *reveals* problems with this challenge to postmodern carelessness and emotional atrophy which it does not seem to be conscious of itself. And that may signal other contexts – ones absent from the text; for in reading any literature, we must be alert to contexts other than those the text itself explicitly invokes, but which are there nevertheless. Jane Austen's novel, *Mansfield Park*, may be primarily concerned with class relationships and responsibilities in early nineteenth-century England, but by sending Sir Thomas Bertram away to the West Indies to sort out his interests there, the novel surely invokes questions of slavery and hence of the economic and ethical basis on which even the most upright English aristocrat's probity rests. In Swift's case, I shall argue, his treatment of the female characters calls up a context his novels otherwise entirely eschew: sexual politics.

Graham Swift's fiction is both very varied and focused around certain recurrent themes, motifs and modes of narration. His first novel, *The Sweet Shop Owner* (1980), sets the characteristic pattern of the novels to follow:

it presents an individual history, of Willy Chapman and his relations with his wife and daughter – principally from Willy's point-of-view – in the context of larger historical and social events from just before the Second World War until the early 1970s – the 'present' of the book. The second, *Shuttlecock* (1981), told in the first person by the protagonist, Prentis, concerns his work in an archive of unsolved past crimes and his unsatisfactory family life in the present; but it is also punctuated by his obsessive pursuit of the truth about whether his father (now in an asylum and completely mute) was a wartime hero or not. *Waterland* – this time narrated in the first person by Tom Crick, a schoolteacher of History who substitutes his own family history for the school syllabus of 'big' historical events – in effect tells the history of the Fens, and of the local Crick and Atkinson families from the eighteenth century through the First and Second World Wars up to the present (1981). Here, 'History' is about to be closed down in Crick's school and his wife Mary has stolen a baby from outside the Safeways supermarket in Lewisham, south-east London: in a sense, the whole book is an attempt to tell the history of this latter event. *Out of this World* is narrated by ex-war-photographer Harry Beech, mentally telling his story ('his-story') to his alienated daughter, Sophie, and by Sophie herself, now based in New York and telling 'her-story' to a psychiatrist, with occasional sections by Harry's dead wife, Anna, and Sophie's husband, Joe. ('His-story' and 'her-story' are useful *double-entendres* for catching up the way private narratives substitute for and reinflect the public narratives of authorised History – a trope Swift uses throughout his fiction.) The novel thus becomes at once a history of the Beech family, whose fortune has been made in arms manufacture, and a history of twentieth-century warfare. *Ever After* uses its narrator, Bill Unwin, an ersatz don at an old university in the present, to tell both his own story (once again from just before the Second World War) and that of his Victorian forebear, Matthew Pearce, a man who lost his faith through modern (Darwinian) science. Finally, *Last Orders* (1996) appears to develop in new directions, being the story of one day's journey to Margate by four East Londoners (Ray, Lennie, Vic and Vince) in order to fulfil their dead friend Jack's wish to have his ashes thrown into the sea there. It is narrated in interspersed fragments by the four men, with sections by the dead man's wife Amy, Vince's wife Mandy, and one short piece by the dead man himself. But the fragments of their stories again coalesce to comprise a narrative of their lives from before the Second World War to the present in 1990 – and that present, as so often in Swift's fiction, is 'explained' by those stories of their past lives.

Amongst the many repeated motifs in these novels, one in particular may have become apparent from my account above. A vestigial but determinate presence in all the novels is the Second World War. In *The Sweet Shop Owner*, much of the earlier sections concerns Willy's tedious, home-based service in an 'Issue of Equipment' unit (ever the shop-keeper). In *Shuttlecock*, it is the silent father's unverifiable experience as a spy working with the French Resistance behind enemy lines, who may or may not have cracked under interrogation by the Germans. In *Waterland*, the war is the peripheral but formative context in which Tom, Mary and their friends grow up in the Fenlands. In *Out of this World*, Harry becomes an aerial war-photographer covering the bombing of German cities and then the Nuremberg trials. In *Ever After*, Bill's supposed father, who kills himself in immediately post-war Paris, has served in some secret capacity and may have been involved in developing nuclear weapons (Aldermaston, the Atomic Weapons Research establishment, is also mentioned, as is the dropping of the first atomic bomb). In *Last Orders*, three of the characters have served in the North Africa campaigns, and a German doodlebug has killed the parents of another in London.

It is as though Swift 'dates' his modern world from the catastrophic events of the mass warfare of the Second World War – one which remains in their shadow and in which the destinies of ordinary lives, even in the 1980s and 1990s, are still determined by them. Or, to put it another way, the postmodern world of the present is in some sense the child or product of that war. Bill Unwin, visiting Aldermaston before war breaks out, sees himself 'as a child of the future' (Swift, *Ever After*, 197), and Tom Crick claims Price, the postmodern schoolboy, to be his 'son' (Swift, *Waterland*, 209), as though his own wartime generation had engendered Price's anomie – thus ironically replacing the aborted child he and Mary might have had. This is a present in which love has withered, reality is displaced by simulacra, images, fantasies and deceptions, curiosity is no more, and a feeling that history (as much a sense of futurity as a sense of the past) has stopped in the face of the wholesale destruction of humanity and civilisation incident on nuclear holocaust. As Martin Amis has suggested in a brilliant essay entitled 'Thinkability': 'the past and the future . . . now huddle in the present. . . . What we are experiencing, in as much as it can be experienced, is the experience of nuclear war. Because the anticipation . . . the anxiety, the suspense, is the only experience of nuclear war that anyone is going to get' (Amis, *Einstein's Monsters*, 17). In other words, when it actually happens, people won't experience it, because they will be obliterated, and *we* only experience it as a threat, beyond which there is no 'thinkability' and hence no future. Such a subliminal recognition of 'the End of History' and the pointlessness of life, postmodern theorists claim, leads to a sense only of a continuous present – what Price, Tom Crick's sixth-form interlocutor in *Waterland*, calls 'the Here and Now' (Swift, *Waterland*, 51). This is a present which perceives no point in moral or political endeavour or agency, and therefore in any systematic value system governing individuals' selfish desires and wants. One inflection of this might be the laissez-faire economics and ego-centred ideology of the Thatcher years and beyond, the demoralisation of the political left, the withering of the 'Nanny' state, the electronic simulations of global information technology, a heritage culture which floods the present with recycled images of the past, and a yuppie 'feel-good' hedonism: 'loads-a-money', live only for yourself and the day. While the present in Swift's novels is never the sole focus of attention, what we see of it is imbued with just such a broad-brush delineation of 'the postmodern condition'.

In *Waterland*, for example, the present (early 1980s) world of Tom and Mary typifies the bourgeois ambience in which Mrs Thatcher came to power, its prosperity and vacuity:

> They settle in Greenwich, in a suburb of London noted for its historical features. . . . They acquire regular habits, spiced with unspectacular variations. . . . A slap-up meal in a restaurant every birthday and wedding anniversary. Trips to the theatre. Weekend excursions. Holidays. . . . Not having a family – and inheriting, in 1969, part of the proceeds of a Fenland farm – they do not lack for money, indeed are almost embarrassingly comfortable: the 'enviable Greenwich home' (Regency, porticoed front door). . . . They acquire regular habits and regular diversions. So much so that three decades pass as if little has happened, as if without event.
>
> (Swift, *Waterland*, 107)

Equally, the Safeways supermarket in Lewisham where Mary steals the baby is described in ironic consumerist detail:

> Long queues at the check-outs; cash registers bleeping. . . . All the mums with families to feed have got their weekend supplies. All the couples with cars to load are eager to be home. They've got all the good things that supermarkets provide. They've got their canned soups and frozen meat, their breakfast cereals and scrubbed vegetables in polythene bags; they've got their cat food, dog food, washing powder, paper tissues, cling film and aluminium foil.
>
> (135–6)

And the postmodern pub where Tom and Price have a drink has the ersatz past and 'virtual' present in anachronistic continuum: 'Mock red velvet. Mock Tudor oak, framing mock Georgian coach-lamps. Amidst the period anomalies, electronic growls, TV-game bleepings. How we advance...' (223). But it is Price who is at the centre of the postmodernity the book identifies, and of the running discourse about 'History' and 'the End of History' which lies at its core. While in his and Crick's school they are 'cutting History' (21), since it seems to have scant 'practical relevance to today's real world' (19), and the headmaster is a burnt-out functionary who believes that 'History breeds pessimism' (135), it is Price who represents the real challenge to Crick's belief in '*historia*' as central to our humanity and civilisation – the word signalling the intimate relationship between 'history' and 'story' (see the first of the novel's epigraphs). For Crick (a year before Jean-François Lyotard's *The Postmodern Condition* [1979] appeared in English [1984] and gave the term its *cachet*), History is 'the Grand Narrative' (53) which 'helps to eliminate fear' (208), and which allows us 'to avoid illusion and make-believe, to lay aside dreams, moonshine, cure-alls, wonder-workings, pie-in-the-sky – to be realistic' (94). Price, founder of the school 'Holocaust Club' (204), interested only in 'the Here and Now' and not the 'irrelevant' past, believes that history, and the world, may be coming to an end (134). The dream he describes to Crick – significantly, in the context of Amis's 'thinkability' above – is of the moment when a nuclear blast has just been announced:

> the main road it's blocked with cars. . . . And I think, this is how it's going to end – we're all going to die in a great big traffic jam . . . they announce it on the telly. You know: you've got four minutes . . . But no one seems to notice. No one moves. My Dad's snoring in his chair. I'm screaming. My mum just sits there wanting to know what's happened to Crossroads . . . all the buildings go red-hot and then they go white and all the people go red too and white . . . ('You couldn't see that – you'd be dead. Stupid') . . . 'Suicide pills, sir. We sit round and all take them together . . .'
>
> (256)

This is 'the postmodern condition', and it causes Crick to question education and by implication History: 'what does it have to offer, when deprived of its necessary partner, the future, and faced instead with – no future at all?' (134). However, the novel nonetheless seeks to counteract the 'recurring nightmare' (134) of Price's postmodernity by affirming the value of reclaiming the past, of 'telling stories', of wanting explanations, of 'curiosity' and of 'love' – convincingly or not, as the case may be.

Christopher Isherwood once coined the phrase 'tea-tabling' for the modern novelist's tendency to shift the emphasis from big public historical and political events onto the small private worlds those big events contextualise (Isherwood, *Lions and Shadows*, 107). The insouciant chatter of the tea-table is the shadowy reflection of the gross happenings going on, and occasionally revealed, outside the drawn curtains of the tea-room. In addition to that already outlined in *Waterland*, a further sample of such tea-tabling throughout Swift's fiction will illustrate how the present postmodern context is summoned into his texts. In *Shuttlecock*, a dominant motif in the Prentis family home is the television which the sons watch endlessly and in particular the programme *The Bionic Man*: 'My sons don't look up to their father. They look up to the Bionic Man. The Bionic Man radiates Californian confidence. The Bionic Man performs impossible feats, solves impossible riddles and bears no relation to anything natural' (Swift, *Shuttlecock*, 9–10). *Out of this World* is set as the Falkland Islands war begins, and focuses on photography as the emblematic mechanical mode in which modern life deceptively reflects and knows itself (the novel also associates it with guns, since 'loading', 'aiming' and 'shooting' are common to both). Harry (pre-empting Jean Baudrillard on the Gulf War [Baudrillard, *Gulf War* . . .]) observes that without the cameras there, it is 'as if . . . [the Falklands war] could not take place', and adds:

> As if the camera no longer recorded but conferred reality. . . . As if the world wanted to be claimed and possessed by the camera. To translate itself, as if afraid it might otherwise vanish, into the new myth of its own authentic-synthetic memory.
>
> (Swift, *Out of this World*, 188–9)

The postmodern simulacrum – 'the separation of the image from the thing. The extraction of the world from the world' (119) – is substituted for, and becomes, reality. Furthermore, the Bronze Age fields which Harry photographs as a peacetime aerial photographer actually show up sites of Ministry of Defence installations, while Sophie's husband, a New York travel agent, specialises in 'sell[ing] dreams' in the form of tours to 1980s England: 'golden memories of the Old World. Thatched cottages and stately homes. . . . Sweet, green visions' (15–16). The ageing Harry, too, living with his beautiful young girlfriend, Jenny, in Wiltshire, is ironically 'facing up to life in a picture-book cottage' (59) – although 'Picture-books aren't real' (79). In fact, he is 'out of this world', since although 'it will seem that England is really only a toy country . . . you mustn't believe that. That things are just toys' (192): the 'real' England discloses its MOD sites and is on its way to the Falklands for '[a] show-case war' (185).

The present world of *Ever After* for Bill Unwin is the cloistered world of an 'old' university college:

> now it is those ancient walls which have become artificial and implausible, like a painstakingly contrived film set. It is everything beyond that is real. If hardly reliable. Out there, . . . the world is falling apart; its social fabric is in tatters, its eco-system is near collapse. Real: that is, flimsy, perishing, stricken, doomed. Whereas here. . . .
>
> (Swift, *Ever After*, 2)

'Whereas here . . .', amongst the 'dodo' dons, the reality is that Bill's fellowship is funded by his stepfather Sam's money, a fortune made after the war in 'plastic' in his drive for 'the polymerization of the world' ('You gotta have *substitoots*': simulacra of 'the real stuff' [7]); and the new breed of academic is the superficial, philandering and rapaciously ambitious telly-don, Potter. Finally, in *Last Orders*, Swift invokes both the robust culture of *The Canterbury Tales* (the 'pilgrims' telling their 'stories' on the way to Canterbury during the 'sweet showers' of April – all the present action of the novel takes place on 2 April 1990), and T. S. Eliot's iconic post-First-World-War text *The Waste Land* ([1922] 1958: indicated below by parenthetical quotations from it) in order to contextualise his own post-Second-World-War materialistic and emotionally vacuous 'Dreamland'. The East London present is one in which wasted postwar lives are lived out in the Coach and Horses pub which is 'never going nowhere' (Swift, *Last Orders*, 210) and where 'last orders' ('HURRY UP PLEASE IT'S TIME') has a more than literal significance; where old family businesses fail in the face of modern commercial competition, a flash car-salesman prostitutes his daughter to an 'Ayrab' City dealer (166), and London's 'St Paul's, London Bridge, the Tower, [are] like things that weren't ever real' (162; 'Unreal City'). Equally, in Margate (where 'I can connect / Nothing with nothing'), Jack's ashes are to be cast into the sea in 'handfuls' (293–4; 'a handful of dust'), and the buildings on its Golden Mile are 'all painted up and decked out like poor man's palaces, except one . . . looming over them all, a bare brick tower with just a few big words on it. It looks more like the way into a prison than a funfair. . . . It's what Margate's famous for, it's what people come here for. *Dreamland*' (273).

The context that Swift's texts invoke, then, is that of the present as a postmodern wasteland – consumerist, careless, dominated by factitious images on film and TV, emotionally null, its 'social fabric in tatters', its eco-system failing, and overshadowed by the necessarily vicarious 'experience' of nuclear holocaust. Our decision about how to respond to this, as I said earlier, is part of the politics of reading a contemporary text. But what is equally a part of this politics is how we react to the challenges the novels posit to the prevailing context, for Swift does not merely identify the wasteland but seems to suggest an antidote to it. Put very simply and crudely, this is 'love' – if only as a minimal and vulnerable possibility.

Whilst the importance of love is continuously *stated* throughout the novels (especially in *Ever After*), a paradoxical index of this is its ubiquitous absence: a powerful sense imbuing the wasteland is of the *failure* of love – lovelessness between heterosexual adults and between parents and children (often, indeed, childlessness). Prentis's relations with his children and particularly his sexual relations with his wife ('Systematically and cold-bloodedly, . . . I am turning my wife into a whore' [Swift, *Shuttlecock*, 75]) are an early example of this, but it is central to all the novels. After their youthful sexual 'explorations' and Mary's aborted pregnancy in *Waterland*, hers and Tom's relationship drifts into childless and sterile routine. Harry Beech's unfaithful wife has been killed in an air crash, and he has sacrificed his love for Sophie to brutalisation by his profession. Bill Unwin and his beloved wife, Ruth, although childless, find 'the real thing', 'romantic love' (Swift, *Ever After*, 148–9), but after she dies of cancer, Bill is 'turned to plastic' (9), while Sam and Bill's mother's marriage is only a 'plausible "substitoot"' (149). Almost all the relationships in *Last Orders* have broken down in one way or another, but most centrally that between Jack and Amy in which for 50 years Jack has refused even to acknowledge the existence of their brain-damaged daughter, June.

Even the minute signs of possible redemption through love are only ever tentative and oblique. Prentis and his wife make love 'naturally' in the sand dunes at the very end of *Shuttlecock*. Crick posits 'curiosity' as the source of love in *Waterland*, linking this to the need for 'explanations', for histories and stories – however inadequate – as a rebuttal of the myopic obsession with 'the Here and Now':

> Children, be curious. . . . Nothing is more repressive than the repression of curiosity. *Curiosity begets love*. It weds us to the world. . . . People die when curiosity goes. People have to find out, people have to know. How can there be any true revolution till we know what we're made of?
>
> (Swift, *Waterland*, 178, my emphasis)

Harry Beech is deeply in love with Jenny in their 'fairy-tale cottage' in *Out of this World*, and there is a possibility of reconciliation with his daughter, Sophie, who is flying back to England as the novel ends. But Harry, too, in the present, is also on a flying trip, having left his pregnant girlfriend below on the ground – so potentially both father and daughter could fall out of the sky: literally 'out of this world'. While *Ever After* constantly posits that

Bill and Ruth achieve 'the real thing . . . the substance of love' (Swift, *Ever After*, 76), it is Bill's mother who derides the notion '*Amor Vincit Omnia*': ' "Love conquers all" If only it were true' (46) in a world of promiscuity and adultery. The novel itself can only close with Bill tenderly remembering Ruth's and his first night together many years before. In *Last Orders*, with the act of redemption achieved (Jack's ashes thrown into the sea in the rain), there is just the possibility that Ray and Amy might make a new life together, and that Ray might fly to Sydney to see his long-separated daughter. But in no sense does the novel confirm this. The *possibility* of love, then – combined with the process of exploring the past through [hi]stories in order to 'explain' how these modern lives have become so damaged – seems to be the minimalist solution to the otherwise sterile and futureless 'Here and Now'.

However, I would suggest that even the proposed potentiality of love in Swift's novels is undercut by a feature of their actual textual realisation which may indicate the determinate absence of another context from the period in which they were written. Swift's women characters, and his treatment of sexual relations, seem to me to be problematical – perhaps signalling an unreconstituted sexism oblivious to the shifts in consciousness brought about by the new feminisms of the last three decades or so. This is not to accuse Swift of mysogyny, but rather of failing to break free from some very conventional male attitudes about women and sex. Once again, of course, we have to bear in mind that these 'attitudes' are strictly those of the novels' narrators. But there is never a moment (except perhaps with Prentis's treatment of his wife) when the reader feels their attitudes are indeed being set up with and for ironic distaste. Either the women characters are largely undeveloped (Marian, Anna, Mandy, Amy – even the wonderfully talented and charismatic Ruth, on whose stated capacity for 'life' and love the moral force of Bill's story depends), or are sexually promiscuous and responsible for harm being done – or both. Mary's teenage 'curiosity' about matters sexual leads to her pregnancy either by Tom or his potato-head brother, Dick, whose own monster 'dick' fascinates her. Following her abortion, she abandons her curiosity, which leads finally to her conversion to 'pie-in-the-sky' religion, a belief in the Second Coming – her theft of a baby is to realise this – and incarceration in an asylum. While curiosity for Tom (and for the author?) is potentially redemptive, Mary's is scapegoated and its punishment in the novel smacks of malevolence. On whose part? Anna goes to bed with a friend of Harry's when the two families are on holiday together, and is shortly afterwards killed in a plane crash; Sophie 'fucks' a Greek plumber in her kitchen shortly after arriving in New York married to Joe; Bill's mother, 'so unscrupulous, so indolent, so heartless' (Swift, *Ever After*, 32) is a 'bitch' (196) whose torrid affair with Sam may have been the cause of Bill's father's suicide (or the latter may not have been Bill's father at all), and she is finally rendered entirely silent. Potter's wife, Katherine, makes an inept attempt to seduce Bill in order to get hold of the manuscript he is editing and thus 'save' her marriage. Amy has an affair with Ray, her husband's best friend; Ray's wife deserts him for another man; and two of the other male characters' daughters effectively become prostitutes.

Furthermore, almost all the (admittedly short and infrequent) scenes of sex read like prurient male fantasies – *especially* when they are being narrated by a woman. A couple of examples will suffice. In *Out of this World*, Sophie describes her seduction of a plumber in New York (he is lying on the floor fixing a pipe):

> I . . . stood nearer so he could look at my legs. . . . He got up . . . and . . . I put my hand on his cock, hard as a pistol, and he hitched up my skirt, right here in this kitchen, with his hands greasy, with the twins upstairs sleeping, and I said, 'C'mon! C'mon fuck me, fuck me good, you great hog!' And after that I was no longer a new-world virgin.
>
> (18)

Apart from the final sentence, that piece of writing could have come from the 'Bored Housewives' section of a 'top-shelf' men's magazine. In *Ever After*, there are moments of gratuitous detail which again suggest a male sexual psyche at work: for example, the telly-don, Potter, in his kitchen during a dinner party with the research student he is currently bedding, is 'observed with his hand on Gabriella's buttock (let us be plain, his hand was thrust beneath the waistband of her distinctly fetching, tight black evening trousers, so we are not talking about the seat of her pants)' (85). Why that unnecessary parenthesis? And in *Last Orders*, Vince and Mandy make love in a camper van: 'she cottoned on . . . soon enough that . . . I liked it cramped and squashed and hasty . . . and I reckon that's how she liked it, too, because it didn't take much coaxing, a look, a nod, and there she'd be with her legs round my neck. . . . She'd sit on my cock . . .' (103). Mandy's own version sounds suspiciously similar: 'I felt his cock stiffening under my hand. . . . He rolled me over and shoved into me and I lifted my knees and gripped him' (160).

The effect of this kind of writing is to make the already uncertain and vulnerable positive of love even less convincing as an antidote to the postmodern malaise than it is in the conscious schema of the books. For if love is only posited in generalised, abstract and one-sided terms, and rendered by a conception of sex which owes its provenance to male fantasy, then redemption solely by '*his*-stories' seems a forlorn hope. A context missing from Swift's otherwise sophisticated and perceptive fiction, perhaps, is that in which the women's movement, from the 1960s onwards, has promulgated the need for political endeavour, both public and personal, and for human agency based on mutual respect and understanding between the sexes, as a means of displacing the stasis at the heart of postmodernity.

I began this essay by proposing that in a contemporary literary work text and context are inseparably 'woven together', that the world to which it alludes is a version of the world in which it is written and read. A notion of historical context, appropriate to the study of past literature, therefore, is replaced by a politics of reading in which the contemporary reader must identify the contexts in which the text locates itself and evaluate the stances it takes to them. Graham Swift's metafiction, I have suggested, at once offers an historical explanation (from the Second World War at least) for the nature of late twentieth-century British society, represents its (postmodern) features in a chilling light, and implies that salvation is only possible if we retain some vestiges of a humanism in which reclaiming the past ('telling [hi]stories') and 'love' are central. These are the contexts which occupy the text, and the way they are presented enunciates the text's own politics. The reader's task is to identify and assess the latter – hence engaging in a politics of reading of their own. Questions we might find ourselves posing are: Is Swift's fictional historiography of the post-modern world convincing? Is his representation of postmodernity a form of cultural despair? Are his solutions to its plight comprehensive and credible – in other words, what *are* the politics of his fiction and how do we react to them? Finally, do their very presence (as, perhaps, a politics of no politics) paradoxically summon up other contexts which the fiction ignores – contexts, for example, in which collective human action seeks to promote change and to replace anomie with agency? I have pointed to sexual politics as one such context which is simultaneously an absence and a haunting presence in Swift's novels. All texts have contexts, but often the most telling ones are those within.

Further Reading

As with many contemporary writers, Graham Swift awaits his critics. There have been, of course, numerous reviews of his novels as they were published, and by now there are also a fair number of critical articles (especially on *Waterland*) scattered through academic books and journals. But as yet, so far as I am aware, no monograph is devoted to his work. I have had recourse to none of this material in writing the present essay, and therefore will not specify individual items for recommendation. Instead, I list some useful general books on postmodernism and on contemporary fiction, indicating, where appropriate, if they contain substantial reference to Swift's work.

Hans Bertens, *The Idea of the Postmodern: A History* (London, Routledge, 1994).

Peter Brooker (ed.), *Modernism/Postmodernism* (Harlow, Longman, 1992) [reprints part of Hutcheon, *The Politics . . .* , below, on *Waterland*].

Steven Connor, *Postmodernist Culture*, 2nd edn (Oxford, Blackwell, 1996).

Terry Eagleton, *The Illusions of Postmodernism* (Oxford, Blackwell, 1996).

Linda Hutcheon, *A Poetics of Postmodernism* (London, Routledge, 1988).

——, *The Politics of Postmodernism* (London, Routledge, 1989) [section on *Waterland*].

Ben Knights, *Writing Masculinities: Male Narratives in Twentieth-Century Fiction* (Basingstoke, Macmillan – now Palgrave, 1999) [section on GS].

Alison Lee, *Realism and Power: Postmodern British Fiction* (London, Routledge, 1990) [section on GS].

Roger Luckhurst and Peter Marks (eds), *Literature and the Contemporary* (Harlow, Longman, 1999) [includes an essay on GS by Wendy Wheeler].

Brian McHale, *Postmodernist Fiction* (London, Routledge, 1987).

Rod Mengham (ed.), *An Introduction to Contemporary Fiction* (Oxford, Polity Press, 1999) [includes an essay on GS by Adrian Poole].

Christopher Nash, *World Postmodern Fiction: a Guide* (Harlow, Longman, 1993).

Joseph Natoli, *A Primer to Postmodernity* (Oxford, Blackwell, 1997).

Madan Sarup, *An Introductory Guide to Post-Structuralism and Postmodernism*, 2nd edn (Hemel Hempstead, Harvester Wheatsheaf, 1993).

Edmund J. Smyth, (ed.), *Postmodernism and Contemporary Fiction* (London, Batsford, 1991).

Patricia Waugh, *Metafiction* (London, Routledge, 1984).

——, *Practising Postmodernism/Reading Modernism* (London, Arnold, 1992).

Nigel Wheale (ed.), *The Postmodern Arts: An Introductory Reader* (London, Routledge, 1995).

References

Martin Amis, *Einstein's Monsters* (London, Penguin Books, 1988).

Jean Baudrillard, *The Gulf War Did Not Take Place*, trans. Paul Patton (London, Power Publications, 1995).

T. S. Eliot, *The Waste Land* (1922), in T. S. Eliot, *Collected Poems 1909–1935* (London, Faber & Faber, 1958).

Christopher Isherwood, *Lions and Shadows* (1938) (London, Four Square Books, 1963).

Jean-François Lyotard, *The Postmodern Condition: A Report on Knowledge* (1979), trans. G. Bennington and B. Massumi (Manchester, Manchester University Press, 1984).

Graham Swift, *The Sweet Shop Owner* ([1980] Harmondsworth, Penguin Books, 1983).

——, *Shuttlecock* ([1981] Harmondsworth, Penguin Books, 1982).

——, *Waterland* ([1983] London, Picador, 1984).

——, *Out of this World* (London, Penguin Books, 1988).

——, *Ever After* (London, Pan Books, 1992).

——, *Last Orders* (London, Picador, 1996).

15 Toni Morrison: *Beloved*

Linden Peach

Portrait of Toni Morrison by Helen Marcus.

Context is an especially complex subject in relation to writers who, like Toni Morrison, draw on a diverse cultural and historical heritage. Morrison was born and brought up in Lorain, Ohio, a midwestern industrial town. Her parents had migrated from the South in the early 1900s; her maternal grandparents were from Greenville, Alabama, and her father's parents from Georgia. Apart from their experiences of the American South, and their families' first-hand knowledge of its history, in writing *Beloved*, a novel about slavery, Morrison was able to draw on her research into black American history, and her own reading in African-American, Euro-American and European literature. She read English with Classics at Howard University, Washington, and wrote a Masters thesis at Cornell University on Virginia Woolf and William Faulkner, Modernist writers whose work was characterised by innovative narrative strategies, multifocal perspectives, constantly shifting internal monologues, and experiments with time.

However, context is an even more complicated subject in the case of writers, again like Morrison, from a people whose history has been obscured and distorted by antagonistic, dominant cultural forces operating from both within and outside their own race. Thus, we also have to take into account the marginalisation of black experience within American history which has largely been written from a white perspective; how black women often felt themselves doubly disadvantaged in being black and women; how black men frequently discriminated against, and abused, black women; Morrison's own experiences as a black woman living in a white-dominated country; and the way in which the civil rights and black nationalist movements of the 1950s and 1960s, when Morrison was a student and university teacher, contributed to the growth of black consciousness.

Thus, there are numerous contexts from which to discuss Morrison's fifth novel. In this essay I want to highlight some of the more important: the verbal narratives adapted in the novel such as the slave narrative, the African spirit tale, the plantation ghost story, and the Bible; its revisioning of the cultural assumptions, perspectives and beliefs associated with these narratives; the interleaving of ideas and perspectives from traditional African and African-American oral cultures with sophisticated literary techniques characteristic of many late twentieth-century novels; the way in which *Beloved* reconfigures American slave history from a black woman's point of view, drawing attention to the sufferings of black women and how slavery distorted and denied notions of womanhood and mothering; and, finally, Morrison's association of the late twentieth-century black American novel with healing.

When Toni Morrison won the Nobel Prize for Literature in 1993, the first African-American woman to do so, some critics alleged that her work was too 'European'. While this was a minority view, it did draw attention to the fact that many African-American writers, who come from mixed cultural backgrounds, usually draw from their African, American and European heritage. Toni Morrison's fiction is especially interesting in this respect because it not only adapts and interweaves verbal narratives of different national and regional origin, but reconfigures the world-views associated with them.

Since *Beloved* is based on the true story of an escaped slave, Margaret Garner, who tried to kill herself and her children rather than return to slavery, the most obvious literary-historical context in which to place the book is the American slave narrative. Moreover, in its concern with slavery many of the principal contexts from which the novel might be discussed come together: literary and cultural influences; the interleaving of oral and literary narrative traditions; black American history; the growth of black consciousness in America from the mid twentieth century onwards; and black American feminism.

The first point that has to be made is that *Beloved* is a very different work from the conventional, nineteenth-century slave story. By the 1850s, the period in which much of *Beloved* is set, the slave narrative had come to be written according to a familiar formula: an initial description by the slave of (usually) his plantation origins, the initiation into hardship and suffering, the escape and the subsequent life in the Northern USA, or in Canada. Not only is *Beloved* structurally different from the formulaic slave stories, it tackles subjects they eschewed for fear of alienating those whose support was needed in abolishing slavery, such as the physical and sexual violence suffered by female slaves.

Ostensibly, *Beloved* has many of the characteristics of late twentieth-century novels to which the label 'postmodern' is usually applied; texts that self-consciously employ complex narrative strategies, multifocal perspectives, and blur the boundaries between fact and fiction and between different kinds of verbal narratives. They are generally much more demanding to read than conventional, third-person, linear novels. Often there is good reason why the writers have chosen to structure their work in such complex ways, for example, to overturn our conventional ways of thinking about a subject, or to challenge our habitual assumptions about how a novel should be written. However, while *Beloved* may employ techniques that are to be found in many 'postmodern' novels, and this is an important context in which to place the book, its complicated structure reflects African-American cultural perspectives; a cyclical rather than linear view of history and of black, especially black female, experience; and Morrison's attempt to revision slavery from a black American woman's world-view.

The 'postmodern' nature of *Beloved* is evident in the way in which the novel fuses the characteristics of slave narrative, elements of traditional oral narrative, and sophisticated literary techniques; in the conflation of biography, history and fiction; and in the impact of late twentieth-century black consciousness and black American feminism on its interpretation of slavery. All these different aspects are anchored in the biography of Sethe, and in Sethe as the product of historical fact, imagination and myth, where the boundary with the real-life Margaret Garner is blurred.

The main events of *Beloved* constitute Sethe's slave past which the reader has to construct piecemeal and which Sethe herself tries to avoid: 'As for the rest, she worked hard to remember as close to nothing as was safe' (*Beloved*, 6). These events include the death of her mother; her marriage to Halle; a whipping which almost kills her; her escape and refuge in the home of her mother-in-law; her recapture and the infanticide of her child; her period of imprisonment; the subsequent years in 124; her sons – Howard and Buglar – being driven away from there by the ghost of Beloved, the child she killed; and her years in an all-female household where the third member is her ghost-daughter.

Beloved begins with Sethe remembering some of the above-mentioned episodes which she would rather forget. But the novel hinges upon what it calls 'rememory', a concept according to which memories have a physical existence beyond the minds of the individuals in whom they originate; it is possible to bump into and inhabit another person's memory. Paul D. is associated with rememory throughout the novel. At the beginning of the book he brings Sethe's 'rememories' of what happened to her husband, Halle, and explanations as to why he did not come to console her. Sethe literally learns to inhabit, and take for herself, these 'rememories' which are Paul D.'s. In doing so, she begins to piece things together, anticipating the experience of the reader in tackling this intricately woven novel. At the end of the book, just before Paul D. returns to reclaim Sethe from death, he is haunted by something he does not understand, something on the edge of consciousness. Suddenly, he realises that it is a memory of Baby Suggs dying, although the memory is not his own because she died nine years earlier in his absence.

The concept of rememory, as it is employed in *Beloved*, is an African-American notion which helps determine the cyclical, 'postmodern' nature of the text which I mentioned above. It also one of many perspectives in the novel arising from a black American view of slavery. It is important to recognise that an awareness of how slavery destroyed not only communities but families was passed down from generation to generation in the black American South. Knowledge of African villages and families as they existed before their destruction by slavery was preserved in stories which slaves told each other. Consequently, many of them relied on the memories of others to give themselves a familial and cultural past.

Thus, the complex structure of *Beloved* acquires significance when placed in the context of Morrison's interest in the 'internal' experience of slavery, usually eschewed in the conventional slave narrative. Unlike the classic mid-nineteenth-century slave narrative, *Beloved* focuses on the 'internal' life of the slaves, and the psychic impact of slavery on black American women. It is clear that although remembering is a painful process for Sethe, she needs to confront, in order to come to terms with, the past. Fleetingly, she recalls the words spoken by Amy, a poor white's daughter, who helped her when she escaped from the plantation: 'Anything dead coming back to life hurts' (*Beloved*, 35). Later in the novel, when Amy's nursing of Sethe for two days is described in detail, her words of reassurance appear to be directed at the reader who by this time has been made familiar with the horrors of slavery: 'Good for you. More it hurt more better it is. Can't nothing heal without pain, you know. What you wiggling for?' (*Beloved*, 78).

Approaching *Beloved* as a slave narrative, then, is more complicated than we might suppose, bringing together as it does so many other contexts and highlighting Morrison's own complex cultural situation and background. However, I want to introduce two further specific contexts that demonstrate how *Beloved* is a sophisticated fusion of literary-historical research and features of traditional African and African-American oral culture.

Although it is well documented that *Beloved* is based on the Margaret Garner story, the fact that it is a response to a specific version of it has often been overlooked. Reverend P. S. Bassett's account of the Margaret Garner story, 'A Visit to the Slave Mother Who Killed Her Child', was published in the *American Baptist* on 12 February 1856, and subsequently included by Morrison herself in *The Black Book* (1974), a collection of memorabilia representing 300 years of black history. The article is not simply an account of what Margaret Garner did, but a record of Reverend Bassett's meeting with her. Several aspects of the essay are adapted in the characterisation and the plot of *Beloved* apart from what actually happened. Reverend Bassett's portrait of Margaret Garner seems to have inspired the characterisation of Sethe: she possesses 'all the passionate tenderness of a mother's love', 'an average amount of kindness', together with 'a vigorous intellect, and much energy of character' (Plasa, *Beloved*, 40). His observation that Margaret Garner's mother-in-law had been a professor of religion for about 20 years was probably the inspiration for Baby Suggs, herself the spiritual centre of *Beloved*. The separation of Sethe and Paul D. appears to have been inspired by Margaret Garner's mother-in-law's story, as reported by Reverend Bassett, of how she and her slave husband were separated from each other for 25 years, during which time she did not even see him in the fields, and did not want him to return to witness her sufferings.

In addition to the important character and plot ideas which Morrison obtained from Reverend Bassett's account of Margaret Garner, his essay profoundly influenced the perspectives on slave history in *Beloved*. The novel's account of the separation of mothers and children on slave plantations was undoubtedly inspired by the mother-in-law's story of how she had never seen most of her eight children. The delineation of the physical violence inflicted on black women slaves in *Beloved* is clearly indebted to Margaret Garner's report of 'her days of suffering, of her night's of unmitigated toil' (Plasa, *Beloved*, 40) and her mother-in-law's admission that she had been a loyal slave until, as she got older and became 'less capable of performing labor, her master became more and more exacting and brutal in his treatment [of her]' (Plasa, *Beloved*, 40). Moreover, Reverend Bassett's reaction to the two women's stories also appears to have influenced the novel. He betrays the naïve, white belief that some slave plantations, such as those in Kentucky, were more benign than others, a view shared by Mr Garner in *Beloved* when Baby Suggs's son, Halle, eventually manages to buy his mother from slavery. But it is a perspective that also misses the crucial point made in the novel by Baby Suggs: from a black slave's perspective, slavery is slavery no matter how the slaves are treated.

However, as I pointed out above, the slave narrative is only one cultural and historical context for this novel. On occasions, for example when the ghost of Beloved in the form of a young woman tries to seduce Paul D., the novel seems to slip into an African spirit tale. At other times, it more obviously recalls the African-American ghost story. As Gladys-Marie Fry has demonstrated, ghost stories have a particular significance in African-American slave history. They were employed by whites in the South to limit the movement of slaves, as a less brutal, and often more effective, alternative to physical violence. The descriptions of haunted places, the return of the dead by night and of attacks on slaves by supernatural beings exploited the slaves' worst fears. In turn, they were reinforced by activities on the part of the plantation owners that were later adopted by the Ku Klux Klan, donning white sheets in pretending to be ghosts, and by rumours spread by the slaves themselves about ghostly happenings. However, the line between the African spirit tale and the African-American ghost story is a thin one. Plantation ghost stories, often embellished by black folklorists, reflect the importance to black Americans, forcibly displaced from their families and their homelands, of traditional African belief in the capacity of their dead ancestors to intervene in the affairs of the living. Thus, Beloved as Sethe's daughter-incarnate makes more sense to us if we recognise the cultural perspective from which Morrison is writing even though, unlike the traditional African spirit incarnate, she acts out of selfish rather than altruistic reasons.

At one level Beloved, as an outraged ghost-daughter intent upon claiming the mother who killed her, subverts the traditional motif in African-American writing of the outraged mother figure. However, she eludes precise definition. Initially, as the spirit ghost of the murdered baby, she is commensurate with the revenging 'undead' of the plantation ghost story, a figure with which the slave owners sought to intimidate the slaves, and the slaves frequently scared themselves. But no sooner has the reader acquired even this view of her then she assumes, or appears to assume, the form of a young woman. Eventually, she seems to represent not a single child but the pain and anguish of the millions of blacks who have been enslaved, tortured and killed. It is in relation to this role that the fragmentary and disjointed nature of many sections of the novel in which Beloved appears makes sense, reflecting the larger chaos and disunity of black slave history.

In *Beloved* Morrison recognises that the history of slavery is much more fractious and contradictory than is conventionally presented, even in many slave narratives. The story of Amy introduces into the novel a subtext of slavery which has often been ignored; in her own tortured body there is literally and metaphorically a history of the slavery endured by poor, working-class whites, whose treatment at the hands of their masters was not so dissimilar, as Sethe discovers, from her own. The introduction of Amy also reminds us that non-European slaves were sought because of their skin colour which prevented them from blending, if they escaped, with the majority population. Similarly, the Cherokee Indians, who befriend runaway slaves, remind us how the Indians were also taken as slaves and how the death of so many, through, for example, European disease, was one of the motivating factors behind the introduction of slaves from Africa and the West Indies. Moreover, when Stamp Paid pulls a red ribbon from the river connected to a piece of a young black girl's scalp, he recovers another alternative narrative to that to be found in many histories of slavery: the way in which emancipation in the South brought not freedom but the widespread slaughter of former slaves. If they were not killed, there was little by way of opportunity for the ex-slaves. When the Federal troops were withdrawn in 1877, many black Americans were left materially, socially, educationally and politically impoverished. Of the three-quarters of them who remained in the Southern states, the majority were in agriculture, locked into a semi-feudal system of tenancy or share-cropping which replaced the slave plantations. The impotence of many of the white liberals to deliver the promise of emancipation is illustrated in the way in which Edward Bodwin constructs a text of his own past as an abolitionist – 'Nothing since was as stimulating as the old days of letters, petitions, meetings, debates, recruitment, quarrels, rescue and downright sedition' (*Beloved*, 260) – serving to underscore the paucity of his present which is epitomised in the image of a man searching for toy soldiers and a watch he had long ago buried in the yard of 124.

Beloved, however, not only reclaims a number of occluded narratives around slavery but suggests that the history in the slave narrative is based on a number of 'texts' within nineteenth-century African-American culture. One of the most significant of these was the North itself, described by Paul D. as the 'Free North. Magical North. Welcoming, benevolent North' (*Beloved*, 112). Once again, however, there is a degree of irony here, for the North was not always as welcoming nor as supportive or effective, as it might have been in its intervention in the South. Generally speaking, however, the myth of the North was an inspirational fantasy for black Americans. Seen often in biblical terms as the Promised Land, the way in which the North was perceived also underscores the importance of the Bible to African Americans. In *Beloved* the words which Sethe uses to claim Beloved – 'Beloved she mine' – and which Beloved uses to claim Sethe – 'I am Beloved and she is mine' – have their source in *The Song of Solomon* which had inspired the title and, in part, the concern with ancestral wisdom in her earlier novel. But, the epigraph of *Beloved* reminds us that its title comes from a part of Paul's epistle to the Romans in which he, in turn, is quoting Hosea from the Old Testament. One of Hosea's three children was called 'not beloved', a representative of the Israelites who had been temporarily rejected as punishment for their own betrayal. After a period of retribution, God reclaims the lost people:

I will call them my people,
which were not my people;
and her beloved,
which was not beloved.

This brings us to another context in which Morrison's novel may be read, not simply the Bible but the way the Bible has been interpreted and used by black Americans. On the slave plantations, religious instruction was intended as a form of social control. The Bible, read from a particular cultural perspective, was one of the means by which colonial authorities tried to introduce Western cultural values to Africa. But while its apparent dualism – 'Black Satan' and 'the snow-white Lamb of God' – appeared to justify slavery, the Bible like all texts is a multilayered narrative. From a black perspective, it was a different work from the one used by whites, providing images appropriate to their condition and history: the delivery of the Righteous, the retribution of the Wicked, Judgement day, Zion, and the Promised Land were especially emphasised. Through its delineation of the history of the Jewish nation, the Bible expounded the trials and miseries of slavery. It offered slaves a source of communal strength through notions of faith, grace and the Holy Spirit, and even a means of achieving healing.

The behaviour of the whites in *Beloved*, too, is anchored in specific histories which we need to recall if we are to understand slavery. Schoolteacher, for example, who makes a study of Sethe, is a student of the pseudo-science of racial hierarchies expounded by Herbert Spencer and Francis Galton. Schoolteacher's equivalents did write treatises on slaves based on putative scientific observation of them and the measurement of various parts of their bodies. They came to rely upon colonial anthropology and eventually vulgar interpretations of Darwinism to give coherence and respectability to popularly held racist myths. One of the most damning effects of white, colonial power structures was the representation and stigmatising of Africans and African-Americans as beasts. This is a stereotype which *Beloved* specifically inverts whilst exposing it as the product of white cultural hegemony and a particular historical narrative of black people:

Whitepeople believed that whatever the manners, under every dark skin was a jungle. Swift unnavigable waters, swinging screaming baboons, sleeping snakes, red gums ready for their sweet white blood . . . But it wasn't the jungle blacks brought with them to this place from the other (livable) place. It was the jungle whitefolks planted in them. And it grew. It spread. In, through and after life, it spread, until it invaded the whites who had made it. Touched them every one. Changed and altered them. Made them bloody, silly, worse than even they wanted to be, so scared were they of the jungle they had made. The screaming baboon lived under their own white skin; the red gums were their own.

(*Beloved*, 198–9)

However, the most significant occluded history that *Beloved* reclaims is the denial and obliteration of motherhood and mothering in slavery, which Morrison's novel suggests distorted the whole notion of womanhood for black women. It is no coincidence that the two main healers in the novel, Baby Suggs and Amy, are women and that Paul D., one of the most sympathetically portrayed black men in Morrison's work, is associated with the feminine. Morrison presents us with a black woman's version of slavery as a counterpoint to a narrative that had until then been told primarily from a male point of view. This is made clear when Stamp Paid visits 124 and hears, indecipherable to him, 'the thoughts of the women of 124, unspeakable thoughts, unspoken' (*Beloved*, 199). The black centre of the novel, associated with the spiritual and with healing, expounds the pain, humiliation and violence endured and, in many cases, transcended by generations of black women.

One of the most powerful 'texts' in the book in this respect is the pattern made by the scars on Sethe's back. Her own reading of them, since she has never actually seen them, is a 'rememory' of Amy's reading of them:

> Whitegirl. That's what she called it. I've never seen it and never will. But that's what she said it looked like. A chokecherry tree. Trunk, branches, and even leaves. Tiny little chokecherry leaves.
>
> (*Beloved*, 16)

Characteristically, there are different 'texts' on Sethe's back depending upon how the scars are read. Amy's reading imaginatively transforms the pain and humiliation of slavery. Later Sethe does the same in remembering the Sweet Home boys: 'Boys hanging from the most beautiful sycamores in the world. It shamed her – remembering the wonderful soughing trees rather than the boys' (*Beloved*, 6). When Sethe and Paul D. make love unsuccessfully because they are both carrying too much guilt and pain, Paul sees the scars differently from Amy and Sethe: they are 'a revolting clump of scars' (*Beloved*, 21).

The novel presents the reader with insights into the suffering of black women. In piecing together the structure of the novel, we weave these perceptions together as well, so that the novel becomes a history of black female slavery. Indeed, the suffering of black women under slavery is so inextricably a part of the book as to give its language a particular impact. This is evident, for example, in Sethe's account of her own mother to Beloved:

> I didn't see her but a few times out in the fields and once when she was working indigo. By the time I woke up in the morning, she was in line.

If the moon was bright they worked by its light. Sunday she slept like a stick. She must of nursed me two or three weeks – that's the way the others did. Then she went back in rice and I sucked from another woman whose job it was. So to answer you, no. I reckon not. She never fixed my hair nor nothing. She didn't even sleep in the same cabin most nights I remember. Too far from the line-up, I guess.

(*Beloved*, 60–1)

For the women to be forced to work by the light of the moon, the traditional symbol of the female, underlines their brutalisation. The use of the verb 'sucked' emphasises how the white man's system has reduced black women to breeding stock – as does the stealing of Sethe's milk. Coupled with the noun 'job', it also reinforces the denial of the closest of emotional bonds, that between mother and child, and how slavery was based on a systemised form of breeding. 'Line' and 'line-up' emphasise the factory-like nature of the system while betraying its role in supporting a capitalist, industrial society. The word 'stick' emphasises the life-denying nature of the whole process. A stick, like a slave, has been broken off from its life source and is thereby dry and dead.

Healing is at the centre of *Beloved* and is centred on Sethe since Amy, Baby Suggs and, finally, Paul D. all contribute to her healing process. In traditional African society, moral judgement was invariably a matter for the community to which the individual was answerable. In *Beloved* the community which initially betrays Sethe significantly comes together at the end of the novel and rescues her from killing Edward Bodwin. They, too, of course, can only achieve absolution for betraying Baby Suggs and Sethe by saving her. Although at one level the fragmentary structure of the novel reflects the disunity of recent African-American history and the chaos which slavery created in the lives of black people, at another level the black experience is seen as a cycle which returns to the shared suffering that should consolidate the black community. This is the Word to which Hi Man refers and of which Baby Suggs speaks. In a sense, then, the sermon which Baby Suggs preaches in the clearing, which in the novel is itself emblematic of a homogeneous black community, is the really important text which lies buried in this novel.

Morrison herself associates the late-twentieth-century African-American novel with healing: 'For a long time, the art form that was healing for Black people was music. That music is no longer exclusively ours; we don't have exclusive rights to it . . . So another form has to take that place, and it seems to me that the novel is needed by African-Americans in a way that it was not needed before' (*The Ancestor as Foundation*, 340). But *Beloved* does not underestimate the enormity of the fracture which slavery and white racialism created. Although it concludes on a note of healing, there is no definitive sense of closure. We do not know how completely Sethe will be healed or whether she and Paul D. have been sufficiently successful in exorcising their respective pasts that they will be able to make a life together. Their particular narrative ends with Sethe's incredulity – 'Me? Me?' (*Beloved*, 273) – while the novel concludes with a pain that's 'an inside kind – wrapped tight like skin . . . No rocking can hold it down' (*Beloved*, 274).

Beloved, then, is not only a novel with a patchwork quilt structure which the reader has to piece together, but a text which literally demonstrates how any narrative has the potential to conceal a myriad of other narratives. More specifically, it challenges and reconfigures the world-views associated with a number of African-American and Euro-American verbal narratives – the slave narrative, the plantation ghost story, black folk tales, and the romance – and is rooted in a realisation that black slave history, like the Bible to which black slaves frequently turned for solace and inspiration, is a multilayered text. Ultimately, *Beloved* develops narratives which have been occluded in most histories of slavery, such as the psychic and physical violence suffered by black women and, especially, the brutalisation of the black mother. At the end of the novel the narrator admits ambiguously that the Margaret Garner/Sethe story, with all its attendant histories, is not one to 'pass on'. This may suggest that this is not a story to relay to future generations, but more likely it means that this is not one to avoid.

Further Reading

Toni Morrison's own very readable essay on the significance of African-Americans for the American literary imagination, *Playing in the Dark: Whiteness and the Literary Imagination* (Cambridge, MA, and London, Harvard University Press, 1992), provides a compelling context from which to read *Beloved*.

The 1990s produced a number of book-length studies of Toni Morrison's work and *Beloved* itself is the subject of numerous articles in scholarly journals.

Two critical introductions to Morrison's work which include chapters on *Beloved*, written with the student in mind, are Jill Matus, *Toni Morrison* (Manchester, Manchester University Press, 1998) and Linden Peach, *Toni Morrison* (1995; 2nd edn, Basingstoke, Macmillan – now Palgrave, 2000). Both these books are primarily concerned with Morrison's work in relation to obscured or erased African-American history.

Further essays on this aspect of *Beloved* are: Marilyn Saunders Mobley, 'A Different Remembering: Memory, History and Meaning in Toni Morrison's *Beloved*', in *Toni Morrison*, ed. Harold Bloom (New York, Chelsea House, 1990), 189–99; and Rebecca Ferguson, 'History, Memory and Language in Toni Morrison's *Beloved*', in *Feminist Criticism: Theory and Practice*, ed. Susan Sellers and Linda Hutcheon (Toronto, Toronto University Press, 1991), 109–27.

An accessible overview of the different critical approaches that have been taken to the novel, including studies of its supernatural elements, its treatment of the self and the complex nature of the narrative, can be found in Carl Plasa, *Beloved*, Icon Critical Guides (Cambridge, Icon Books, 1998).

Another accessible work on the physical self in *Beloved* is Laura Doyle, '"To Get to a Place": Intercorporeality in *Beloved*', in Laura Doyle, *Bordering on the Body: The Racial Matrix of Modern Fiction and Culture* (Oxford, Oxford University Press, 1994), 206–30. A rewarding study of Morrison's fiction in the light of contemporary feminist critical theory is Barbara Rigney, *The Voices of Toni Morrison* (Columbus, Ohio State University Press, 1991).

Accounts of how Morrison's work has furthered the development of the African-American novel and contributed to debates about African-American identity can be found in Linden Peach (ed.), *Toni Morrison: Contemporary Critical Essays*, New Casebook (Basingstoke, Macmillan – now Palgrave, 1998). This collection includes extracts from a stimulating psychoanalytic study of *Beloved*: Jennifer FitzGerald, 'Selfhood and Community: Psychoanalysis and Discourse in *Beloved*'; and from a discussion of *Beloved* as a 'postmodern' novel: Rafael Pérez-Torres, 'Knitting and Knotting the Narrative Thread – *Beloved* as Postmodern Novel'. There is also a substantial extract from a study of *Beloved* in relation to black history by Ashraf H. A. Rushdy: 'Daughters Signifyin(g) History: The Example of Toni Morrison's *Beloved*'. Essays published in scholarly journals can sometimes argue from critical perspectives and use terms with which the student may not be familiar. The book includes introductory notes on the critical concepts employed in these essays.

The reader who would like to pursue Morrison's use of the Margaret Garner story should consult Cynthia Griffin Woolf, '"Margaret Garner": A Cincinnati Story', *Massachusetts Review*, 32 (1991), 417–40. Morrison's use of the ghost story is discussed in: Barbara Hill Rigney, '"A Story to Pass On": Ghosts and the Significance of History in Toni Morrison's *Beloved*', in *Haunting the House of Fiction: Feminist Perspectives on Ghost Stories by American Women*, ed. Lynette Carpenter and Wendy K. Kolmar (Knoxville, University of Tennessee Press, 1991), 229–35; and Elizabeth B. House, 'Toni Morrison's Ghost: The Beloved Who is Not Beloved', *Studies in American Fiction*, 18 (1990), 17–26.

References

Reverend P. S. Bassett, 'A Visit to the Slave Mother Who Killed Her Child', *American Baptist*, 12 February 1856, rpt. in Carl Plasa, *Beloved*, Icon Critical Guides (Cambridge, Icon Books, 1998), 39–41.

Gladys-Marie Fry, *Night Riders in Black Folk History* (Knoxville, University of Tennessee Press, 1975).

Toni Morrison, *Beloved* (1987; rpt. London, Picador, 1988).

——, 'The Ancestor as Foundation', in *Black Women Writers 1950–1980: A Critical Evaluation*, ed. Mari Evans (New York Books, 1984).

Index

Ackroyd, Peter, 88
aesthetics, 59, 100, 151, 156, 168; *see also* visual arts; aesthetic judgement, 150
Allott, Miriam, 109, 110, 111, 113, 116
Alvarez, A., 177
American Baptist, The, 229
Amis, Martin, 214, 216
Arbuthnot, John, 65, 70
Austen, Jane, 91–104, 156; *Emma*, 92; *Mansfield Park*, 96, 97, 212; *Northanger Abbey*, 98; *Persuasion*, 46, 93–104; *Pride and Prejudice*, 92

Barker, Juliet, 106
Barnes, Djuna, 166
Barnes, Julian, 132
Bassett, Reverend P. S., 229–30
Bath, 97–9
Baudrillard, Jean, 217
Beckett, Samuel, 188, 194, 204
Bell, Clive, 159
Bennett, Arnold, 164
Bettey, J. H., 148
Bible, The, 83, 89, 128, 138–9, 143, 145, 226, 232–3, 236; *The Song of Solomon*, 232; biblical references, 83, 138–9, 143, 232
Billington, Michael, 189
biography/biographical context, 2, 48–9, 52, 65–6, 68, 80, 88, 95, 97, 123, 136, 139–40, 156–8, 173–5, 212, 226, 228
Blake, William, 46, 79–90;

America, A Prophecy, 80–1, 87; 'The Chimney Sweeper', 81–6; 'Jerusalem', 88; 'The Little Vagabond', 86; *Prophetic Books*, 87–9; *Proverbs of Hell*, 88; *Songs of Innocence and of Experience*, 81–8
Blakemore Evans, G., 19, 23, 29
Boleyn, Ann, 54
Book of the Duchess, The, 12
Boumelha, Penny, 147
Bowen, Elizabeth, 160
Boyer, Abel, 71
Bradley, A. C., 35, 150
Brecht, Bertolt, 151
Brontë, Charlotte, 105–18, 156, 158, 162, 167, 168; *Jane Eyre*, 105–18, 161
Brontë, Emily, 111
Bunyan, John, 138, 174
Burbage, Richard, 36
Byron, Lord George Gordon Noel, 101; Byronic, 115

Carlyle, Sir Thomas, 123, 130; *Past and Present*, 123; *Sartor Resartus*, 130
Carpenter, Richard, 146
Carrington, Dora, 159
Carter, Angela, 106
Cézanne, Paul, 141
Chartier, Roger, 47
Chaucer, Geoffrey, *The Canterbury Tales*, 1–14, 212, 218
childhood, 82–4, 111–12, 160
class, 5–7, 22, 84–6, 92, 95–8, 112–13, 121–2, 126, 139, 140, 142, 147, 149, 162, 212